Implementing Operations Management Suite

A Practical Guide to OMS, Azure Site Recovery, and Azure Backup

Peter De Tender

Apress®

Implementing Operations Management Suite: A Practical Guide to OMS, Azure Site Recovery, and Azure Backup

Peter De Tender
Daknam, Belgium

ISBN-13 (pbk): 978-1-4842-1825-9   ISBN-13 (electronic): 978-1-4842-1979-9
DOI 10.1007/978-1-4842-1979-9

Library of Congress Control Number: 2016958436

Managing Director: Welmoed Spahr
Lead Editor: Gwenan Spearing
Technical Reviewer: Newton Sheikh
Editorial Board: Steve Anglin, Pramila Balan, Laura Berendson, Aaron Black, Louise Corrigan,
    Jonathan Gennick, Robert Hutchinson, Celestin Suresh John, Nikhil Karkal, James Markham,
    Susan McDermott, Matthew Moodie, Natalie Pao, Gwenan Spearing
Coordinating Editor: Mark Powers
Copy Editor: Kezia Endsley
Compositor: SPi Global
Indexer: SPi Global
Artist: SPi Global

Distributed to the book trade worldwide by Springer Science+Business Media New York, 233 Spring Street, 6th Floor, New York, NY 10013. Phone 1-800-SPRINGER, fax (201) 348-4505, e-mail orders-ny@springer-sbm.com, or visit www.springeronline.com. Apress Media, LLC is a California LLC and the sole member (owner) is Springer Science + Business Media Finance Inc (SSBM Finance Inc). SSBM Finance Inc is a **Delaware** corporation.

For information on translations, please e-mail rights@apress.com, or visit www.apress.com.

Apress and friends of ED books may be purchased in bulk for academic, corporate, or promotional use. eBook versions and licenses are also available for most titles. For more information, reference our Special Bulk Sales–eBook Licensing web page at www.apress.com/bulk-sales.

Any source code or other supplementary materials referenced by the author in this text are available to readers at www.apress.com. For detailed information about how to locate your book's source code, go to www.apress.com/source-code/. Readers can also access source code at SpringerLink in the Supplementary Material section for each chapter.

Printed on acid-free paper

To my wife Els, my source of inspiration and support. I'm blessed being your "Petie".

To my two wonderful teenage girls Kaylee and Kitana. I'm proud to be your dad.

To my dad, taken away too soon. You taught me how to be successful, only by working hard and loving what you do.

Contents at a Glance

Contents

About the Author

Peter DeTender has 20 years of professional expertise in the Microsoft Infrastructure segment, with a main focus on Microsoft Cloud technologies (Azure, Enterprise Mobility Suite, Office 365, and more) After working for some of the top Microsoft partners in Belgium, he ran his own successful business for several years, mainly providing Infrastructure and Cloud Architect training and readiness in a passionate and enthusiastic way. Peter coached several Microsoft Partners all over the world in doing more Microsoft business, both from a technical and business angle.

Just recently, as of June 2016 to be exact, Peter joined Microsoft Corp as an FTE Azure Architect/ Program Manager in the global AzureCAT GSI team, part of Azure engineering, where his role consists of providing Azure-focused readiness training and Cloud practice building coaching to the TOP15 Microsoft Global System Integrators. This role allows Peter to combine his two passions—working on the latest and greatest up-to-date technologies and cooperating with people from all over the globe.

His valued credentials are Microsoft Certified Trainer, Azure Certified Architect, and—before he joined Microsoft—Peter was also recognized as a Microsoft MVP, first on Windows IT Pro (2013-2014) and switched to the Azure category in 2015.

In his free time, Peter loves speaking at (inter)national conferences and community events and is a technical writer and courseware creator.

You can contact Peter on twitter as @pdtit, or visit his website http://www.pdtit.be

About the Technical Reviewer

Newton Sheikh is a consultant for Cloud and distributed computing with a focus on Microsoft Azure. He is a .NET developer and a security expert for infrastructure services running on the Cloud. Newton has been writing codes on .NET and for the web for five years. His keen interests are mathematics and algorithms.

Newton enjoys coding, designing, architecting solutions for the Web and the Cloud. With a keen interest in game designing, he has worked on multiple platforms, including XNA, Android, and iOS. He loves to try new, lightweight, yet powerful game engines.

Most recently he has developed a hobby for photography and loves to carry his camera on his travels.

About the Technical Reviewer

Acknowledgments

The first idea for writing this book came up after meeting with Apress at Microsoft Ignite Chicago in May 2015. So here we are, 18 months and several updates later, providing you with the most up-to-date knowledge and experiences I could share. Azure Backup and Azure Site Recovery became part of OMS, and is now available in Azure Resource Manager. The current version at the time of completing this book has no resemblance to what it was when I started the writing process back in June 2015.

My first words of thanks go to the wonderful team at Apress who guided me through sometimes challenging and hard times. The public Cloud cadence is here, and it only goes faster and faster. This brought the necessary frustrations and missing deadlines to the table. Mark, Gwenan, and Laura managed it all well and professionally, guaranteeing that this book got published in the end.

Three books and four years later, I promised my wife and kids I would never write another book. Knowing how much time they must miss me when I'm building—and destroying—another lab, sitting quietly at my desk, writing another chapter on my computer, not always giving them the attention they deserve... there is no way I can thank them enough for all their understanding and patience for letting me do this. Els, while you are not reading my books, you are my biggest fan and motivation to become better in everything I do. You are a great support and push me through hard times. Kaylee and Kitana, my two loving and beautiful girls, you are both so much fun to see growing up, knowing what wonderful women you will become.

I want to thank anybody who ever attended one of my public speaking sessions, attended one of my many training gigs anywhere in the world, or was one of my customers. It is thanks to you that I love this job, and I will continue pushing myself beyond my own limits.

And lastly, a huge "thank you" goes out to you, the reader of this book. I hope you like it and use it when implementing these great technologies. Enjoy the journey as much as I did when writing it.

Introduction

Learn how to protect, back up, recover, and monitor your data and infrastructure in the Cloud with Microsoft's Operations Management Suite (OMS), Azure Backup, and Azure Site Recovery.

Implementing Operations Management Suite starts with an overview of the Operations Management Suite, followed by several chapters that uncover Azure Backup and how to configure it, followed by deep dives into aspects of Azure Site Recovery (ASR). This includes how it works, how to configure it, how to streamline your disaster recovery failover from on-premises to Azure, as well as how ASR can be used to migrate (lift-and-shift) from Amazon's AWS or VMware infrastructures. Learn about protection groups, how to perform planned and unplanned failover, and more.

The author, Peter De Tender, Microsoft infrastructure expert with 20 years of experience and who recently joined Microsoft Corp's AzureCAT GSI team as Azure Architect/Program Manager, takes you through the necessary theory and background on each topic, along with clear, hands-on step-by-step lab guides to help you implement and configure each feature yourself. You'll also find out how to estimate your platform costs when using Azure infrastructure components, making this book your one-stop guide to the latest disaster recovery services in Microsoft Azure.

By going through this book, you will learn:

- How to understand current concepts and challenges in IT disaster recovery

- How to monitor your IT infrastructure, both running on-premises or in a hybrid/public Cloud by using Operations Management Suite

- How to protect your data by leveraging the powers of Azure Backup and its configuration options

- How to protect, recover, and monitor your environment with Azure Site Recovery, and the configuration options available

This book is especially for IT professionals and IT decision makers who are interested in learning about Operations Management Suite, Azure Backup, and Azure Site Recovery, in order to build and/or optimize their IT disaster recovery scenarios.

CHAPTER 1

■ ■ ■

Introduction to OMS

The way IT infrastructure has been managed in the last decade is undergoing a serious change, based on the following domains:

- Businesses require a faster time to market

- More and more IT assets, resources, and applications are shifting to a "Cloud" infrastructure

- IT needs to provide more detailed insights, support predictability, and control of IT

- Businesses are adopting micro-services and containers

- IT "management as a service" is a reality

Now, if we think about modern IT management, what should this look like? At first, it should support different infrastructures. Starting from an organization's own datacenter, integrating with service providers' datacenters, and providing monitoring information from public Cloud infrastructures like Microsoft Azure, Amazon AWS, and others. On a more technical layer, it should support both Windows Servers and Linux, whether installed as physical servers or running on virtualization technologies like Microsoft Hyper-V, VMware, or other hypervisors.

And this is exactly what makes Microsoft Operations Management Suite an ideal candidate, as it perfectly answers these needs.

If you are wondering how Microsoft Operations Management Suite can be of help, know that more and more business departments are turning their heads towards *shadow-IT,* public Cloud IaaS (Infrastructure as a Service), and SaaS (Software as a Service) solutions that can be acquired almost in the same easy way as installing an app on your mobile device; so basically, there is no longer a need to the support the internal IT departments anymore.

Some organizations already recognize this issue and are taking the necessary steps to create a more agile IT alternative within the organization. IT departments need to get back in the game by investigating new innovations that support applications and services that drive business needs and support business growth.

Microsoft OMS (Operations Management Suite) is a Cloud-based monitoring and management solution for any IT environment. They can be small or big, and primarily run Microsoft technologies or a combination of multiple operating systems like Linux, VMware, and OpenStack. Whether your assets are running in a local datacenter or completely in a public Cloud infrastructure like Microsoft Azure or Amazon AWS or in a hybrid topology, it doesn't matter. Each provides different insights into your organization's IT landscape.

Before going into more detail about each of these, there is something else I want to talk about first.

When I heard of Microsoft Operations Management Suite the first time, about two years back, I immediately thought it was the Cloud replacement for the other famous Microsoft monitoring solution, System Center Operations Manager (SCOM). To be honest, up to a certain level, there is a lot of overlap when only thinking about the monitoring features. However, the interesting thing is that OMS actually

P. De Tender, *Implementing Operations Management Suite*, DOI 10.1007/978-1-4842-1979-9_1

allows for a tight integration with System Center Operations Manager in your datacenter, as well as providing automation, in a similar way as System Center Orchestrator provides in an on-premises configuration.

■ **Note**   To set things straight from the beginning, Microsoft Operations Management Suite is *not* the Cloud replacement of System Center Operations Manager, but more about that later on.

Now that this main misconception has been clarified, I'm sure I have your full attention to continue reading and learning all the great things that the Operations Management Suite offers you.

Shifting Needs in IT Management

As I already mentioned in the first paragraphs, there is a continuous change in the way IT management is shifting:

- Third-party companies are offering Management as a Service (MaaS).

- Customers want a faster time to market when they are deploying new IT assets and applications.

- More and more companies are executing Cloud migrations; and not just Microsoft Cloud, but "any Cloud," whether public, private, or hybrid.

- Organizations always want to get a better view of IT management, mainly from a business perspective.

- Nowadays, applications and Cloud services are more and more offered as so-called micro-services and containers, taking some or all of the control away from the IT department. And they don't want to give up control.

Then again, management should be available from any Cloud, no matter what resources or services are running there. On-premises datacenter management should provide a centralized support mechanism, taking all components in the monitoring and management stack. To optimize IT services, automation and orchestrated operations are becoming critical. If the organization is using resources from the public Cloud—think of Microsoft Azure, Microsoft Office 365, or Amazon Web Services to name just a few—IT organizations still require an almost identical level of management and reporting about the overall health state of these public Cloud resources, no matter where they are running.

Why Use OMS?

I hope the first few paragraphs made you wonder about different issues or challenges in the modern IT management operations, showing you how Operations Management Suite can be of help here.

Some of these challenges can easily be solved (or at least up to a certain level, which is probably different for each individual organization) by understanding some of the core characteristics of Microsoft OMS.

Easy to Use

OMS management runs from an administrative portal, running in a browser as shown in Figure 1-1. This not only avoids conflicts and issues with certain other applications running on the management station, it also allows for remote management. As long as an IT admin has an Internet connection, it should be possible to log on to the portal. Another advantage is that you don't need to prepare a complex infrastructure in your local datacenter to allow for providing management.

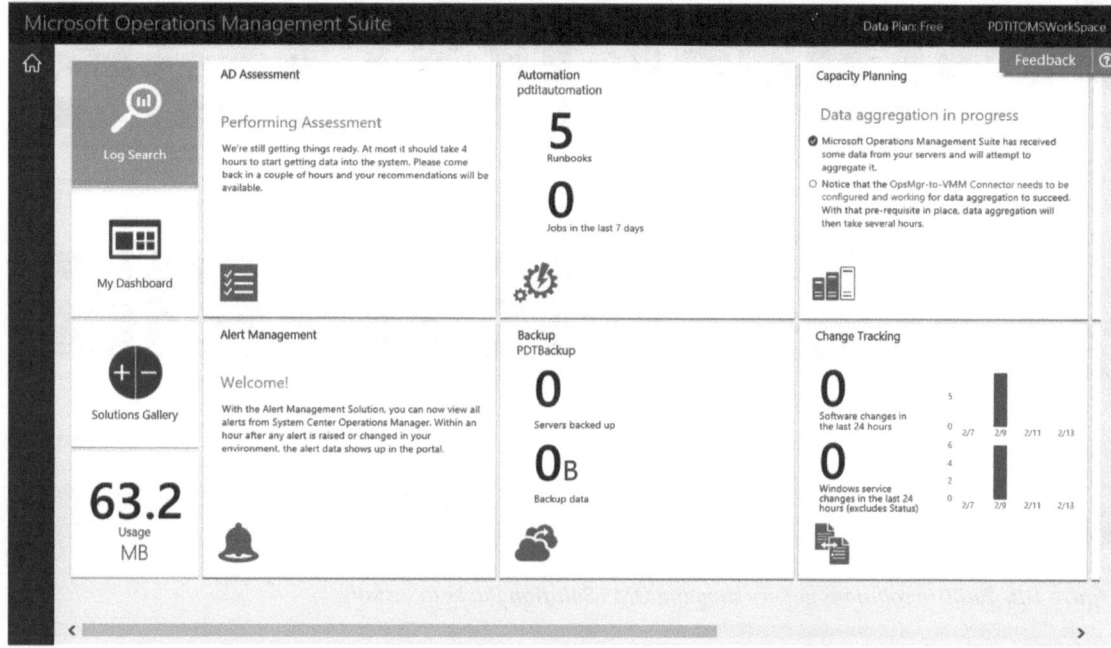

Figure 1-1. *Microsoft Operations Management Suite dashboard*

Next to the administrative portal from a browser, the OMS product team also built a mobile client, which is working on iOS, Android, and Windows Mobile. For more information on the mobile app features and download links for the different platforms, have a look at the following URL:

```
https://www.microsoft.com/en-us/cloud-platform/operations-management-suite-mobile-apps
```

Easy to Deploy

OMS can be deployed in minutes instead of days (or even weeks in certain more complex environments). Basically, all information is coming from an OMS agent, which can be installed locally on a Windows or Linux machine, or you can configure a direct integration with an already running System Center Operations Manager in your datacenter. The OMS management and monitoring portal is build around "tiles," which refer to so-called Solution Packs (see Figure 1-2).

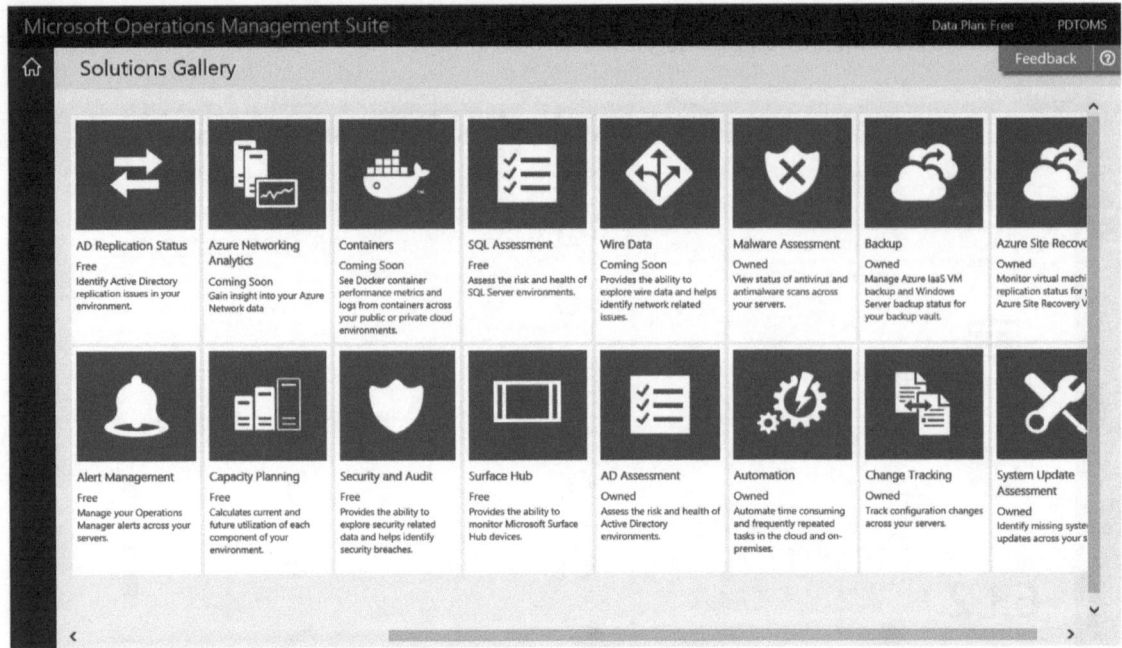

Figure 1-2. *Built-in solutions gallery showing OMS Solution Packs to install*

It is by using these Solution Packs that your logged information gets translated to an easy-to-understand dashboard. When your infrastructure is growing, whether on-premises or in some Cloud, it should be enough to deploy an OMS agent on the additional Windows or Linux machine, to immediately start receiving logging information from it.

In the next chapter, I show you how these OMS agents can be deployed in different ways.

Ready for Hybridization

As I already pointed out in the first few paragraphs, OMS supports multiple Clouds, multiple operating systems, and can also integrate with System Center Operations Manager. While this is not a must, as you will find out in the next chapter, it somehow is built to integrate with an existing System Center Operations Manager infrastructure, if you want to get all details about your on-premises infrastructure. The alternative is deploying OMS agents to your Hyper-V hosts or individual virtual machine guests.

I have deployed the Operations Management Suite already in a Cloud-only setup, relying on the provided Solution Packs and by installing agents on Hyper-V hosts, where other setups are based on the System Center Operations Manager integration.

Directly from within the Operations Management Suite dashboard, an administrator can download and install the OMS agent for Windows or Linux server platforms or configure the integration with System Center Operations Manager (see Figure 1-3).

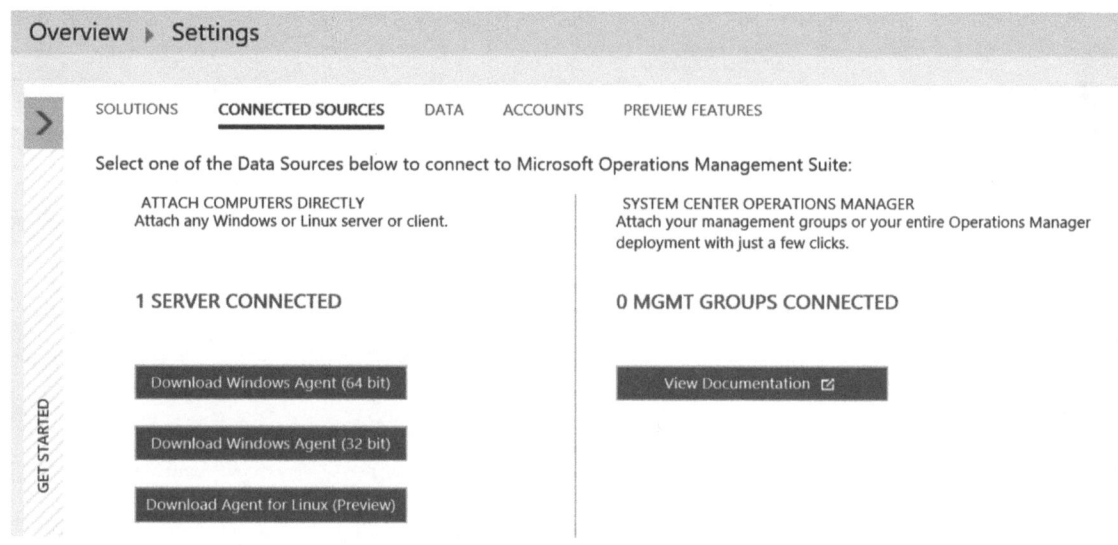

Figure 1-3. *OMS settings, where you can download the agents*

Integration is provided in System Center Operations Manager 2012 SP1 RU6 or 2012 R2 RU2; however, note that it is still called Operations Insights in this version.

What Features and Functionalities Does OMS Provide?

Microsoft Operations Management Suite is not a single product as such, but a collection of solutions:

- Log Analytics
- IT automation
- Backup and recovery
- Security and compliance

Log Analytics

Log Analytics is the key component of OMS, especially when you only think of it as a monitoring solution. The deployed OMS agents collect all information from the resource servers, storing it in the configured Azure Cloud storage location, where it will be retained per your OMS subscription plan (more on that later). All logged and collected information can be retrieved by using a powerful Log Search feature, providing you all details and insights in your environment. Filtered log search results can be saved for later consulting or exported to an Excel sheet, or you can create a dashboard tile for it to show real-time information on the centralized dashboard in the portal.

A sample screenshot from the Log Search possibilities is shown in Figure 1-4.

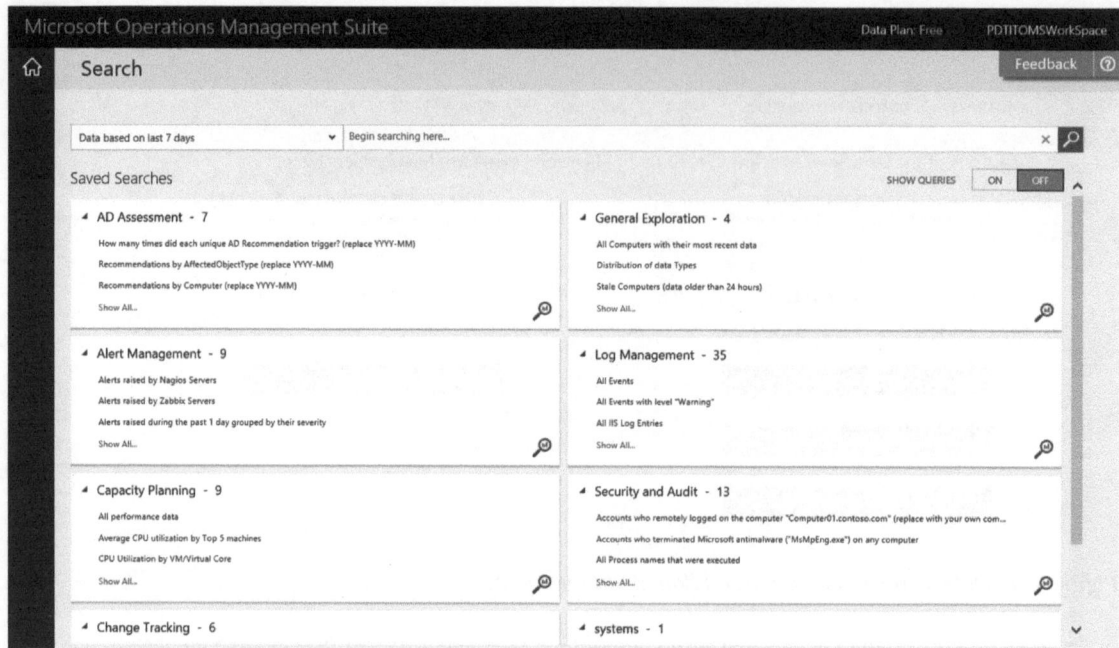

Figure 1-4. *OMS Log Search possibilities*

While the Log Search is very powerful, it requires some "getting used to" in terms of learning how to build the filter queries to retrieve your logged information. In the next chapter, I guide you through several examples so you become an OMS Log Analytics expert.

IT Automation

The automation engine in OMS is based on the Azure Automation engine, allowing full automating about anything you can think of in the Azure world, as well as your on-premises infrastructure. Automating tasks mainly relies on PowerShell scripting. You could use PowerShell ISE to author scripts or use the graphical authoring tool that is provided in the Azure portal.

Typical use cases for automation is shutting down test/dev virtual machines in Azure to save on cost, or automating the deployment of new resources; then again, there is no real limitation to automating tasks, so you could use OMS Automation to orchestrate about any manual repetitive task you have been executing or will execute in your datacenter or in Azure.

A high-level architecture of the Azure integration is shown in Figure 1-5.

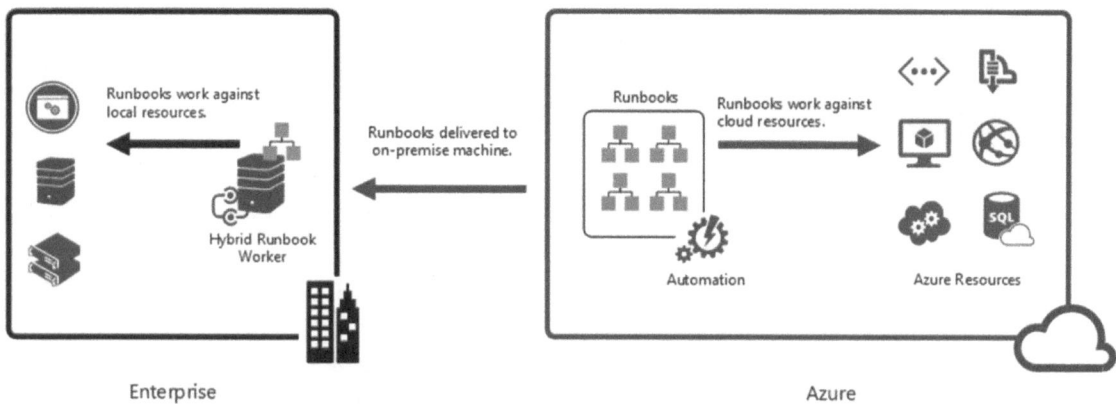

Figure 1-5. *Showing the integration of OMS Automation to both Azure and an on-premises infrastructure*

Backup and Recovery

Azure Backup

Azure Backup and Azure Site Recovery are two core Infrastructure as a Service (IaaS) features of Azure, also known as *business continuity* features; this is because they allow you to continue running your business applications in case of a disaster, or at least perform a quick recovery. Where both components existed as stand-alone Azure features before, they are now available as a bundled offering together with OMS monitoring and management. (The bundled offering mainly points to the licensing aspect though, not to the technical side of things.)

And to make it already a bit more confusing, Azure Backup currently exists in three different flavors:

- Azure Backup (an agent that can be installed on a Windows machine, allowing backups of files and folders to the Azure Backup Vault)

- Azure Backup Server (a full-fledged enterprise oriented backup solution, completely based on the System Center Data Protection Manager concepts, providing backups from on-premises workloads like Exchange, SharePoint, SQL Server, and so on, to the Azure Backup Vault)

- Azure Backup (backup of Azure running VMs to Azure Backup Vault)

Azure Backup was introduced in the Azure Classic mode, but since May 2016, the feature has been migrated to the Azure Resource Manager as well. If you were using the Azure Backup Classic approach, it only allowed you to manage backups from classic VMs; where now in the Azure Resource Manager way, it recognizes both Azure Resource Manager Virtual Machines to be backed up, as well as Azure Classic Virtual Machines. Another interesting aspect is that it also provides full support for taking backups of on-premises running virtual machines.

Obviously, each of these flavors is discussed a lot more in detail in the Azure Backup chapter. For each flavor, a step-by-step configuration is required from the Azure portal, as is shown in Figure 1-6.

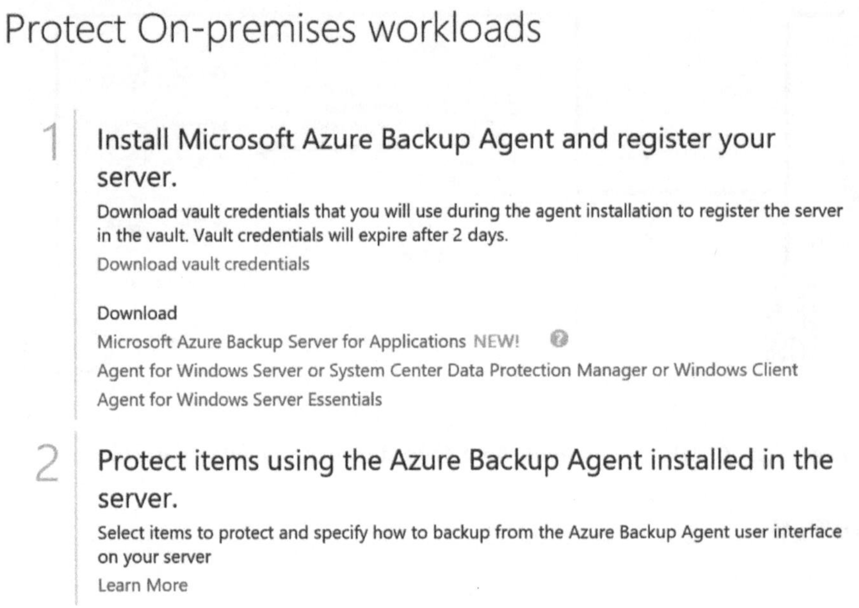

Protect On-premises workloads

1 | **Install Microsoft Azure Backup Agent and register your server.**

Download vault credentials that you will use during the agent installation to register the server in the vault. Vault credentials will expire after 2 days.

Download vault credentials

Download
Microsoft Azure Backup Server for Applications NEW! ❓
Agent for Windows Server or System Center Data Protection Manager or Windows Client
Agent for Windows Server Essentials

2 | **Protect items using the Azure Backup Agent installed in the server.**

Select items to protect and specify how to backup from the Azure Backup Agent user interface on your server

Learn More

Figure 1-6. Showing the different Azure Backup configuration options available from the Azure portal

Azure Site Recovery

Honestly, Azure Site Recovery is one of my personal favorite features of Azure, for several reasons. Most importantly, it's because disaster recovery, being the core reason of existence of Azure Site Recovery, is an important feature in any organization, big or small. Second is that it's a complete solution, it's easy to set up, and it "just works".

What do I mean by being a complete solution? This refers to the fact that Azure Site Recovery allows you to replicate virtual machines to Azure VMs, from basically any source (such as physical server operating systems, Hyper-V or System Center Virtual Machine Manager-based VMs or VMware ESX, or ESXi based VMs). As long as the operating system is supported in Azure, Azure Site Recovery can do the trick.

Next to replication from/to Azure, it also supports replication between two physical datacenter locations, without replicating any data to Azure whatsoever. In this scenario, you are leveraging on the powers and intelligence of Azure Site Recovery as the control mechanism (the orchestration), but the virtual machine data itself is being replicated directly on Hyper-V or VMware host level or on physical storage level. (See Figure 1-7 for high-level overview.)

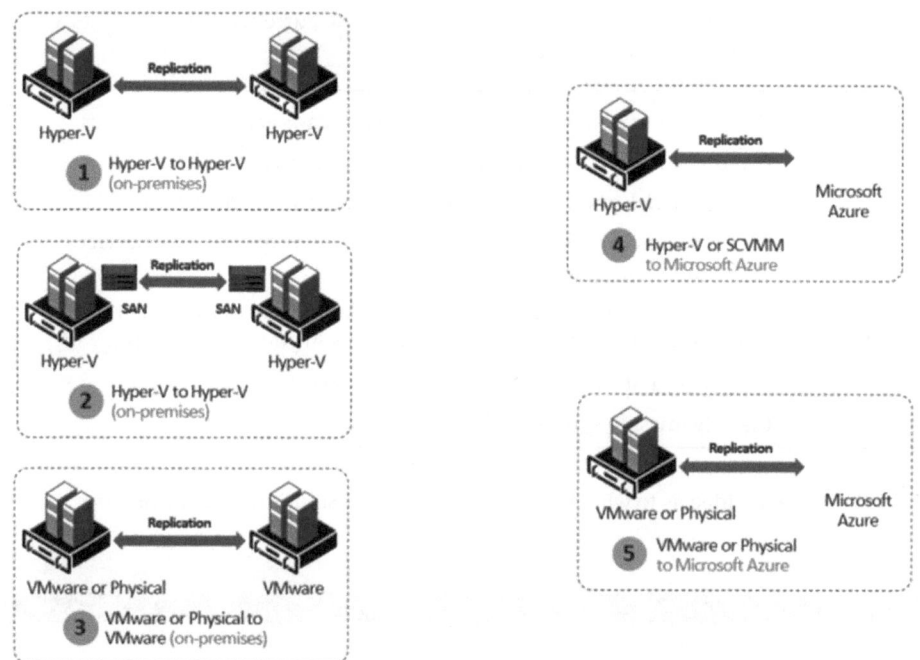

Figure 1-7. *Quick overview of the different ASR topologies, both on-premises and to Azure (Image source: https://azure.microsoft.com/en-us/documentation/articles/site-recovery-overview/Security and Compliance)*

It's interesting that more and more Microsoft partners and customers are using Azure Site Recovery as a "migration" tool to help them easily migrating on-premises virtual machines toward Azure VMs. So, while it never was designed and built to be a migration tool, it certainly can be used for that.

Security and Compliance

Security and Compliance is the last big family of features provided by OMS. Out of the detailed logging and analytics we slightly talked about in the Introduction, a core component is understanding critical security and compliance data. In this way, OMS can really help you get a good view of security risks within your IT infrastructure; again, irrelevant from running on-premises or in a hosted datacenter or in a public Cloud scenario. If the infrastructure, applications, and services are monitored by an OMS agent, security and compliance data will be collected and can be analyzed.

From a technical view, OMS provides several Solution Packs, of which the current collection offers a couple of different ones related to security and compliance:

Malware Assessment	View status of antivirus and anti-malware scans across your servers.
Security and Audit	Explore security related data and identify security breaches.
SQL Assessment	Assess the risk and health of your SQL Server infrastructure.
AD Assessment	Assess the risk and health of your Active Directory Directory Services environments.
Alert Management	View or Operations Manager and OMS alerts easily to triage alerts, as well as identify the root causes of problems in your environment.
Change Tracking	Track configuration changes across your servers.
System Update Assessment	Identify missing system updates across your servers.

(See Figures 1-8 and 1-9 to get an idea as to what the Security and Audit Solution Pack dashboard looks like.)

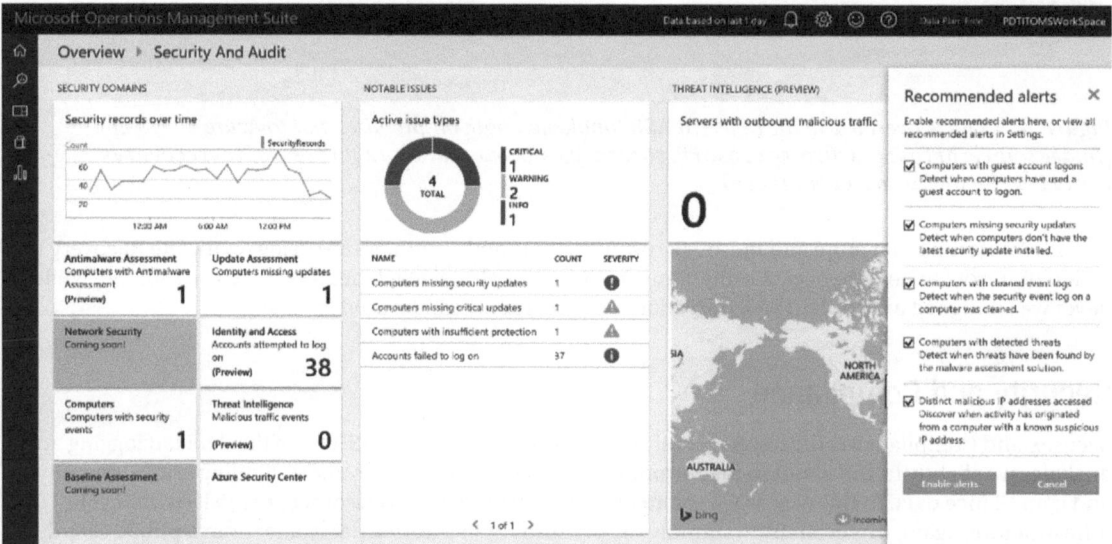

Figure 1-8. *Sample dashboard from the OMS/Security and Audit Solution Pack in my OMS subscription*

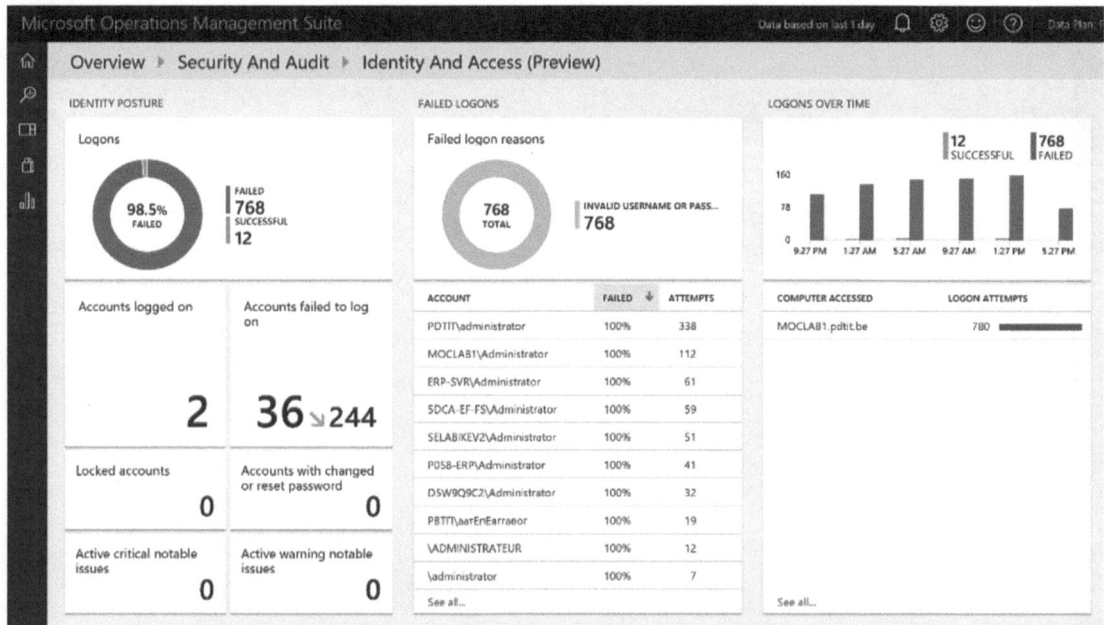

Figure 1-9. *Sample dashboard from the OMS/Security and Audit/Identity and Access tile in my OMS subscription*

It should not be a surprise that this list will get outdated quick, knowing OMS is a Cloud-based product and has a quarterly update cycle. Or even faster. That said, there is a natural overlap between the already mentioned Log Analytics and some of the security and compliance topics. In the end, it doesn't matter that much where exactly you get the information.

While it is not 100% correct, understanding it as Log Analytics gives you access to *all data* gathered by OMS, whereas the Solution Packs—like the security ones mentioned in the table before—could be understood as filtered data. The result will be the same, but it is easier to go to the filtered view than having to create your own custom search queries to find the same data (although it doesn't block you from doing that).

Continuing with this example of the Security and Audit Solution Pack, I could show you how easy it is to use this dashboard. At this top root view, the tiles on the left side contain the condensed information, which is already complete and accurate. If I'm interested in getting more detailed feedback on one of the tiles, it suffices to select one of them (Identity and Access is the example in Figure 1-9), which will bring up another dashboard, exposing more details.

I can now select the Accounts Failed To Log On tile, opening another layer of the dashboard, and giving me an even more granular view (see Figure 1-10).

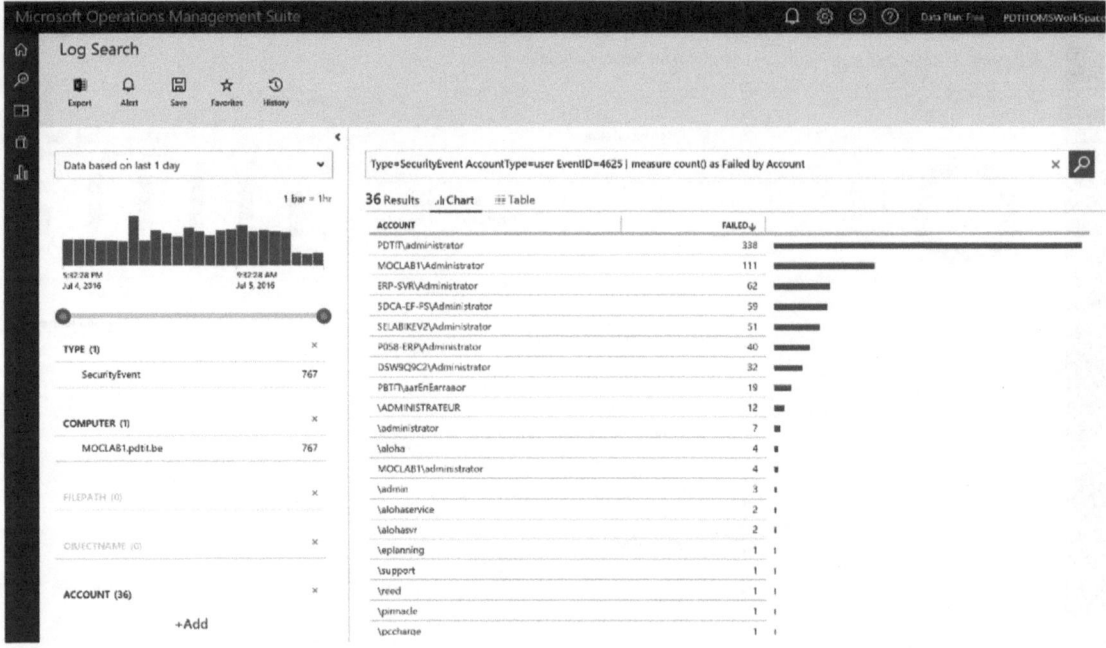

Figure 1-10. *Sample dashboard from the OMS/Security and Audit/Identity and Access/Accounts Failed to Log On tile in my OMS subscription*

■ **Note** As you can see, I'm now at the "lowest" level of detail here, basically using the Log Analytics component of OMS again, which falls back to the following Log Analytics query:

```
Type=SecurityEvent AccountType=user EventID=4625 | measure count() as Failed by Account
```

This shows the beauty and—more important—the ease of use of the Operations Management Suite, its very powerful Log Analytics, and the Solution Packs, and how these all collect and represent data in nice looking and very useful dashboards.

The Operations Management Suite Architecture

Now that I have introduced you to the overall concept of Operations Management Suite and its core capabilities, let's take it one step further and walk through the generic OMS architecture, as outlined in Figure 1-11.

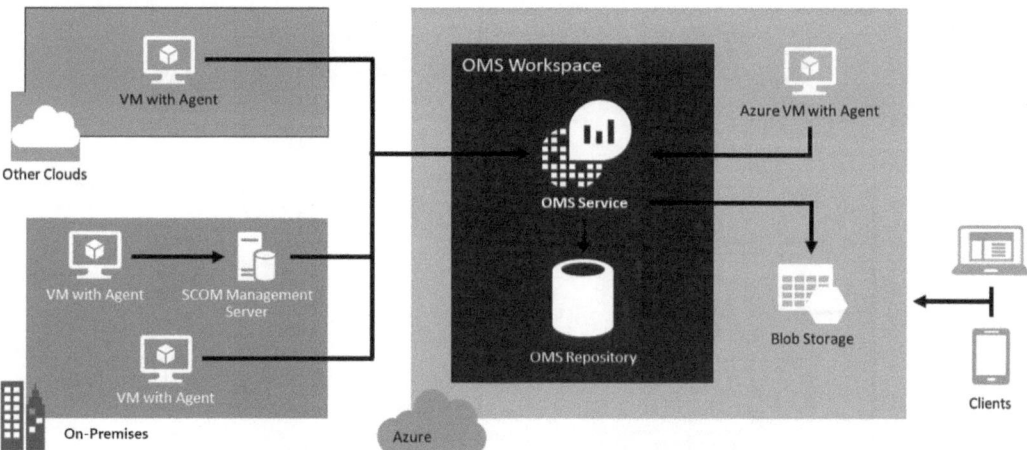

Figure 1-11. *Generic overview of the OMS architecture and its components*

Starting from a conceptual overview, there are three different "data source environments":

- Azure public Cloud providing the OMS Cloud-based service, as well as monitoring VMs that are running in Azure, by using the OMS agent. Another source of data can be an Azure storage account, collecting diagnostics logging from Azure PaaS components like web roles, worker roles, or other components.

- On-premises infrastructure, where the VMs are monitored by using the OMS agent or by integrating with the System Center Operations Manager.

- Third-party Cloud, where the VMs are monitored by using the OMS agent.

Upon starting to use the Operations Management Suite, the first thing you have to do is create an OMS Workspace. This is a unique OMS environment, linked to your Azure administrative account and a pricing schema (see the pricing section at the end of this chapter for more details). Within this OMS Workspace, you define the OMS Repository, different data sources you want to use, the dashboards, and the Solution Packs. It is also possible to create multiple OMS Workspaces to, for example, split Log Analytics data collection and outputs between test/dev/production system environments.

Once the OMS Workspace is set up and the data sources are configured (OMS agents deployed), all data that is being generated by the different connected sources is centrally stored in the OMS Repository, which is hosted in Azure. It is this OMS Repository that is being accessed by the Log Analytics service, giving you real-time insights by using powerful queries and custom dashboards. The Azure architecture "under the hood" looks like the topology in Figure 1-12.

13

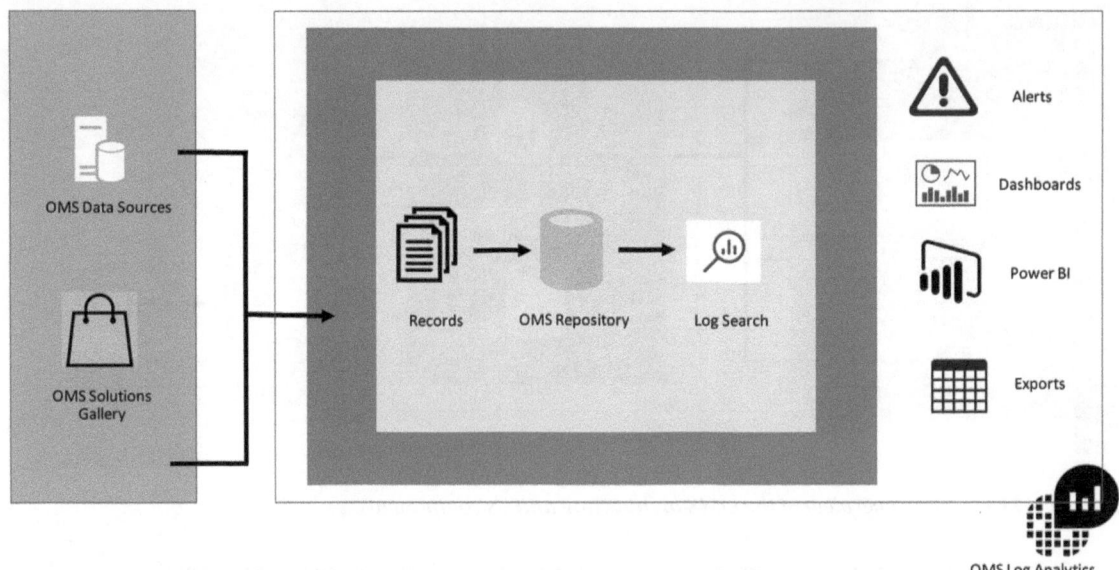

Figure 1-12. *OMS Log Analytics components overview*

The OMS Data Sources point to the server machines (physical servers, virtual machines, or running Windows OS or Linux OS) and other sources (web role, worker role, and so on) generating data, which gets collected by the OMS Repository. These data sources are a combination of events and performance data from the server machines, as well as IIS log files or any other custom log files. It is up to you as the sysadmin to define what information you want to collect. This is configurable during the deployment of the OMS Monitoring Agent on the server machine, or directly from the Azure resource component Log Analytics configuration settings.

Depending on your OMS subscription (see the last section in this chapter for more details on pricing), Log Analytics data is retained in the OMS Repository for seven days, one month, or one year. The output and true analysis of this data is mostly done from the OMS portal, by using preconfigured or custom-built Log Analytics query search functionalities, by using one of the many Solution Packs, or by running detailed data analysis from Power BI or Excel. There is also a Log Search API available if you want to build or integrate with custom solutions in third-party monitoring tools.

Operations Management Suite Pricing

If you are a bit familiar with the Microsoft world of applications and especially with licensing and software agreements, it should not come as a surprise that it is one of the hardest exercises in the overall IT tasks.

Determining the correct licensing and pricing for Operations Management Suite is no different.

To avoid making any mistakes in this section, I recommend consulting the official Operations Management Suite Pricing web site from the following URL:

```
https://www.microsoft.com/en-us/cloud-platform/operations-management-suite-pricing
```

In short, there are two major differences in determining the OMS pricing:

- Operations Management Suite Add-On for System Center

- Operations Management Suite Stand-Alone

OMS Add-On for System Center

If you are already using the Microsoft System Center (2012 R2) Suite, you can immediately benefit from the OMS Add-On, which was announced initially to be valid until July 2015, but got renewed until July 2016.

■ **Caution**   Since this book will be published after July 2016, no guarantee can be given this discounted offer is still valid as you are reading this book.

By licensing this System Center (Standard or DataCenter edition) OMS add-on, you get access to all the new services within OMS, at a convenient step-up price. In short, there is about 25% discount for the System Center OMS add-on compared to the stand-alone licensing cost. With the aforementioned promotional discount, the difference is even 50%. In this scenario of the System Center add-on, you are entitled to use all the OMS components (Log Analytics, Backup, Recovery, and Automation), according to the respective license model you have (see Table 1-1).

Table 1-1. *OMS Licensing Offerings*

	Details on included entitlements	For System Center Standard License	For System Center Datacenter License
Operational Insights	Includes the premium tier, which retains your data for 12 months.	100GB per year	500GB per year
	The annual entitlements listed to the right are prorated monthly. After exceeding the prorated monthly entitlement, overage charges apply at the rates listed below in the stand-alone pricing.		
Backup	Storage is charged separately.	2 VMs	10 VMs
	Backup entitlement can be used for backing up VMs, application servers like Microsoft SQL Server, Exchange, SharePoint, Dynamics, and file servers.		
Site Recovery	Storage, storage transactions, and outbound data transfer are charged separately.	2 VMs	10 VMs
	With the free tier, prices are automatically applied from the 32nd day onward.		
	When purchased during the promotional period ending June 30, 2016, the Operations Management Suite add-on will also include Site Recovery to Azure. Outside the promotional period, it will only include site recovery to customer owned sites.		

(continued)

Table 1-1. (*continued*)

	Details on included entitlements	For System Center Standard License	For System Center Datacenter License
Process Automation	The annual entitlements listed to the right are prorated monthly. After exceeding the prorated monthly entitlement, overage charges apply at the rates listed below in the stand-alone pricing.	10,000 min per year	50,000 min per year
Desired State Configuration	The annual entitlements listed to the right are prorated monthly. After exceeding the prorated monthly entitlement, overage charges apply at the rates listed below in the stand-alone pricing.	2 VMs	10 VMs
	Suite price*	$717 per year	$3,585 per year
	40% promotional offer available until June 30, 2016 only.	$430 per year	$2,150 per year
	When purchased separately	$1,138 per year	$5,690 per year

OMS Stand-Alone Pricing

While there are certain benefits of integrating the OMS Cloud service with an on-premises System Center Suite solution, there is nothing wrong in using it as a stand-alone product.

From a pricing perspective, the cost model looks a bit different than when using the OMS System Center add-on approach. Instead of getting access to all OMS features at once, it is up to you to decide what feature(s) you want to use, and the licensing is more of a "per item" level, as shown in Table 1-2.

Table 1-2. *OMS Stand-Alone Pricing Overview*

Operational Insights (Premium Tier)	$3.50 per GB
Backup	Starting at $10 per VM/month
Site Recovery to Customer Owned Sites	$16 per VM/month
Site Recovery to Azure	$54 per VM/month
Process Automation	$0.002 per min
Desired State Configuration	$6 per VM/month

(Each service is priced either per virtual machine, per GB of ingested data, or per minute of service consumption.)

OMS Components Free licensing

What I also wanted to mention here is the fact that certain OMS components are available in a free tiered licensing model as well. This is the ideal way to start using OMS immediately as a trial, to see what features and components can be of use in your specific situation.

In most cases, you can use the full feature set of OMS, where the limitation is set on the amount of ingested data, the retention setting on how long the data is kept in the OMS Repository (seven days in case of the free tier) or the number of VMs involved. For more details, look at Table 1-3.

Table 1-3. *OMS Component Overview for the "Free" Edition*

Operational Insights	Includes the premium tier, which retains your data for 12 months.	500MB per day with a seven-day retention period
	The annual entitlements listed to the right are prorated monthly. After exceeding the prorated monthly entitlement, overage charges apply at the rates listed below in the stand-alone pricing.	
Site Recovery	Storage, storage transactions, and outbound data transfer are charged separately.	First 31 days of every protected instance
	With the free tier, prices are automatically applied from the 32nd day onward.	
	When purchased during the promotional period ending June 30, 2016, the Operations Management Suite add-on will also include Site Recovery to Azure. Outside the promotional period, it will only include site recovery to customer owned sites.	
Process Automation	The annual entitlements listed to the right are prorated monthly. After exceeding the prorated monthly entitlement, overage charges apply at the rates listed below in the stand-alone pricing.	500 min per month
Desired State Configuration	The annual entitlements listed to the right are prorated monthly. After exceeding the prorated monthly entitlement, overage charges apply at the rates listed below in the stand-alone pricing.	5 nodes per month

■ **Note**   OMS Backup is not available in the Free tier.

In this first chapter, I introduced you to Operations Management Suite (OMS), including what features it can provide, and why monitoring and management of your IT infrastructure in general is critical to the business.

I explained the different components that are available in the current OMS suite, described the OMS solution architecture, and guided you through the highlights of licensing.

In the next chapter, we will take it a lot more technical. I describe how you can start using OMS, by creating an OMS Workspace, guiding you through the deployment of OMS agents and configuring Azure data sources. Lastly, I will show you how to use the Log Analytics Search functionality, how to enable different Solution Packs, and how to use the OMS dashboards.

CHAPTER 2

■ ■ ■

Deploying OMS: Monitoring in the Cloud

After the introduction to Operations Management Suite (OMS from this point on) in the previous chapter, I can imagine you are eager to dive into the technology and start deploying OMS right away. If you skipped Chapter 1, I recommend you at least take some time to go through it, as it contains interesting information about the different features OMS can provide, its architecture, and how licensing works. Being a technical guy myself, I know how tempting it is to skip the introduction and boring licensing information, but as an architect, I understand how important that aspect is for the overall success of the technical implementation.

Anyway, I promised a more technical chapter, so here we go...

In this chapter, I will guide you through the technical deployment of OMS in several ways. Obviously, I will show you how to create your own OMS Workspace, followed by showing you how to deploy the OMS agent on both a Windows Operating System and a Linux server. Next to that, I will guide you through the configuration of Log Analytics for an Azure component like Web Apps.

Once we have the OMS Log Analytics components running, we move over to the Solution Packs area. I will show you how you can add several of these Solution Packs to your OMS Workspace. Next to the preconfigured ones, I will also guide you through the basics of creating your own custom Solution Packs.

When all that is up and running, we will dive into using the Log Analytics query search, showing you first of all how easy it is, but also how intuitive and powerful. You will become more and more familiar with the Log Search by going through the examples I use Log Analytics results into Visual Studio OMS Mobile App.

■ **Note** The examples I use throughout this book for both OMS and Azure VMs can all be executed by using the free/trial versions. So no more excuses! That said, don't forget you can also use OMS against on-premises running VMs, so there is no specific need to use Azure VMs. It's just easier if you don't have an on-premises environment available.

© Peter De Tender 2016
P. De Tender, *Implementing Operations Management Suite*, DOI 10.1007/978-1-4842-1979-9_2

Creating the OMS Workspace

Although this might sound obvious, you need an active Azure subscription, as well as administrative access to this subscription, before being able to create the OMS Workspace following these steps.

1. Once the Azure subscription is configured, or if you already have an Azure administrative account available, connect to the Microsoft OMS landing page:

   `http://www.microsoft.com/oms`

   It should look something like Figure 2-1 (unless Microsoft changes the web site in meantime).

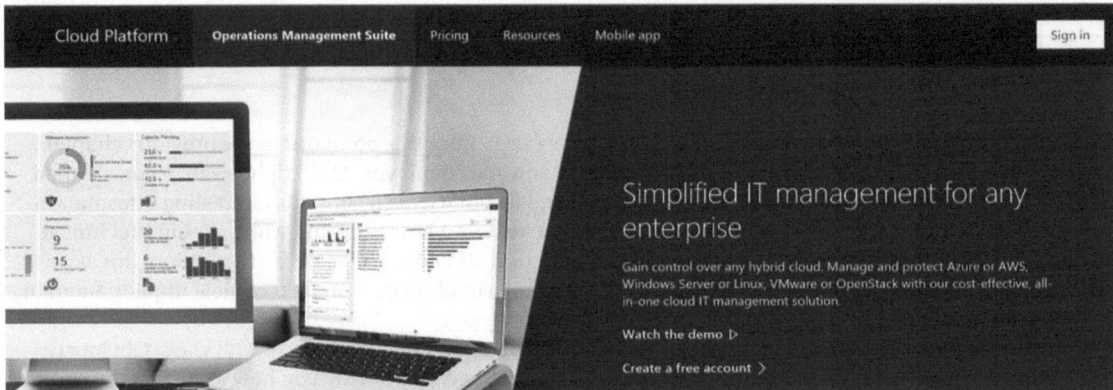

Figure 2-1. *Microsoft Operations Management Suite landing web page*

2. From here, click Create a Free Account.

3. This will redirect you to the Azure login form; after successfully logging in with the Azure admin credentials, you are redirected to the Create New Workspace form, where you have to enter some personal and company related info, as shown in Figure 2-2.

Figure 2-2. Create New Workspace form

4. After completing this form and clicking the Create button, you are asked to select the Azure subscription you want to link to this OMS Workspace, as shown in Figure 2-3.

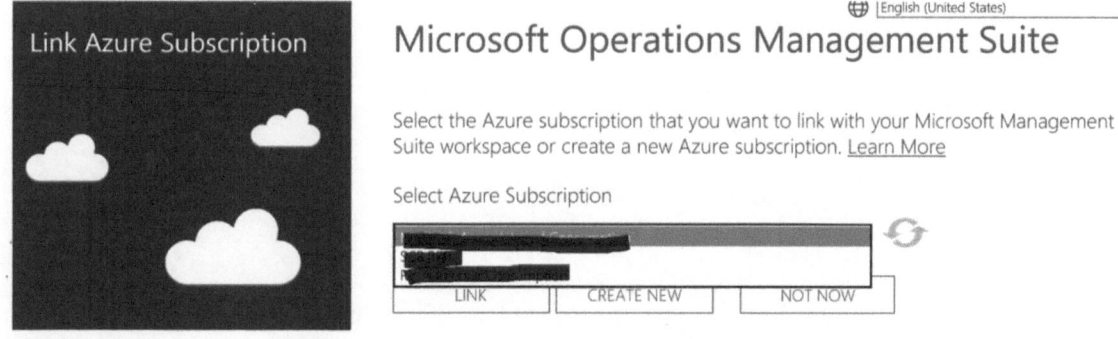

Figure 2-3. Link Azure Subscription page

■ **Note**   You can use any name you want for the OMS Workspace, as long as it is unique to OMS. If the name is already in use, the portal will block you from using it.

5.   Click the Link button. This is the final step in creating your OMS Workspace. After a few seconds, you are redirected to your OMS dashboard, which should look like the one in Figure 2-4.

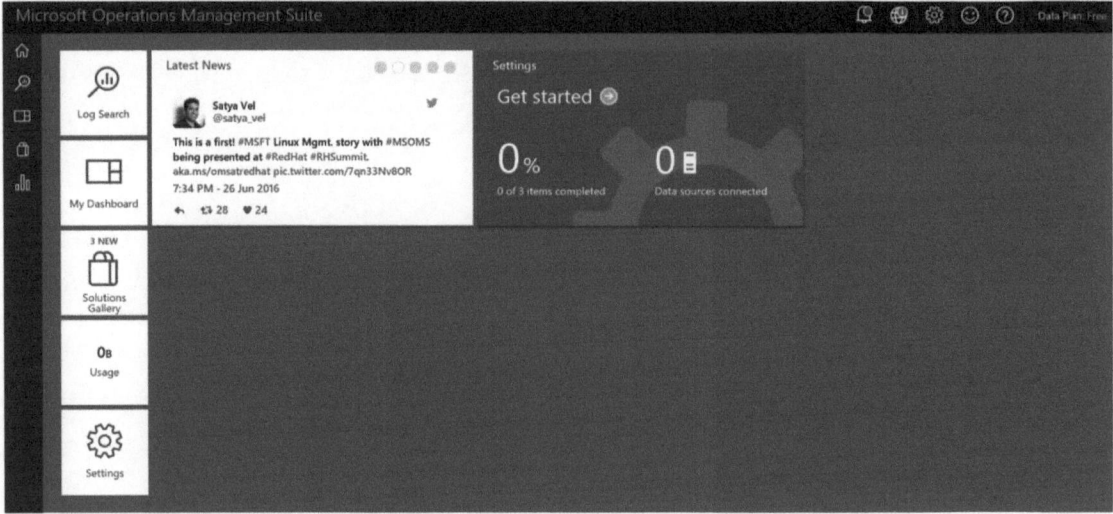

Figure 2-4. Newly created OMS dashboard

Besides the creation of the OMS Workspace and fresh dashboard, you should also have received an e-mail to the mailbox account that is linked to your Azure subscription, asking you to confirm the e-mail address to the OMS Workspace. Look at Figure 2-5 for the e-mail I received (sender was noreply@oms. microsoft.com in my case).

Hey Peter

We have received a request to add this email address
to a Microsoft Operations Management Suite account.
Please click "Confirm Now" to let us know that is okay
to add this email address to this account.

Confirm Now (→)

The Microsoft Operations Management Suite Team

Microsoft

Microsoft respects your privacy. Please read our online **Privacy Statement**.
This message from Microsoft is an important part of a program, service, or
product that you or your company purchased to participate in.

Microsoft Corporation, One Microsoft Way, Redmond, WA 98052 USA

Figure 2-5. *E-mail address needs to be confirmed*

6. Clicking the Confirm Now button in the e-mail will also redirect you to the OMS
   Workspace. It is required to do so, even though the OMS Workspace is already
   created successfully from the previous steps.

This completes the steps that are needed to successfully create an OMS Workspace.

Initial Configuration of the OMS Workspace

Now the OMS Workspace is successfully created, you can continue the configuration of the OMS Workspace
by going through some basic settings that need to be defined first, before you start using the solution.

1. From the OMS Workspace dashboard (see Figure 2-4), click the Settings - Getting
   Started tile.

   This brings you to the Settings dashboard, as you can see in Figure 2-6.

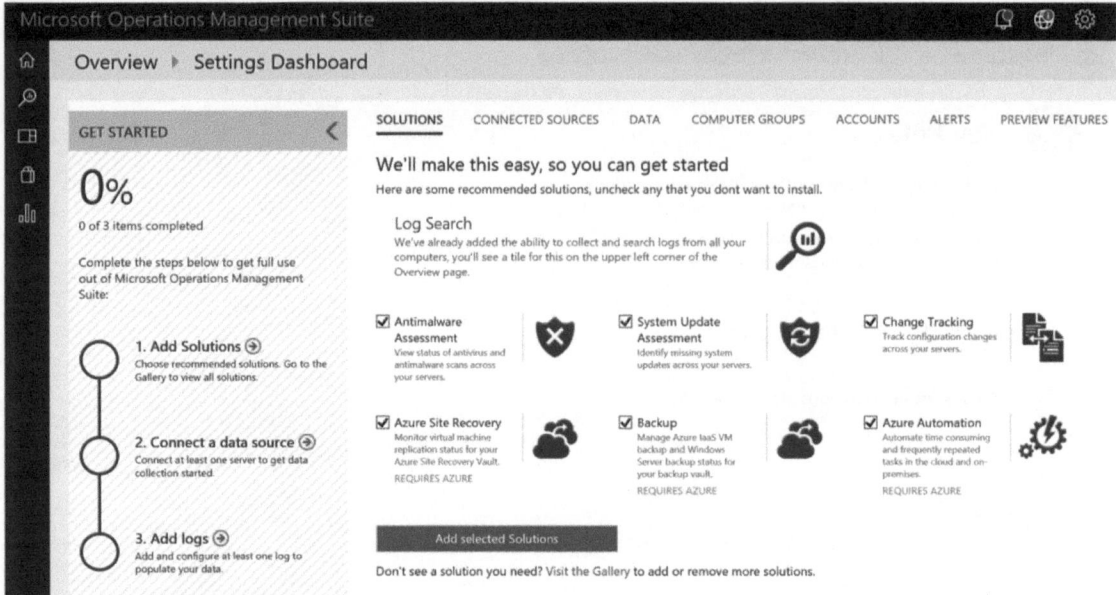

Figure 2-6. *OMS Settings dashboard*

Here, you must go through a three-step based scenario, as you can see in Figure 2-7, to complete the base configuration. In the first step, you add several solutions to the Workspace, followed by connecting with multiple data sources. In the last step, you define how and which logs need to be saved for retrieval later.

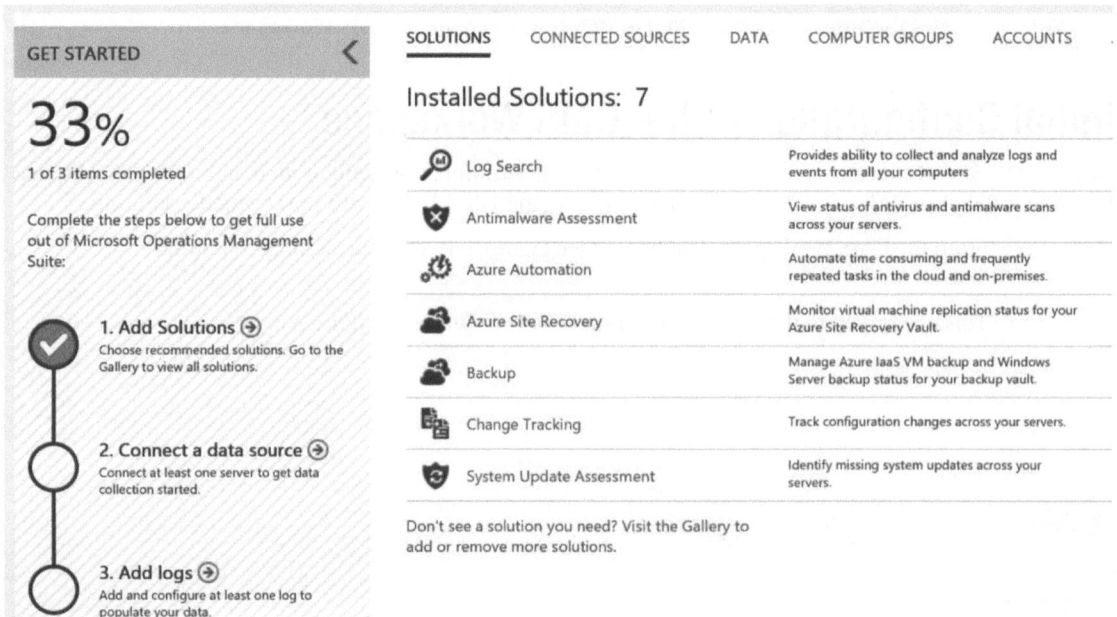

Figure 2-7. *OMS Workspace settings—solutions have been added to the Workspace*

Notice several solutions, like Antimalware Assessment, Change Tracking, Backup, and some others that are already selected so they can be added to your Workspace.

2. Confirm the addition of these solutions by clicking the Add Selected Solutions button.

This will result in a green marked step for Step 1 - Add Solutions, as well as a switched view in the OMS Console, as shown in Figure 2-7.

We will skip Step 2 (connect a data source) for now, as this will be covered in the next section. (In a real-life scenario, it would be logical to deploy the agent first and then configure the log settings in Step 3.)

This brings us to Step 3, where we will define parameters and settings related to log files. This shows the different log counters that can be retrieved and stored in the backend database. Notice the Windows and Linux Performance counters; they are selected by default already.

1. Select IIS Logs and activate the option to Collect W3C format IIS Logs.

2. Go back to Windows Event Logs; notice that nothing is selected yet.

3. In the Enter the Name of an Event Log to Monitor field, enter `Microsoft-` (be sure to include the dash). This will present a full list of Microsoft-related event logs, as you can see in Figure 2-8.

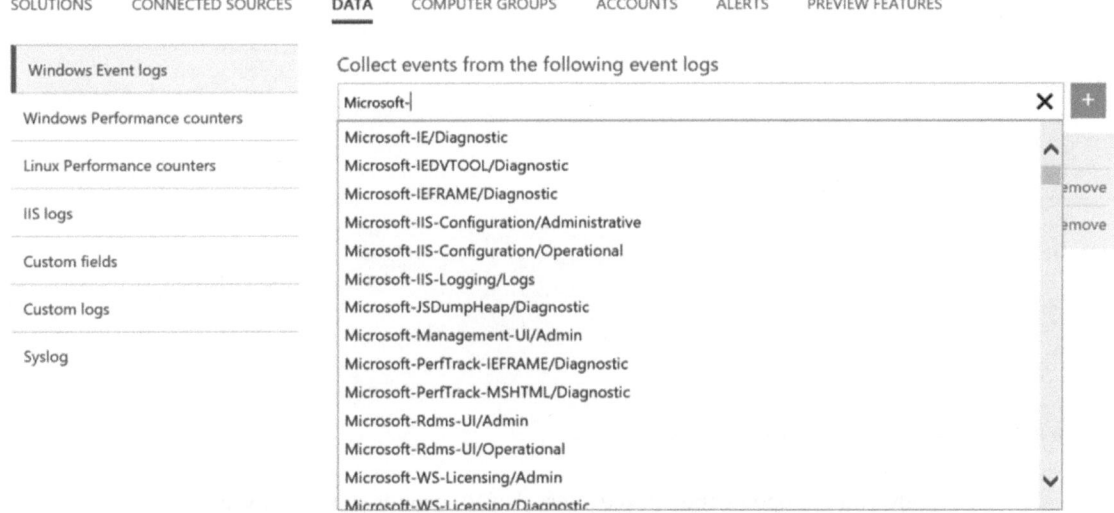

Figure 2-8. *Selecting the Microsoft event logs you want to collect events from*

4. Select an event from the list so it is completed in the text box, and click the blue + sign. This will add it to the list of selected event logs. Optionally, you can deselect the Error or Warning or Information events from being logged.

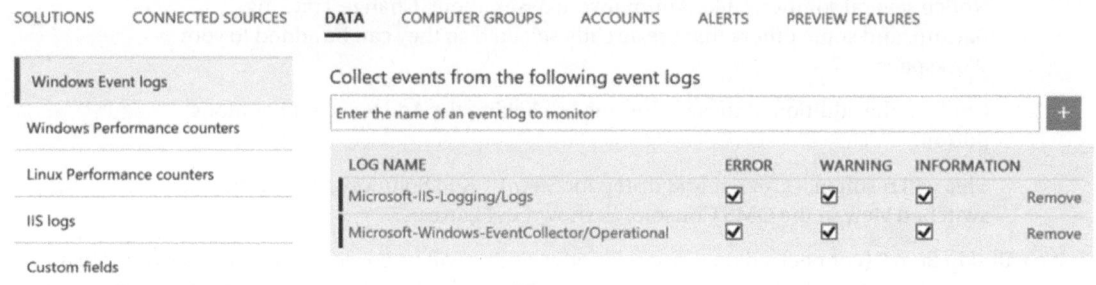

Figure 2-9. *Adding Windows event logs*

5. Feel free to add several event logs to the list.

6. Select Windows Performance Counters. Notice that all the counters that are available are selected by default. Click the Add the Selected Performance Counters button, as shown in Figure 2-10.

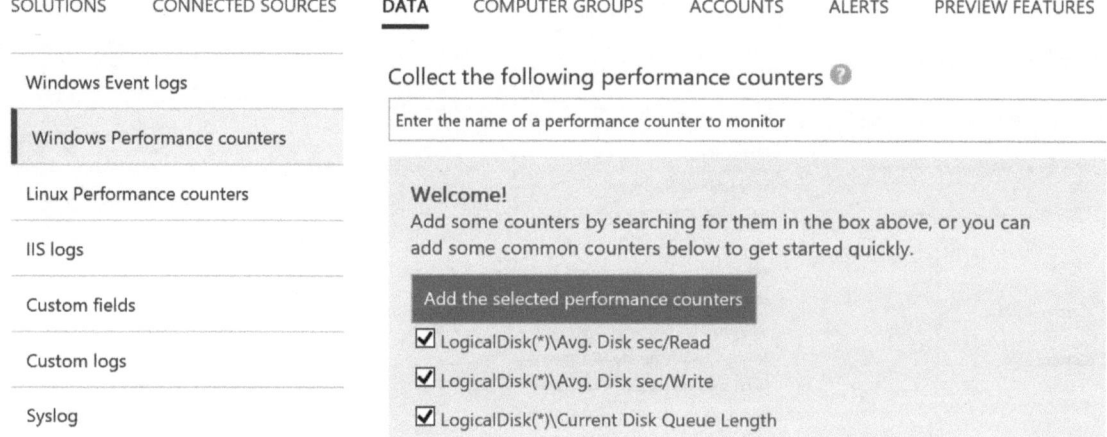

Figure 2-10. *Selecting performance counters*

7. Optionally, you can update the sample interval of 10 seconds to another value, but it is not required.

8. Select the Linux Performance counters. Notice that all counters that are available are selected by default. Click the Add the Selected Performance Counters button.

9. Make sure to save your settings by clicking the Save button in the upper-left corner of the window (see Figure 2-11).

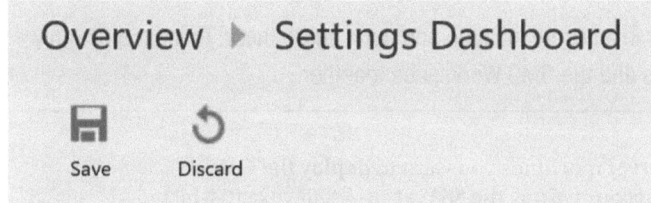

Figure 2-11. *Save the selected event log settings you have configured*

This completes the initial configuration settings walkthrough of the OMS Workspace settings.

Deploying the OMS Agent to a Windows Server

In this section, you log in to one of your Windows Server machines you have available and deploy the OMS agent.

1. From the OMS dashboard, go to Settings. Select Connected Sources in the top menu.

2. Download the Windows and/or Linux agents to your management workstation. Also take note of the Workspace ID and the Primary and Secondary keys. (See Figure 2-12 for an example.)

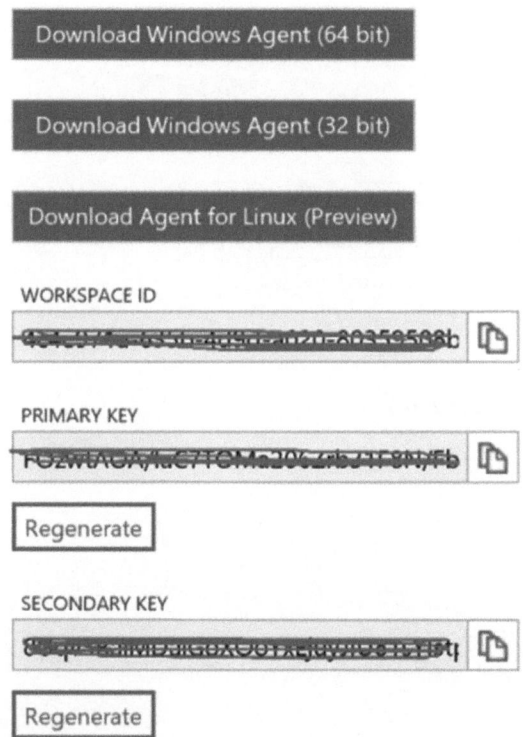

Figure 2-12. *OMS agent download options, including Workspace ID and keys*

■ **Tip**   Store your Workspace ID and both keys in a secure location and don't share them. These are the only parameters needed to link both managed clients and the OMS Workspace together.

3. Log on to one of your Windows Server machines you want to deploy the OMS agent to, using an administrative account. Copy the MMASetup-AMD64.exe (64-bit) or MMASetup-i386.exe (32-bit) to this server.

4. Run the MMASetup-exe file with administrative rights (see Figure 2-13).

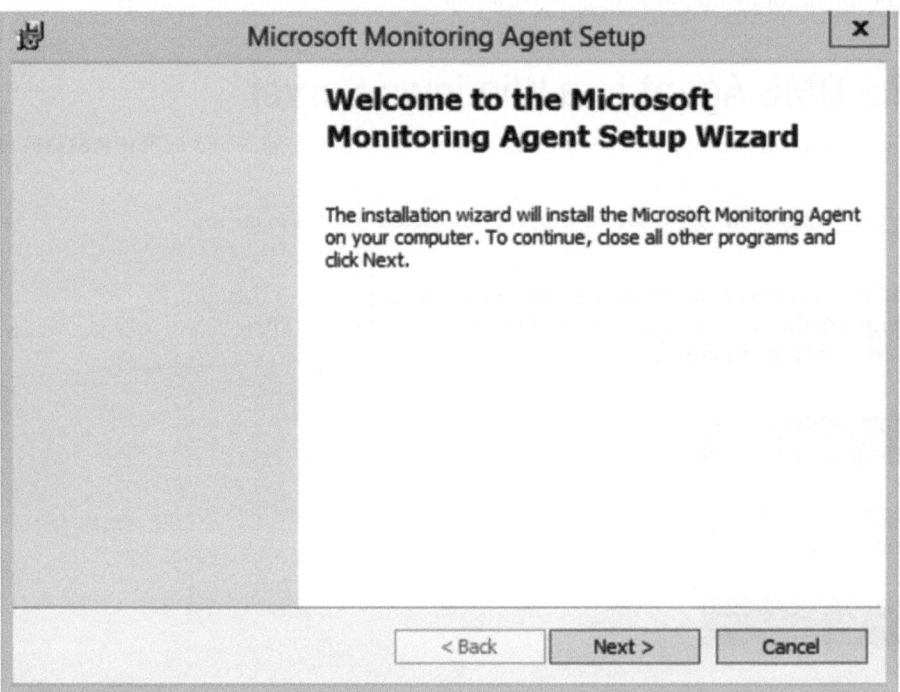

Figure 2-13. Starting the MMASetup.exe

5. Click Next, which shows the license terms (see Figure 2-14).

Figure 2-14. *Agree with Microsoft Software License Terms*

6. Click the I Agree button.

7. Click Next, which shows you the default installation folder, as shown in Figure 2-15.

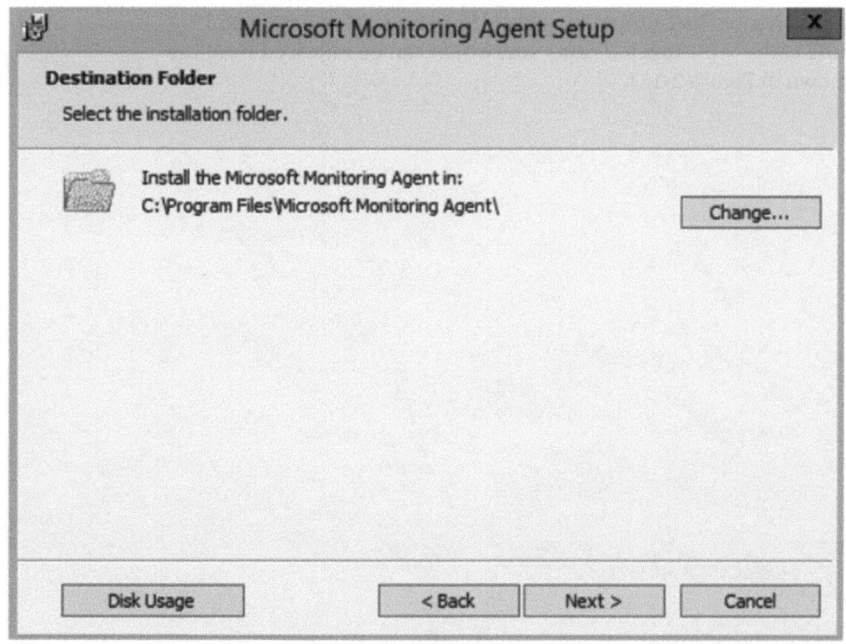

Figure 2-15. *Select the OMS Agent Installation folder of your choice*

8. When you click Next, the Agent Setup Options are shown. Here you define if it is an OMS stand-alone agent or is integrated with SCOM (see Figure 2-16).

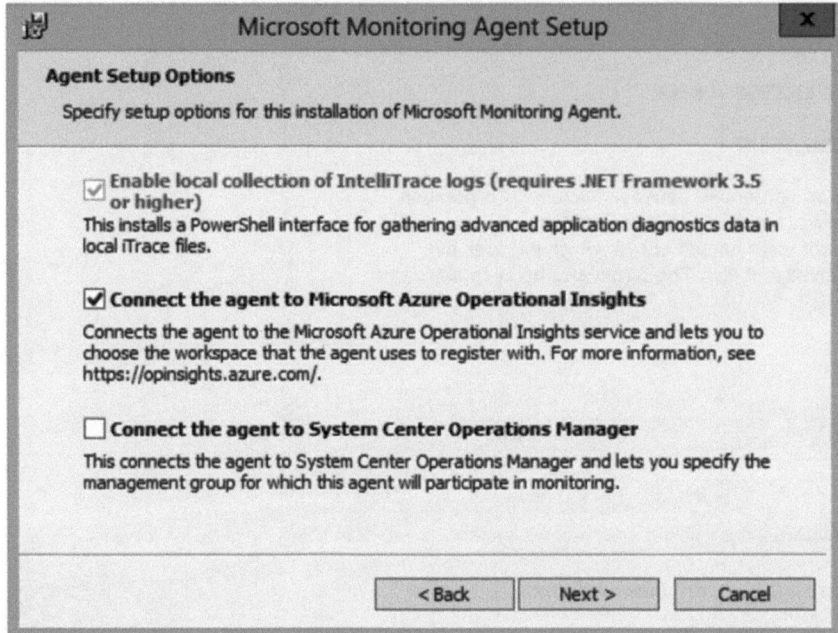

Figure 2-16. *Make sure Connect the Agent to Microsoft Azure Operational Insights is selected*

9. Click Next to see the Azure Operational Insights information. Most important here is taking note of the Workspace ID and Key, which can be retrieved from the Azure portal (shown in Figure 2-17).

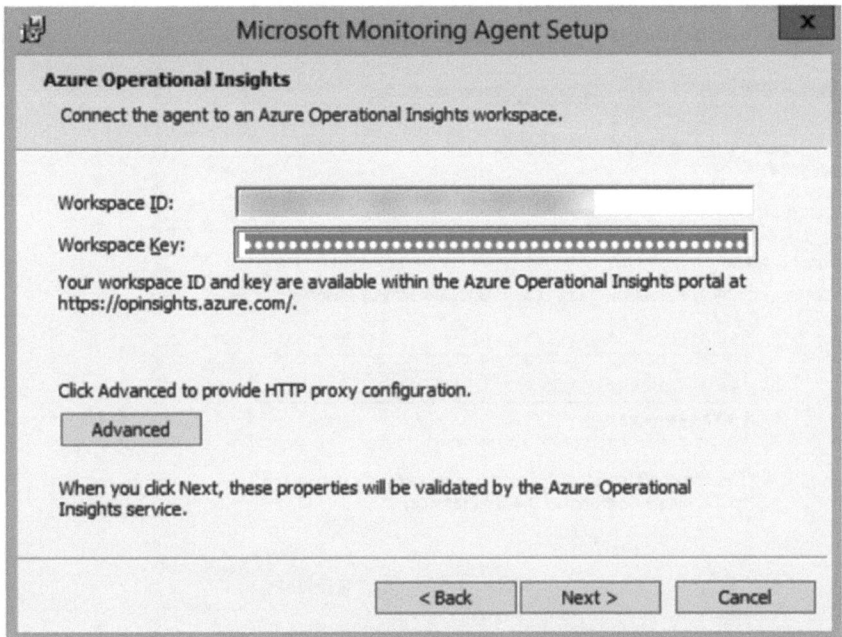

Figure 2-17. *Enter your OMS Workspace ID and primary key*

10. Click Install and wait for the setup to be completed.

11. Click Finish to close the installation wizard.

This completes the installation of the OMS agent on a Windows Server machine.

■ **Note**   At the time of writing, the OMS Agent for Linux was in technical preview. If you are interested in deploying it in your environment, look at the section "Deploying the OMS Agent on Linux Server Operating System" later in this chapter.

Verifying the OMS Agent Settings on a Windows Server

To verify the configuration settings of an already installed OMS agent, or to find out what Workspace ID it is connecting to, use the following steps:

1. From the Windows Server machine, open the Control Panel in the classic view. (If you can't find it under Control Panel, the default installation path is c:\ Program Files\Microsoft Monitoring Agent, from where you can launch the exe file.)

2. Click Microsoft Monitoring Agent.

3. Click the Azure Operational Insights tab.

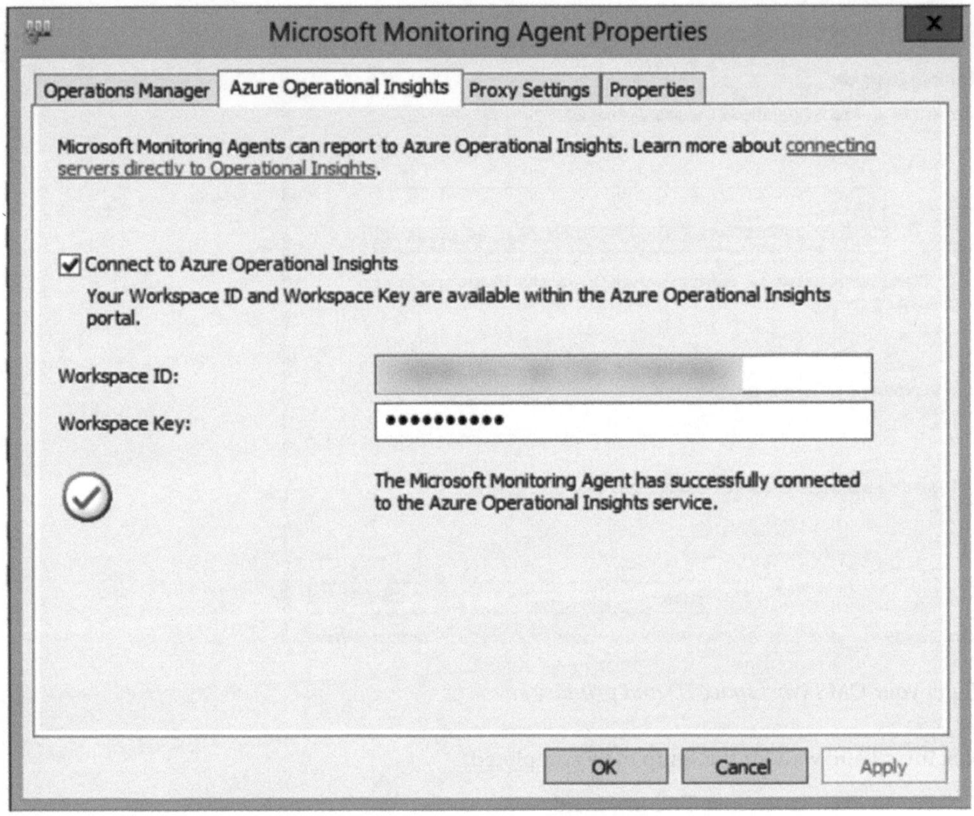

Figure 2-18. Make sure Connect to Azure Operational Insights is checked

As long as your monitored servers are having an HTTPS connection to the OMS Workspace environment, they should report fine to the OMS backend. Sometimes a page refresh might be required to verify that the agent connects to OMS.

To verify this from within the OMS Workspace, using the following steps:

1. Log on to the OMS Workspace and go to Settings.

2. Select Connected Sources in the top menu.

3. Notice the number of servers that are connected.

4. Click on the connected server.

5. This brings you to the detailed view dashboard for this particular machine(s), as is visible in Figure 2-19.

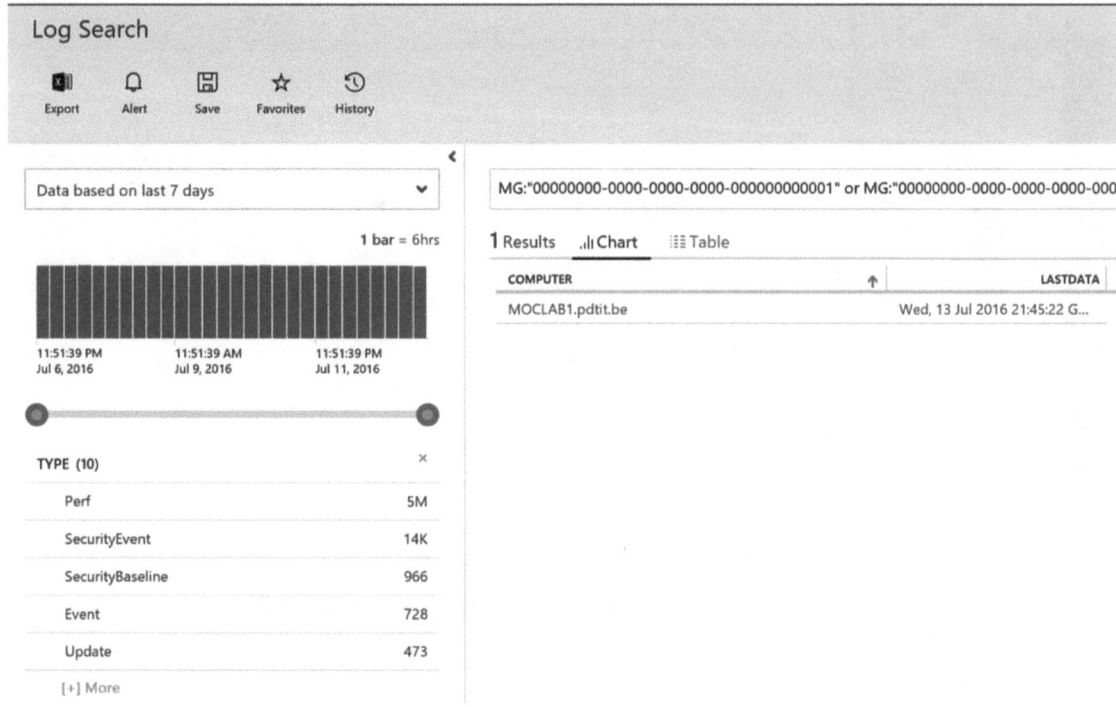

Figure 2-19. *Detailed view of connected server(s) to the OMS Workspace*

Adding OMS Solution Packs to the Dashboard

At this stage, you have a working OMS Workspace, you have configured several event log settings, and have deployed an OMS Agent to a Windows Server machine. Before analyzing the Log Search functionality of OMS, I will show you how to add OMS Solution Packs (tiles and filters) to the OMS dashboard.

1. From within the OMS dashboard, select Solutions Gallery.

2. This will show you a full list of currently available Solution Packs, as shown in Figure 2-20.

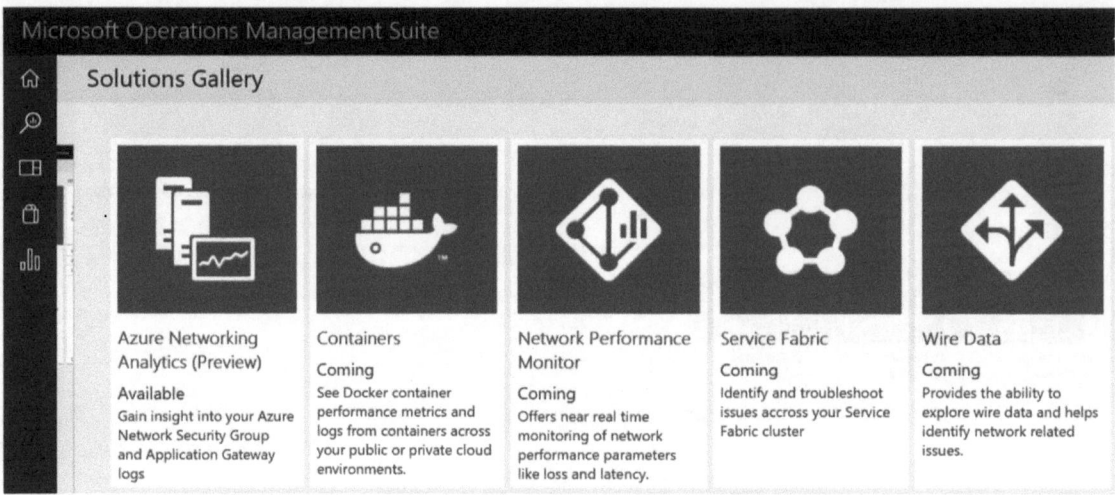

Figure 2-20. Solutions Gallery

3. Select any of the available Solution Packs, which will open a more detailed information page about this Solution Pack.

4. Click the Add button.

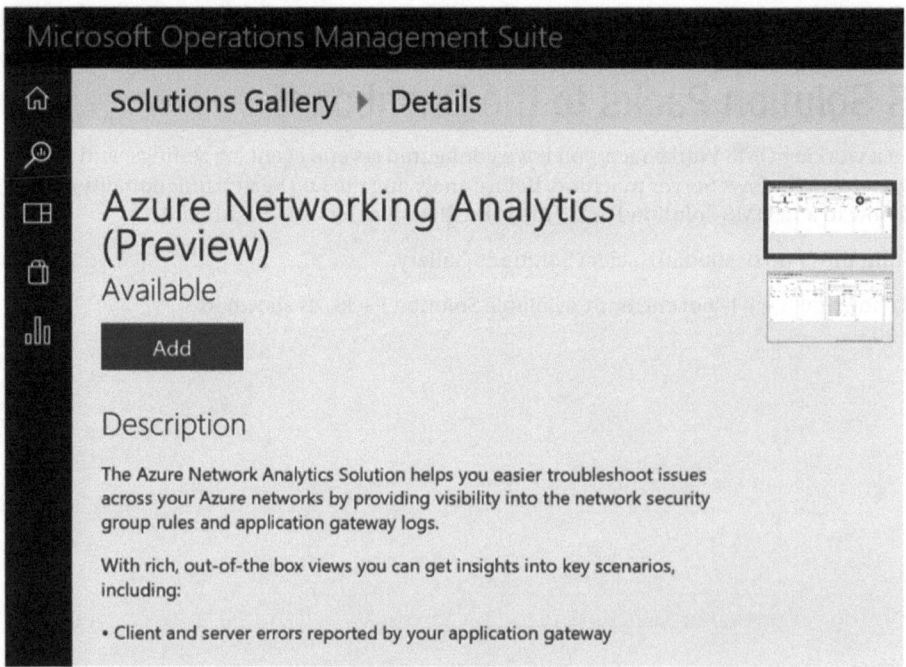

Figure 2-21. Solution Pack details and installation

5.   Select a few other Solution Packs from the list and add them to your OMS
     Workspace. The result should look similar to my demo configuration in Figure 2-22.

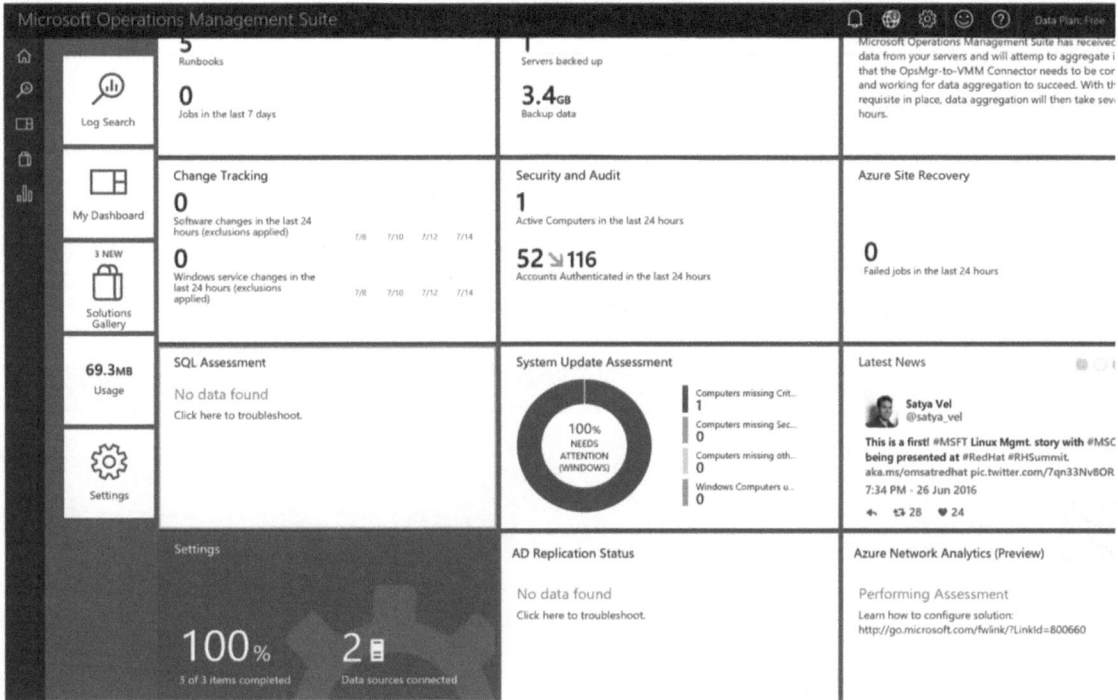

Figure 2-22. *Customized OMS Workspace with several Solution Packs*

This completes the configuration of the OMS Workspace and adding Solution Packs.

Analyzing OMS Information and Using Log Search

Log Search

From the previous steps, you now have a fully working OMS environment set up, which is gathering event log information from different sources in your network.

■ **Note**   I explained before how to deploy the OMS agent to a single Windows server machine, but nothing blocks you from deploying OMS agents to multiple servers in your environment, running on-premises, in Microsoft Azure, or anywhere else. The only communication required is HTTPS from the OMS-managed machine to Azure.

In this section, I guide you through several examples on how to use the powerful OMS Log Search function to perform detailed OMS data analysis. For that, I will start from the Log Search option, digging deeper into the analysis feature by going over several "typical" Solution Packs and showing you how to analyze the data from them.

■ **Note**   These examples will never be complete, as it all depends on what Solution Packs you deployed and what operating systems you are running in your environment. However, they should give you more than enough information to go out and explore the power of OMS, Log Search, and data analysis yourself.

1. Log on to the OMS Workspace dashboard.

2. Click the Log Search button.

3. Become familiar with several sample queries that are documented there.

4. In the search field, type `Computer="name of a Windows Server machine running an OMS agent in your environment"`, where "name..." is the FQDN of the machine. An example from my demo environment is shown in Figure 2-23.

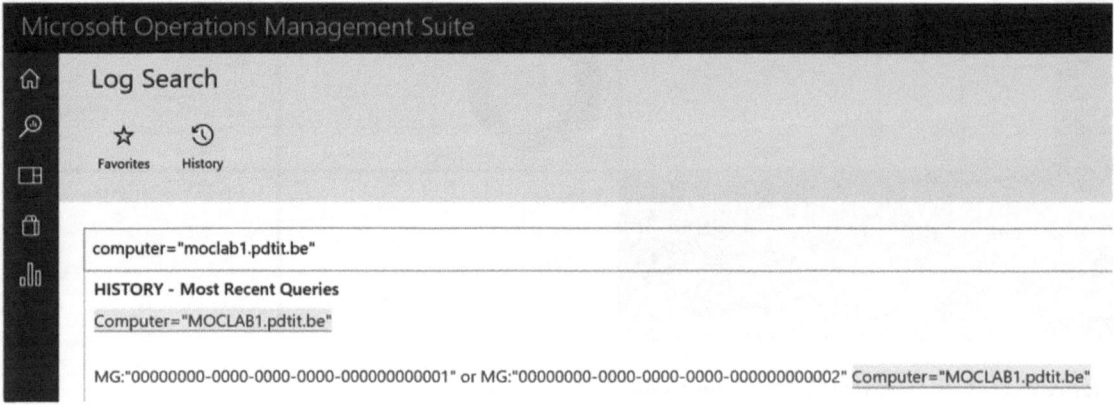

Figure 2-23. *Log Search for a specific computer*

5. Click the Search button.

6. This brings you to the detailed Log Search results for the given Windows machine, as shown in Figure 2-24.

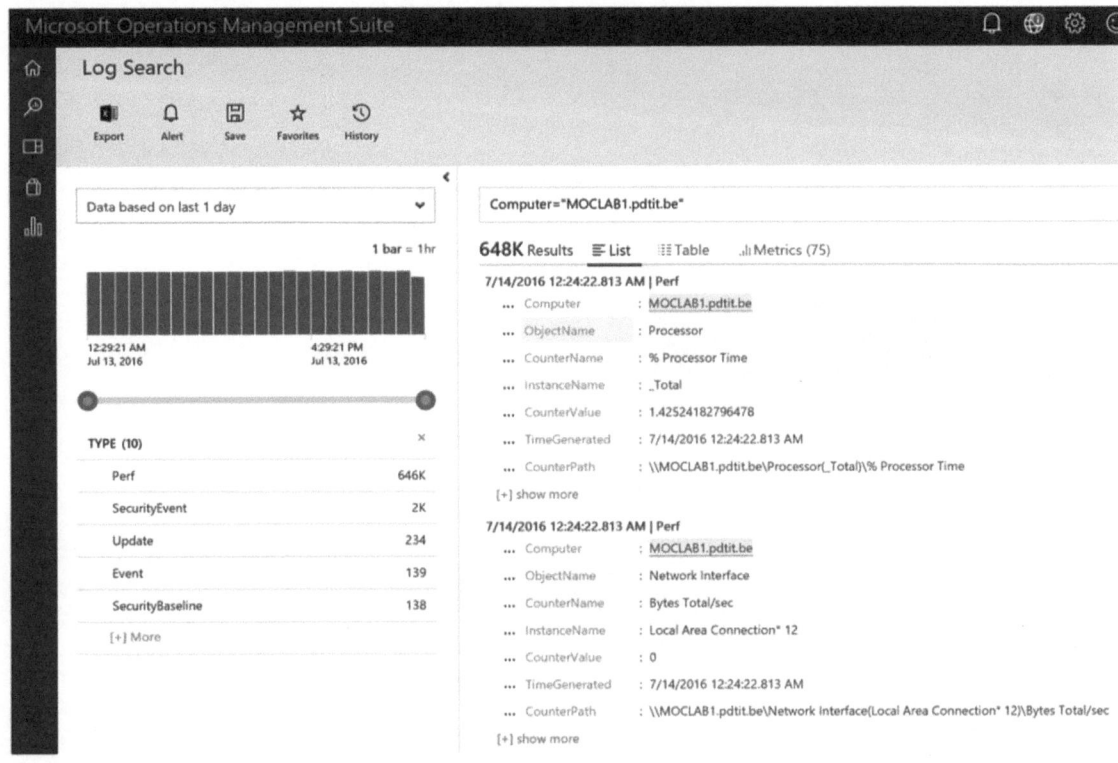

Figure 2-24. *Log results for computer=<servername>*

7. From the detailed list view, select Metrics. This brings up all the details for all available counters you selected, with their logged event information.

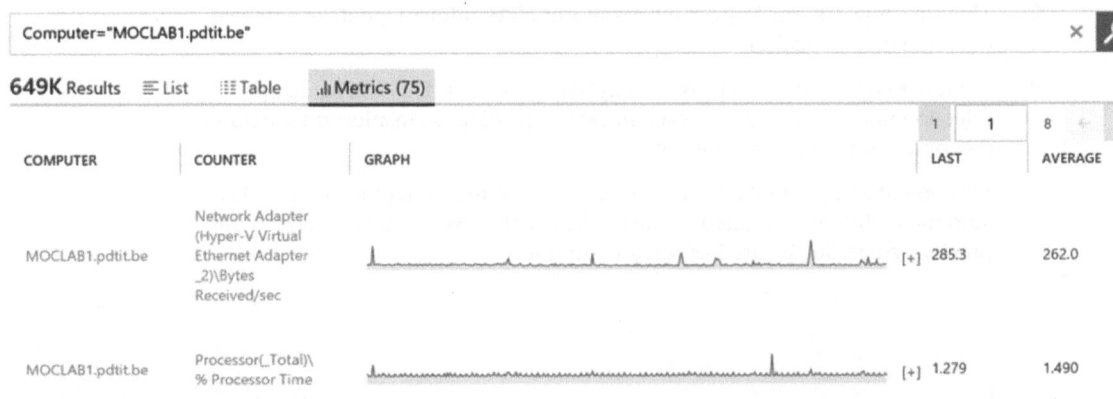

Figure 2-25. *Log Search: metrics for counters*

8. From within the same Log Search result window, select Update in the Type section of the screen (left side) and then click Apply. As this might look a bit different in your environment, look at Figure 2-26 to get an idea as to what to expect.

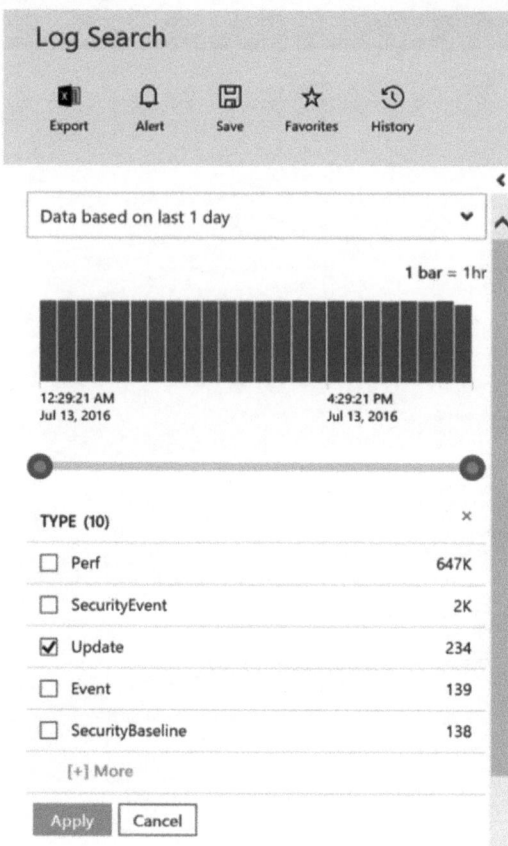

Figure 2-26. *Log Search for the Update Type filter*

9. This will show you the Log Search results for all Windows Update events that occurred on the machine.

10. From the Log Search results, select any field you want. This will bring up selection filters on the left side again. Select any of these results and see how the outcome is immediately different.

11. Also note that the initial Log Search query we started from (computer=...) is automatically being updated too, according to the selections we made in the previous steps. See Figure 2-27 for an example.

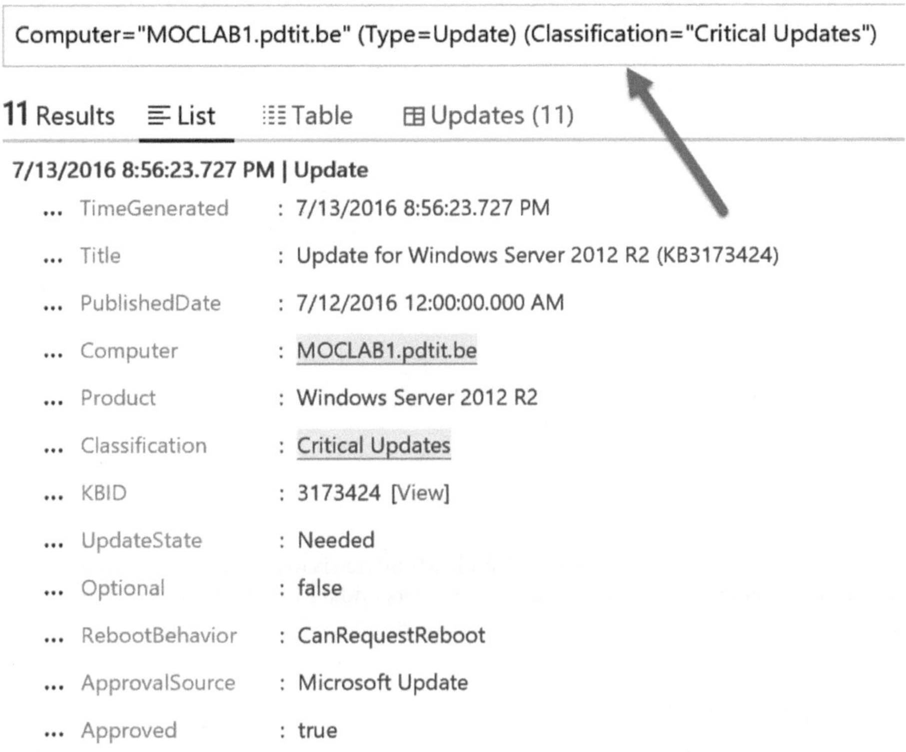

Computer="MOCLAB1.pdtit.be" (Type=Update) (Classification="Critical Updates")

11 Results   ≡ List   ⋮⋮⋮ Table   ⊞ Updates (11)

7/13/2016 8:56:23.727 PM | Update

... TimeGenerated   : 7/13/2016 8:56:23.727 PM

... Title   : Update for Windows Server 2012 R2 (KB3173424)

... PublishedDate   : 7/12/2016 12:00:00.000 AM

... Computer   : MOCLAB1.pdtit.be

... Product   : Windows Server 2012 R2

... Classification   : Critical Updates

... KBID   : 3173424 [View]

... UpdateState   : Needed

... Optional   : false

... RebootBehavior   : CanRequestReboot

... ApprovalSource   : Microsoft Update

... Approved   : true

Figure 2-27. *Log Search query automatically updates based on selections you make in the output results*

12. To avoid needing to redo this search, you can save this for later retrieval, or as a base for modifying future Log Search queries.

13. From the dashboard, click the Save button. This opens up the save selection fields on the right side.

14. Provide a descriptive name for the query. In the Category field, you can add a random description, or select a preconfigured one, like in my example in Figure 2-28

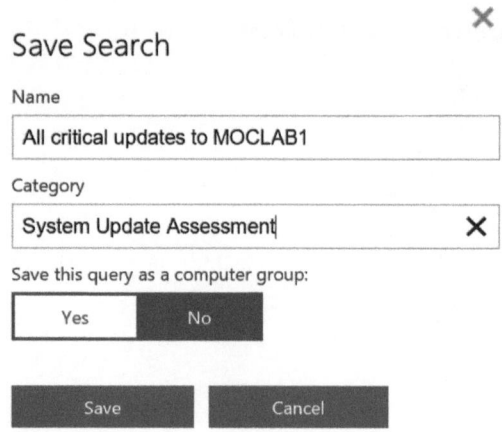

Figure 2-28. *Save Log Search query results for later*

This completes the exercise in which you use the Log Search. My advice is to spend as much time here as possible, clicking around, seeing how the Log Search query gets updated accordingly, and become familiar with the syntax. You'll be amazed with the power!

Solution Packs Data Analysis

Another approach for getting data out of the OMS Repository is by going directly through one of the Solution Packs you installed earlier. In this next example, I will walk you through the Security and Audit Solution Pack as a good example of the strength and level of detail of OMS. Where on the other hand, you will see how easy and intuitive the portal is to work with.

1. From the OMS dashboard, click the Security and Audit Solution Pack tile.

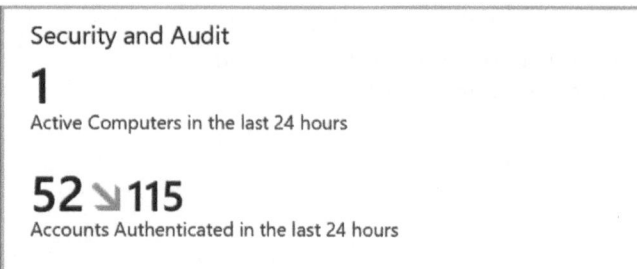

Figure 2-29. *Security and Audit tile*

Notice this tile is already providing you with live data. I can see there is one active computer in my environment, on which 52 accounts performed 115 authentication attempts in the last 24 hours.

Knowing this is a single stand-alone Hyper-V box as demo machine for writing this book, having one administrative user account, this sure looks like we need to investigate a little bit further... let's see what the dashboard exposes as results (see Figure 2-30).

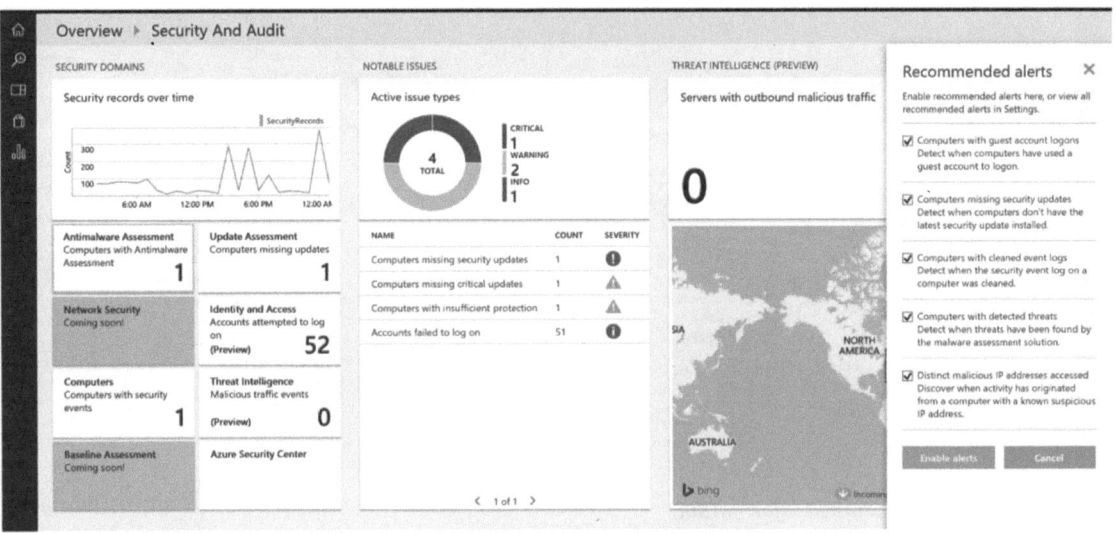

Figure 2-30. *OMS Security and Audit dashboard view*

- On the left side, notice the Security Records Over Time tile, which gives you a clear view of the number of security events logged in the last few days.

- Also on the left side, notice the different tiles with life information. Each of these tiles can be clicked, which will redirect you to a more detailed view.

- In the Notable Issues section in the middle, you see a pie chart with detailed information on different types of activities. Below the pie chart, more information is provided regarding logon attempts. Each of these results can be selected to expose even more granular details.

- Notice the Recommended Alerts section to the right, providing you with several recommended alerts that you can activate by clicking the button.

- Last, you can get a nice view of the world map, detecting from which geographical regions threat attempts occur (this feature was in preview at the time of writing, hence no real data is visible).

2. Select the Account Failed to Log On option in the notable issues section.

3. This redirects automatically to another Log Search query result window, which looks like the example in Figure 2-31.

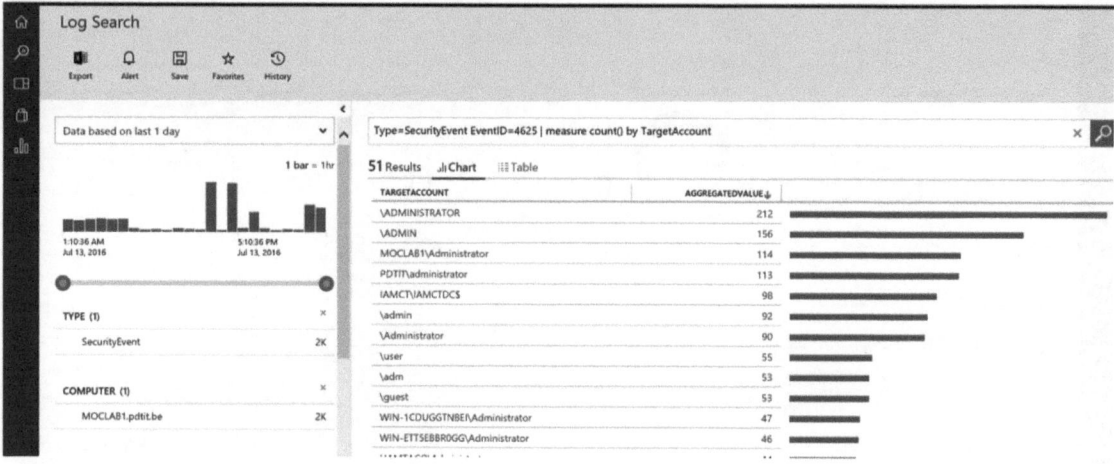

Figure 2-31. *Security detailed information*

4. Go through the output here, and most important, see how the Log Search query is again built up, based on the different selections you made in the different parts of the dashboard within the Security and Audit Solution Pack.

Deploying the OMS Agent to Linux Systems

At the beginning of this chapter, you learned how to deploy the OMS agent to a Windows server and start gathering log information from that machine. As an additional note, I quickly want to walk you through the deployment of the OMS agent on a Linux server system (Ubunto 14.x in my scenario).

1. From the Azure portal, deploy an Ubuntu Server 14.x Virtual Machine (if you don't already have one available).

2. Log on to the Linux server from a Telnet session (I'm using `Putty.exe`), with root admin credentials.

3. Use the following command to download the latest version of the OMS agent for Linux from the GitHub repository (see Figure 2-32 for the output):

   ```
   wget https://github.com/Microsoft/OMS-Agent-for-Linux/releases/download/
   v1.1.0-28/omsagent-1.1.0-28.universal.x64.sh
   ```

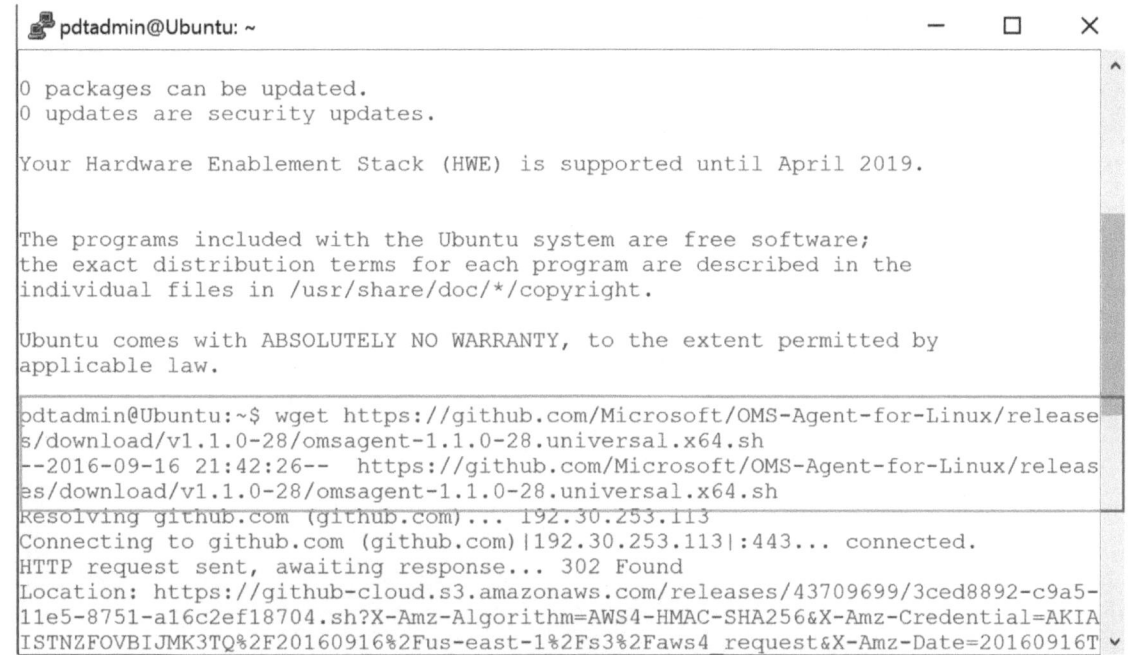

Figure 2-32. Downloading the OMS agent for Linux package on Ubuntu server

4.   Once the download is complete, run the following command to run the actual
     agent installation job. Note you need the OMS Workspace ID and Primary Key
     (which can be retrieved from the OMS/Settings portal). (See Figure 2-33.)

```
sudo sh ./omsagent-1.1.0-28.universal.x64.sh --upgrade -w <YOUR OMS
WORKSPACE ID> -s <YOUR OMS WORKSPACE PRIMARY KEY>
```

```
pdtadmin@Ubuntu: ~                                          —    □    ×

2016-09-16 21:42:30 (25.0 MB/s) - 'omsagent-1.1.0-28.universal.x64.sh' saved [87
664534/87664534]

pdtadmin@Ubuntu:~$ sudo sh ./omsagent-1.1.0-28.universal.x64.sh --upgrade -w  4c
4e971a-63                      } -s zNH2Ad2QwbB0dgGIp
                                                         =
Checking for ctypes python module ...
Extracting...
Updating OMS agent ...
----- Updating package: omi (omi-1.0.8-4.universal.x64) -----
(Reading database ... 28585 files and directories currently installed.)
Preparing to unpack .../omi-1.0.8-4.universal.x64.deb ...
 * Shutting down Open Group OMI Server:                          [ OK ]
Unconfiguring omid service ...
 Removing any system startup links for /etc/init.d/omid ...
   /etc/rc0.d/K20omid
   /etc/rc1.d/K20omid
   /etc/rc2.d/S20omid
   /etc/rc3.d/S20omid
   /etc/rc4.d/S20omid
   /etc/rc5.d/S20omid
   /etc/rc6.d/K20omid
Unpacking omi (1.0.8.4) over (1.0.8.4) ...
```

Figure 2-33. *Installing the OMS agent for Linux package on Ubuntu server*

5. Within a few seconds and after refreshing the OMS portal, I can see that the number of connected sources (my servers) has increased to two servers, as can be seen from Figure 2-34.

Linux Servers

Attach any Linux server or client.

2 SERVERS CONNECTED

Figure 2-34. *Number of connected sources has increased to two in seconds*

6. When clicking on the 2 Servers Connected link, I'm redirected to the Log Search, where I can see that my Ubuntu machine is already generating log information (see Figure 2-35).

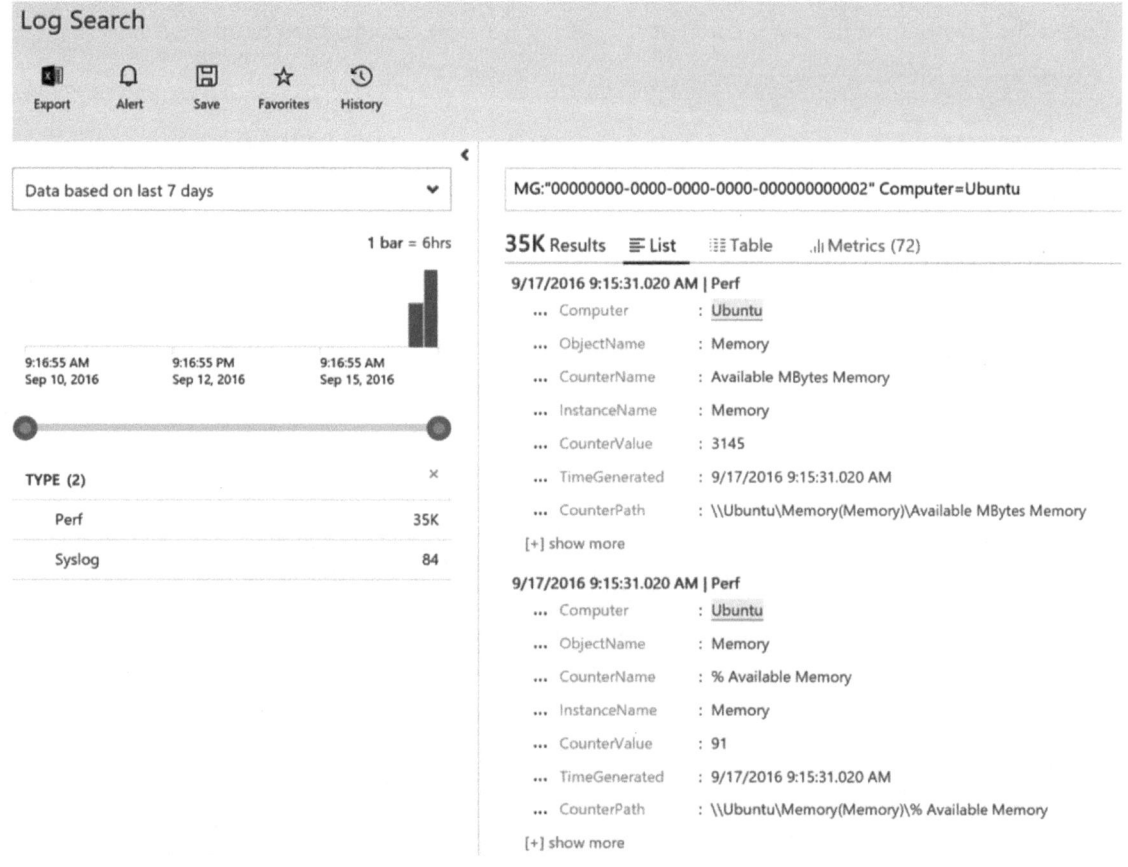

Figure 2-35. *Ubuntu server generating log information*

7. Now how does the OMS agent running on my Ubuntu server know what to capture and send log information for? Just as in the Windows world, you can specify the performance counters that should be used for this. From the OMS Portal/Settings/Data, notice the Linux Performance Counters section, which shows the different performance counters that can be configured, as shown in Figure 2-36.

Collect the following performance counters ❓   ☑ Apply below configuration to my machines

Enter the name of a performance counter to monitor

COUNTER NAME	INSTANCE	SAMPLE INTERVAL	
Logical Disk	*	10 seconds	
% Used Inodes			Remove
Free Megabytes			Remove
% Used Space			Remove
Disk Transfers/sec			Remove
Disk Reads/sec			Remove
Disk Writes/sec			Remove
Memory	*	10 seconds	
Available MBytes Memory			Remove
% Used Memory			Remove
% Used Swap Space			Remove
Processor	*	10 seconds	
% Processor Time			Remove
% Privileged Time			Remove

Figure 2-36. *Linux performance counters that can be configured*

This completes the core configuration of the OMS agent for Linux server operating systems.

The OMS Mobile App

As mentioned in the introduction of this chapter, OMS is not only available from within a web browser, but can also be run from a mobile device (iOS, Android, and Windows Mobile) using a native app.

Obviously, the mobile app doesn't give you 100% functionality as is available from the browser console, bit it does offer a couple of interesting features, up to 90% of the browser portal. (The main difference from the portal version is the mobile app doesn't allow OMS environment configuration changes like adding data sources, for example. It is mainly to be used for consulting and consuming feedback from your environment.)

First of all, there is the quick overview of the monitored infrastructure, showing you a graphical overview of all monitored events. Selecting a data and time shows you all valid results, on to which filters can be applied to fine-tune the search results (see Figure 2-37) and allowing you to dig into Log Search as well.

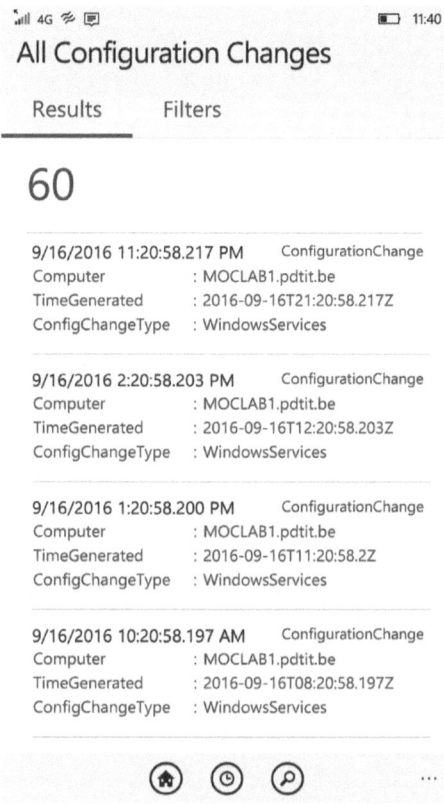

Figure 2-37. *OMS Mobile App log search*

The Solution Pack tiles you have available in the browser portal are identical in the mobile app, visible from the Overview menu. (see Figures 2-38 and 2-39). Selecting one of the Solution Pack tiles will show you a more detailed status (see Figure 2-40).

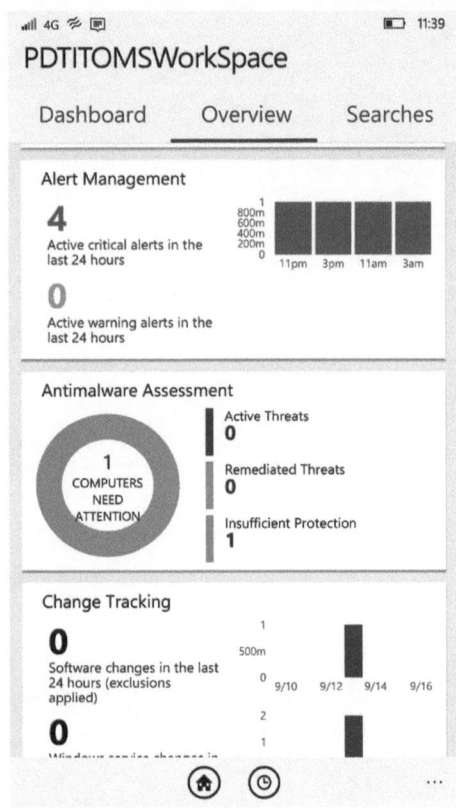

Figure 2-38. *OMS Mobile App Solution Pack tiles*

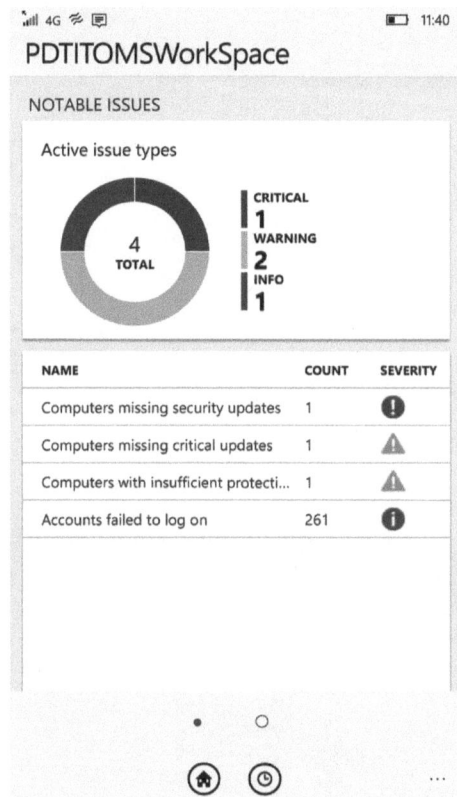

Figure 2-39. *OMS Mobile App Solution Pack tile, detailed view*

Figure 2-40. *Drilling down on the Accounts Failed to Log On option*

While the OMS Mobile App is not the "be all, end all" of the OMS solution, it is a welcome additional and nifty tool for system administrators wanting to get a view on their monitored environment while on the road.

Summary

I assume by now you have a good understanding of the base features and functionalities of OMS, including how the Solution Packs can be integrated and how the Log Search queries can be of help.

There is a lot more to tell about the OMS dashboard and overall monitoring aspects and powerful features, for which I would need another 400 pages to describe all the possibilities.

If you have any specific questions related to OMS, do not hesitate to reach out to me and I'll be happy to answer them.

In the next chapter, I step away a bit from OMS dashboards, guiding you through Azure Backup, which is one of the other core components of OMS.

CHAPTER 3

■ ■ ■

Deploying and Configuring Azure Backup

Welcome to the second big component of the Operations Management Suite, Azure Backup.

When I talk about Azure Backup, I actually should refer to the different kinds of backup, all driven by and integrating with Azure:

- ***Agent-based backup of a Windows machine.*** This can both be a Windows Server Operating System and Windows Client Operating System. This solution plugs into the native Windows Backup application. It can also integrate in an existing System Center Data Protection Manager (SCDPM) infrastructure, where Azure Backup Vault can be selected as the target for backups.

- *Agent-based Enterprise-targeted backup solution for on-premises workloads.* These include Windows Server and Linux, as well as complex application workloads like Exchange, SQL, or SharePoint. This solution is also known as ***Azure Backup Server***, and has a lot of similarities to SCDPM.

- *Full system backup of Azure virtual machines to an Azure Backup Vault, by using Azure-based snapshots and using the Azure VM extensions.* This works for both Windows VMs and Linux VMs.

To make it even a bit more complex to understand, Microsoft refers to this solution as *Recovery*, where they make a distinction between Backup Recovery and Disaster Recovery. Both of them are part of the OMS suite, as discussed in the previous two chapters.

In this chapter, I will start with a general overview section, in which I describe the concepts of Azure Backup, including what is supported and what not. After that, I walk you through the technical deployment and configuration of each "kind of Azure Backup" mentioned here, so you learn by yourself how the technology works.

This chapter will handle the deployment of the Azure Backup agent, where Chapter 4 will discuss Azure Backup Server, and finally in Chapter 5, you will learn about configuring Azure VM backups by using the Azure VM extension.

Introduction to Azure Backup

I started investigating Azure Backup about three years ago, when it was first available in preview in the Azure classic portal. I dedicated numerous workshops to it, spoke about it at conferences all over the world, developed courseware on the subject, and have updated the draft version of this chapter for the third time, making sure I can share the latest information available as close to publishing date of this book as possible.

© Peter De Tender 2016

P. De Tender, *Implementing Operations Management Suite*, DOI 10.1007/978-1-4842-1979-9_3

While I will cover Azure Backup only as part of Azure Resource Manager here, know that 85% of the overall Azure Backup functionality is the same in the Azure classic portal. If you are new to using Azure Backup, I encourage you to use the new Azure portal, thus Azure Resource Manager. Obviously because it is the newest way of working.

Backup as a solution is nothing new, and neither is "Cloud backup". So what makes Azure Backup so interesting?

The way Azure Backup is developed and integrated in Azure makes it really easy to deploy, configure, and use. It can replace your current on-premises backup solution or become an extension to it. It can also provide backups of virtual machines running in Azure.

What sets Azure Backup apart from a lot of the other Cloud backup solutions is that most of the others think of the Cloud as an endpoint or target for the backup files. They are mainly replacing only part of the traditional backup solution, by replacing tape drives and local storage by Cloud storage. Azure Backup is different, in a way that it can be seen as a Cloud storage backup target, but it also incorporates a full backup agent and backup software solution, as mentioned.

Some additional advantages I see in using Azure Backup are:

- *Automatic storage management* by leveraging on Azure Storage, providing a pay-per-use cost model, as well as Local Redundant (LRS) or Geo-Redundant Storage (GRS).

- *Unlimited scalability* of Azure Storage for backup.

- *No cost* related to *ingress* (backup to Azure) data or *egress* (restore from Azure), which is different than typical Azure outgoing data (which comes with a cost, although pushing data to Azure is always free).

- *Encryption by default*; all data being backed up to Azure is encrypted with AES 256 standard and stored in the Azure Backup Vault in an encrypted way, by using an encryption key.

- The Azure Backup agent and Azure Backup Server can provide *application consistent backups* for Exchange, SharePoint, and SQL Server.

- *99-year long-term retention*, which points to archiving capabilities.

- *Incremental backup* is available as a backup option, allowing you to speed up the process of the backup job itself, by limiting the amount of data that needs to be backed up.

- Except from Azure virtual machine backups (by using the extension), all other Azure Backup solutions support *data compression*. This limits the amount of storage that is required in Azure.

■ **Note**   Although this is an interesting feature in some other backup products, Azure Backup does not provide deduplication.

Supported Environments

Before walking you through a step-by-step deployment and configuration exercise, I want you to understand the different supported environments for Azure Backup, again in the three different scenarios I mentioned at the start of this chapter.

Supported Operating Systems for Azure Backup (Agent)

Azure Backup supports the following operating systems for backup:

- Windows 7, 8, 8.1, and 10

- Windows Server 2012 and 2012 R2

- Windows Server 2008 SP2 and 2008 R2 SP1

■ **Note**   Always make sure you install the latest Service Packs and/or Roll Up updates to avoid issues.

There are certain differences in specific Operating System SKUs, where some are not supported by Azure Backup (agent). For the latest "official" Microsoft update of this table, check out the URL `https://azure.microsoft.com/en-in/documentation/articles/backup-azure-backup-faq/`.

Up to some minor limitations, all current Windows Server and Client Operating Systems are supported. Again, don't forget I am talking about the agent-based version of Azure Backup, which means *files and folders only*.

Supported Operating Systems for Azure Backup Server

Azure Backup supports the following operating systems for backup:

- Windows Server 2012 and 2012 R2

■ **Note**   Windows Server 2008 R2 SP1 is *not* supported for running Azure Backup Server, and the Windows 2012 or 2012 R2 server cannot be a domain controller.

Supported Operating Systems for Azure VM Backup

The following operating systems are supported for backup by Azure VM Backup, leveraging on the virtual machine agent and backup extensions:

- Windows Server 2012 and 2012 R2

- Windows Server 2008 SP2 and 2008 R2 SP1

- Linux Operating Systems:

    - CentOS 6.3+ and 7.0+

    - Debian 7.9+ and 8.2+

    - Oracle Linux 6.4+ and 7.0+

    - Red Hat Enterprise Linux 6.7+ and 7.1+

    - SUSE Linux Enterprise 11 SP4, 12+, and 11.3+ (SAP specific)

    - Ubuntu 12.04 LTS, 14.04 LTS, and 16.04 LTS

That's not to say that it won't work on other versions of these platforms, but these are the supported ones. For Windows Server, it is obvious, as those are the only Windows Server versions running on Azure (not taking Server 2016 Technical Preview into account). As there are many different custom flavors of Linux, it could be that it is not working, although this would be more the exception in my opinion.

Now you know what platforms are supported, I jump back into the technology and walk you through the different solutions and configurations step-by-step.

Deploying and Configuring Azure Backup (Agent)

In this first scenario, I guide you through the deployment and configuration of Azure Backup, by using the Azure Backup agent.

The advantage of this solution is that it is the closest to the "typical" approach we have been using for on-premises backups for many years. You install a backup server and then deploy agents for the different servers and operating systems and application workloads. On the backup server, you create scheduled jobs and have centralized monitoring.

And that's exactly the beauty of using Azure Backup by using the agent. It can integrate in almost any scenario, without needing to dramatically change your current backup approach. Talk about a flexible way of migrating on-premises workloads like backup to the Azure Cloud!

By going through the exercises in this section, you will learn how to:

- Configure an Azure Backup Vault

- Deploy the Azure Backup agent to a Windows machine

- Configure an Azure Backup policy

- Perform a backup and restore of a Windows machine

Configuring an Azure Backup Vault

In this first part, you will learn how to set up and configure an Azure Backup Vault by using the Azure Resource Manager portal.

1.   From the Azure portal, click + New and search for backup. From the list of search results, select Backup and Site Recovery (OMS) (see Figure 3-1).

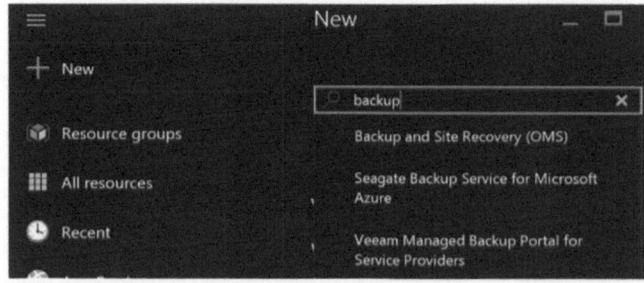

Figure 3-1. *Backup and Site Recovery (OMS)*

2.   Select it again in the Results blade (see Figure 3-2). Once it's selected, click the Create button.

NAME	PUBLISHER	CATEGORY
Backup and Site Recovery (OMS)	Microsoft	Management

Figure 3-2. *Backup and Site Recovery (OMS) result*

3. This opens the Recovery Services Vault, where you create the vault (see Figure 3-3).

   - Provide a unique vault name

   - Select the Azure subscription you want to use for this vault

   - Create a new resource group

   - Choose the location (Azure region) where you want the vault to be created

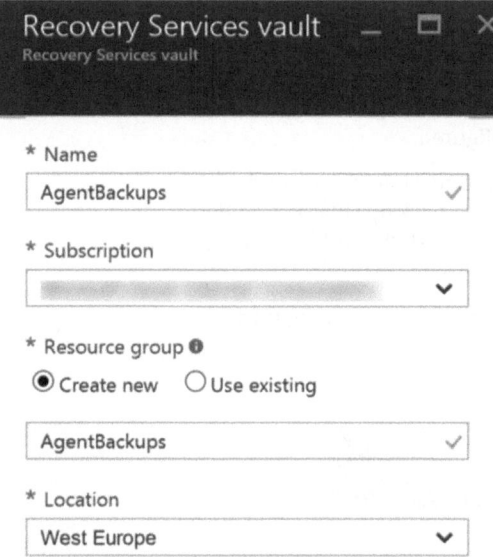

Recovery Services vault

Recovery Services vault

* Name

AgentBackups

* Subscription

* Resource group ❶
◉ Create new   ○ Use existing

AgentBackups

* Location

West Europe

Figure 3-3. *Creating a new Recovery Services vault*

4. Click the Create button to get the Recovery Services vault you created. Wait for the notification regarding the successful creation of the vault.

5. Once the vault is created, head back to the Azure portal, select Resource Groups, and notice the new Resource Group called AgentBackups. Select the resource group and notice the AgentBackups vault being created in here (see Figure 3-4).

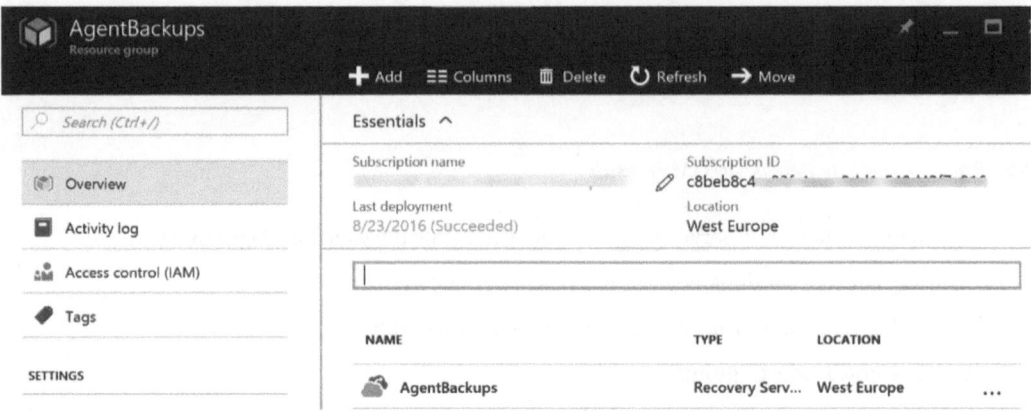

Figure 3-4. *Azure Recovery Services vault created in a new resource group*

6. Select the Azure Recovery Service vault. This will open the vault settings blade. From the settings, browse to Getting Started and then click Backup. This opens the Getting Started with Backup blade, where you have to go through a three-step scenario in getting most of what is required configured.

7. In Step 1, you select the backup goal. Here you define where your workload is running (Azure on-premises) and what you want to back up (files and folders, Hyper-V virtual machine backups, or more complex workloads like Exchange, SharePoint, and SQL Server).

    - Select On-Premises and Files and Folders for this exercise (see Figure 3-5).

    - Click OK to confirm the selection.

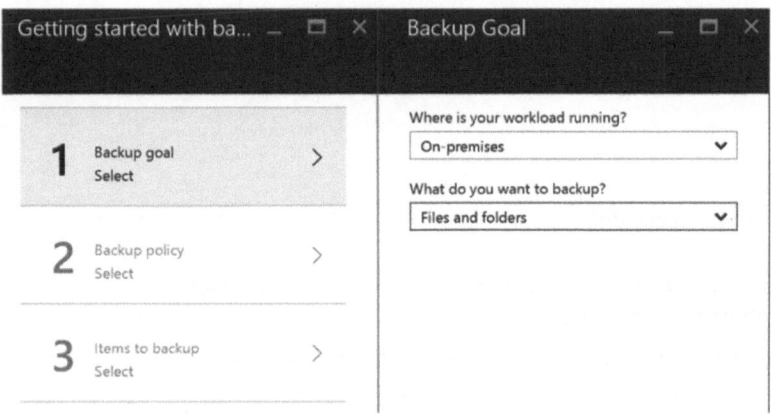

Figure 3-5. *Configuring the Azure Backup*

8. In Step 2, you download the Azure Backup agent and vault credentials. Use those files to install the agent on the backup source server (see Figure 3-6).

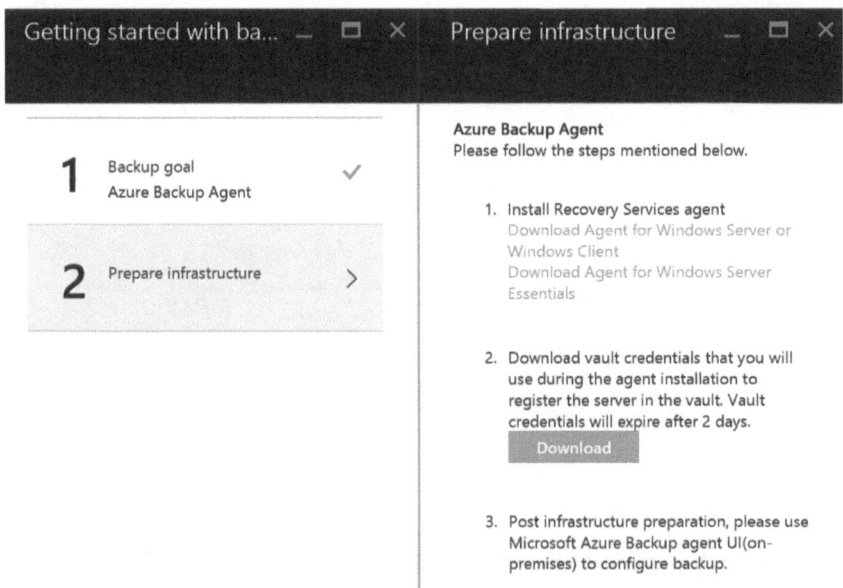

Figure 3-6. *Preparing the infrastructure—download the Azure Backup agent*

■ **Note** There is a different Azure Backup agent for Windows Server Essentials. It's a specific version of Windows Server targeted at the SMB market (it replaces the former Small Business Server—SBS.)

Deploying the Azure Backup Agent to a Windows Machine

To continue the installation of the Azure Backup agent, log on to the on-premises Windows machine (this can be a physical or virtual machine) using administrative credentials. Copy the two download files (MARSInstaller.exe and the vault credentials file) to the server or make sure you can access them remotely.

1. Start MARSInstaller.exe, which launches the Azure Backup installation wizard. You can change the installation folder or accept the default folder (see Figure 3-7).

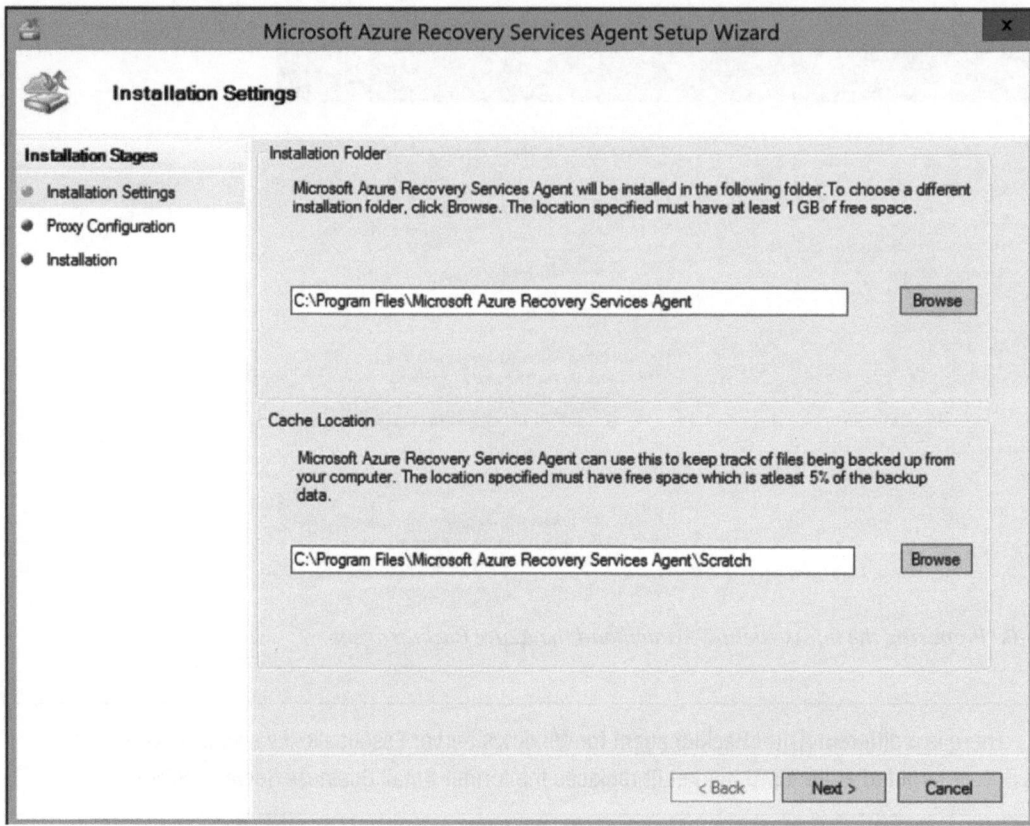

Figure 3-7. *Installation settings for the Azure Backup agent*

2. In the next step, you have the option to define your proxy settings if needed. In my lab environment, servers have a direct Internet connection, so nothing needs to be changed here.

3. In the Installation step, a check is done on additional Windows operating system components like Windows PowerShell and .NET Framework. If these components are missing, the installation will fail.

    Click the Install button to continue the installation. This shouldn't take too long. A notification will appear saying that the installation has completed successfully (see Figure 3-8).

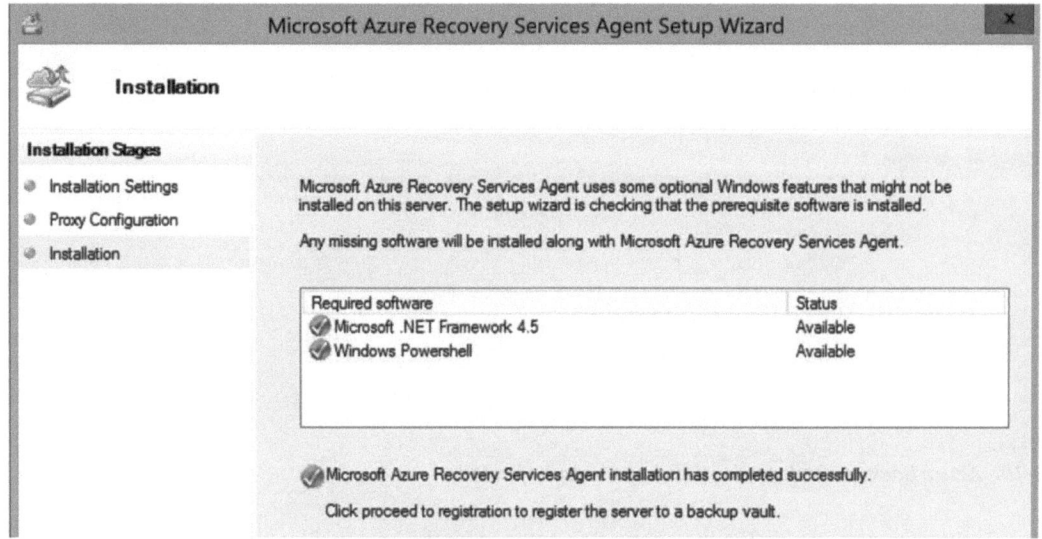

Figure 3-8. Installation has completed successfully

4.   Click the Proceed to Registration button to continue.

5.   This is where you have to import the Azure Backup Vault credentials file that you downloaded earlier, which will link this server's setup to the correct vault (see Figure 3-9).

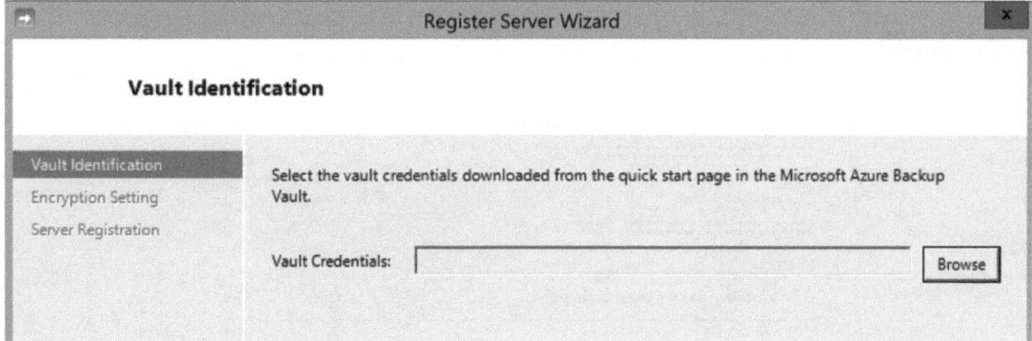

Figure 3-9. Import the vault credentials file

6.   Browse and import the file; the results should look like Figure 3-10.

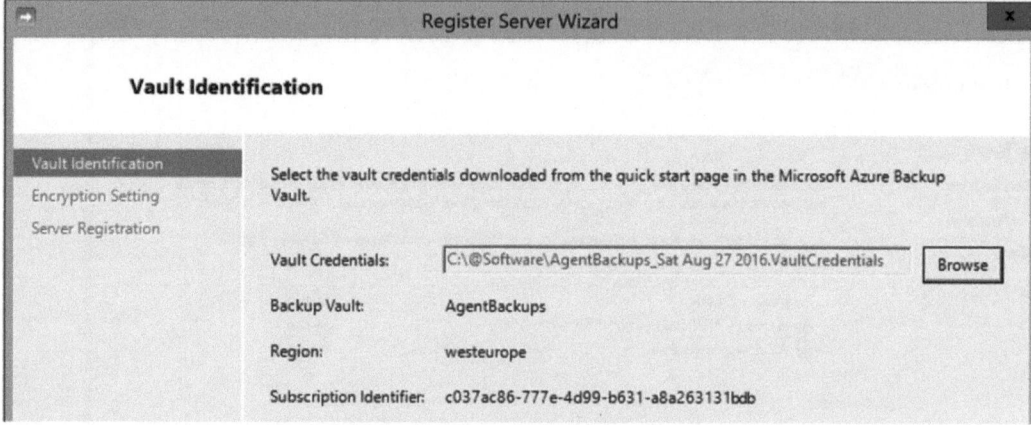

Figure 3-10. *Azure Backup Vault credentials have been imported*

7. In the next step, you define the encryption settings for the backup files-in-transit, as well as in-rest. Without this encryption key, data cannot be restored from the backup vault, so keep this credentials file in a secured place (see Figure 3-11).

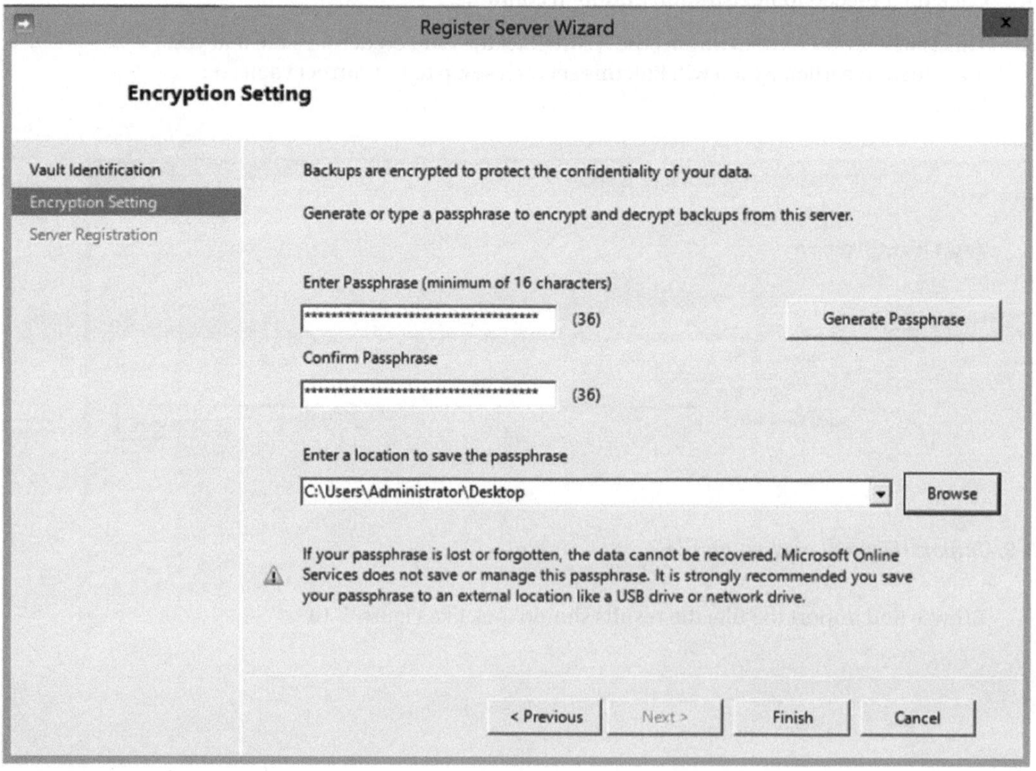

Figure 3-11. *Specify the backup encryption settings*

8. The encryption passphrase is also saved to a file, as you can see in Figure 3-12.

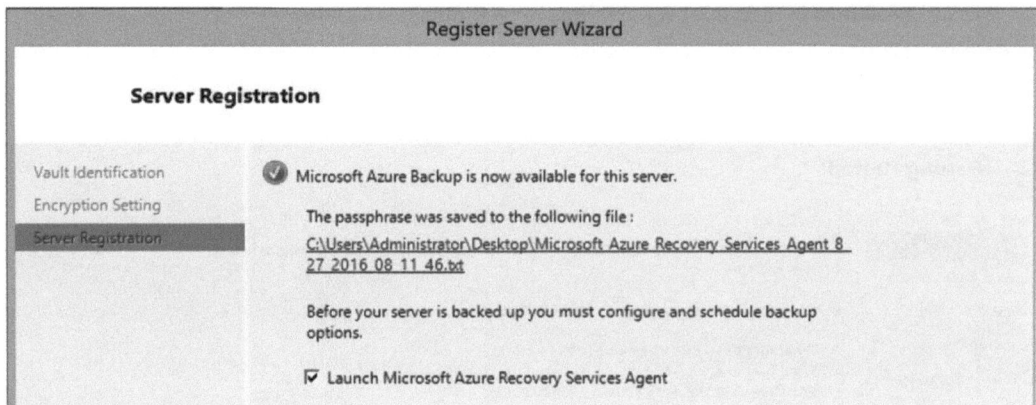

Figure 3-12. *Encryption passphrase is saved to a text file*

Configuring an Azure Backup Job on a Windows Machine

Follow these steps to configure an Azure Backup job on a Windows Machine:

1. After closing the Backup agent registration wizard, the Microsoft Azure Recovery Services console will be launched. Notice in Figure 3-13 that the program is called Microsoft Azure Backup.

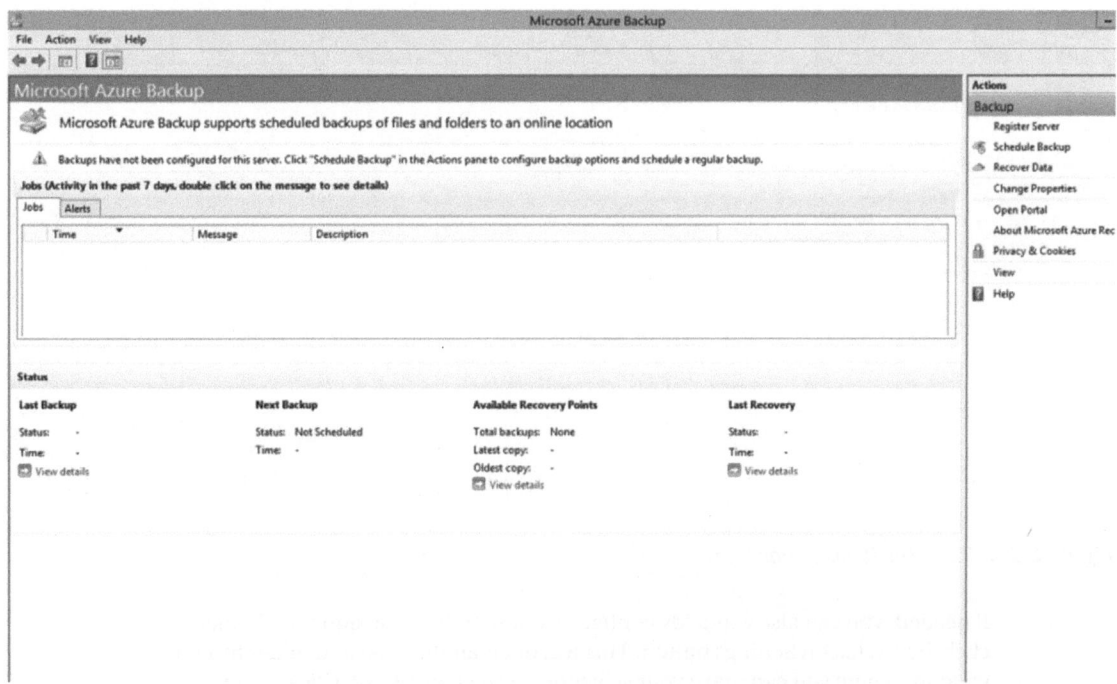

Figure 3-13. *Microsoft Azure Backup console*

2. From within the Microsoft Azure Backup console, navigate to the action pane to the right and select Schedule Backup. This will launch the Schedule Backup Wizard, as shown in Figure 3-14. Click Next to continue.

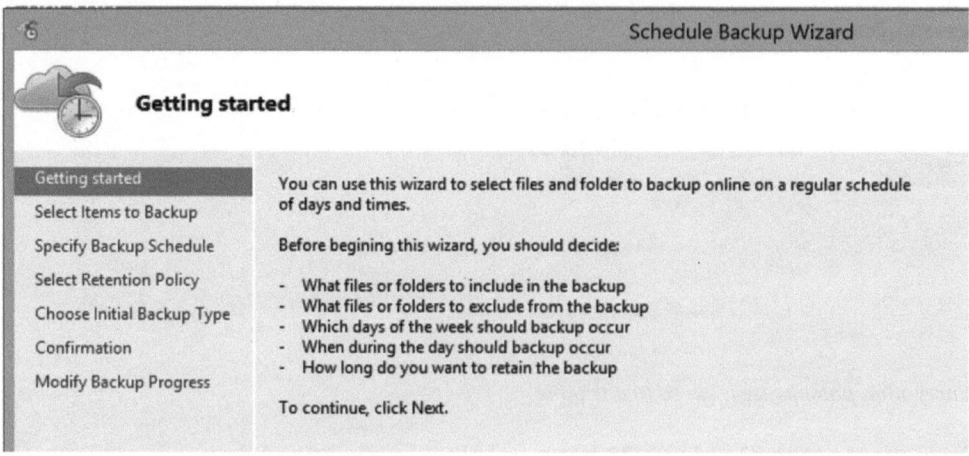

Figure 3-14. *Schedule Backup Wizard*

3. Configuring the backup job is straightforward. You start by selecting the items you want to back up. Open the browser to select the folders and files you want to include, as shown in Figure 3-15. Click Next to continue to the next step.

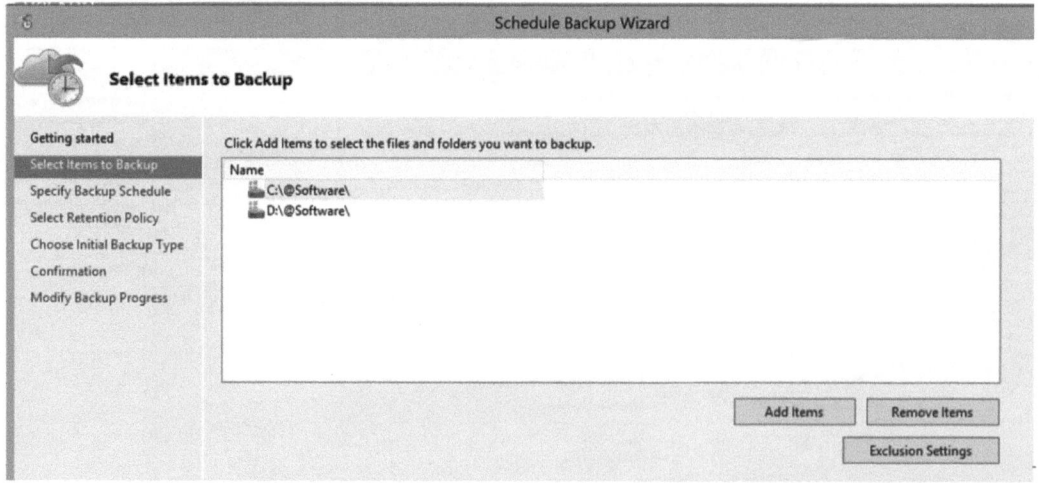

Figure 3-15. *Select the items to back up*

4. If needed, you can also explicitly configure folder or file exclusions. To do that, click the Exclusion Settings button. This will open another file and folder browser window, where you can make your selections (see Figure 3-16). Click Next to continue.

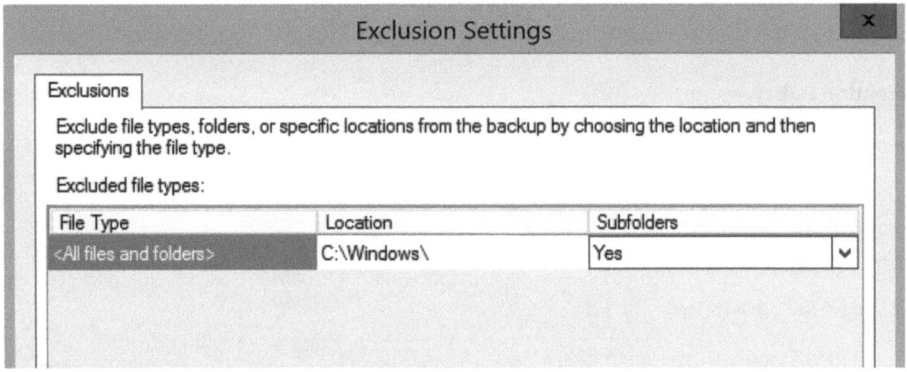

Figure 3-16. Set the exclusion settings

5. The next step involves defining your backup schedule (see Figure 3-17). You have the option between configuring a daily or weekly backup. Next to that, you define up to three timeslots for taking backups, which is done as an incremental, to save on data transit to Azure. Click Next to continue.

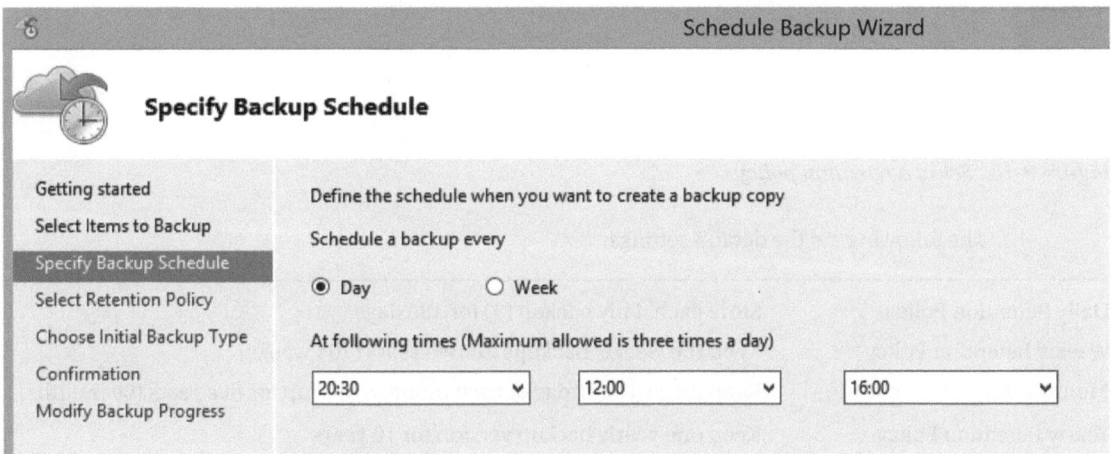

Figure 3-17. Specify the backup schedule

6. After setting up the backup schedule, you define a retention policy. This points to the number of days/weeks/months/years the backup data has to be stored in Azure (see Figure 3-18).

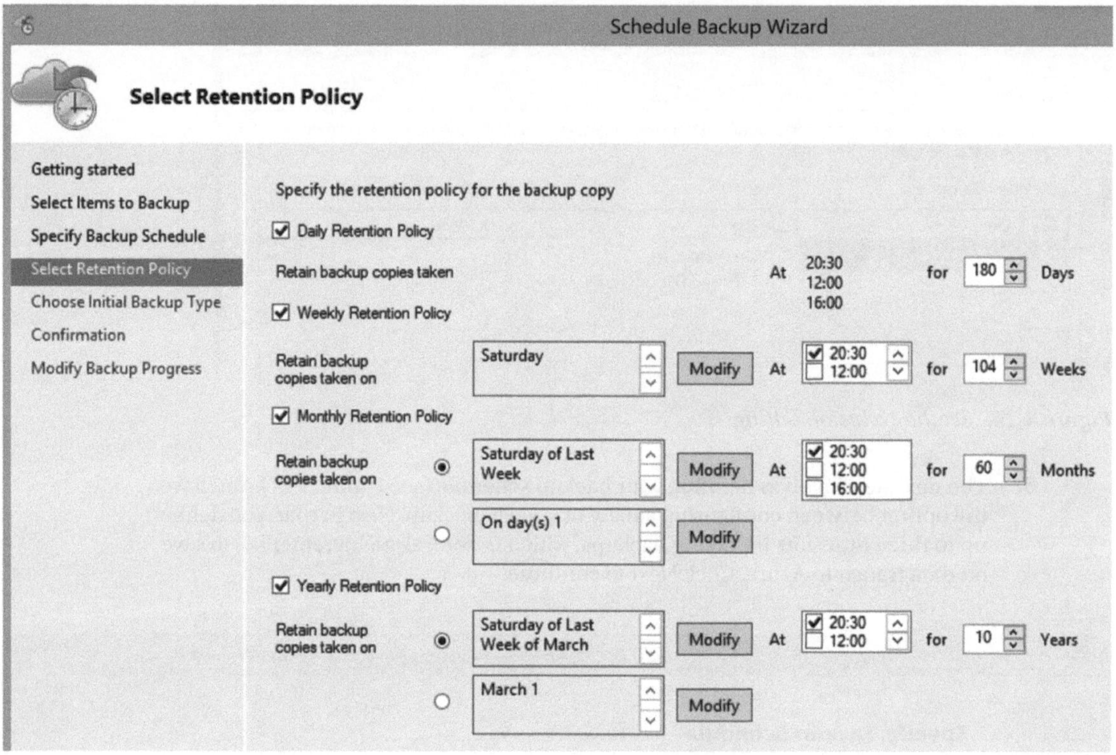

Figure 3-18. *Select a retention policy*

The following are the default settings:

Daily Retention Policy	Store each daily backup (3) for 180 days
Weekly Retention Policy	Keep the weekly backups for two years (104 weeks)
Monthly Retention Policy	Keep the last Saturday of each month's backup for five years (60 months)
Yearly Retention Policy	Keep one yearly backup version for 10 years

7. In the next step, you define how to transfer the backup data to Azure. There are two options:

    • Directly taking the initial backup over the Internet (encrypted, port 443)

    • Using offline data disk shipments to the Azure datacenter

When choosing the offline data disk shipment, you have to provide several parameters regarding your Azure subscription, such as your Azure subscription ID, Azure storage account, and the storage container where you want these backups to be stored. See Figure 3-19.

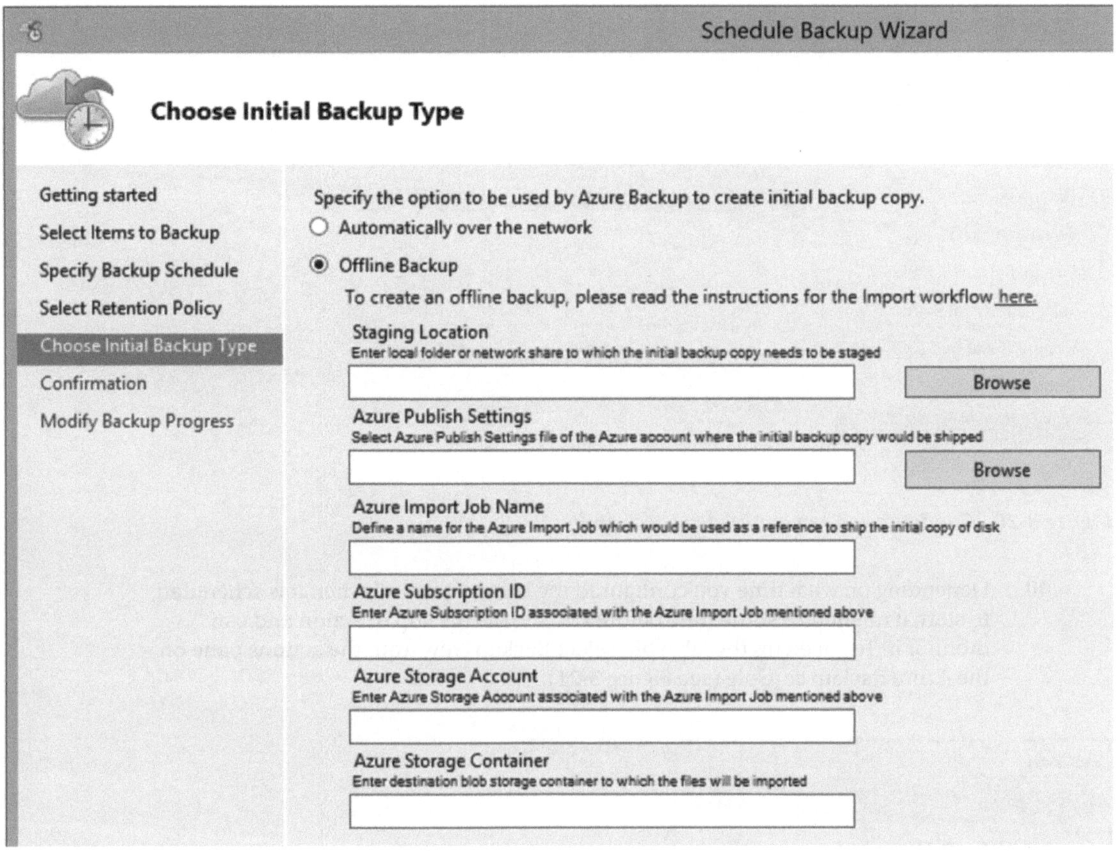

Figure 3-19. *Choose an initial backup type—offline*

■ **Note** For more detailed information regarding the offline backup import and export procedure, read the following Azure documentation: `https://azure.microsoft.com/en-gb/documentation/articles/backup-azure-backup-import-export/`.

---

8. In this exercise, select Automatically Over the Network and click Next to continue.

9. The backup job is created and scheduled, and we are at the end of the wizard, having successfully configured the backup schedule (see Figure 3-20).

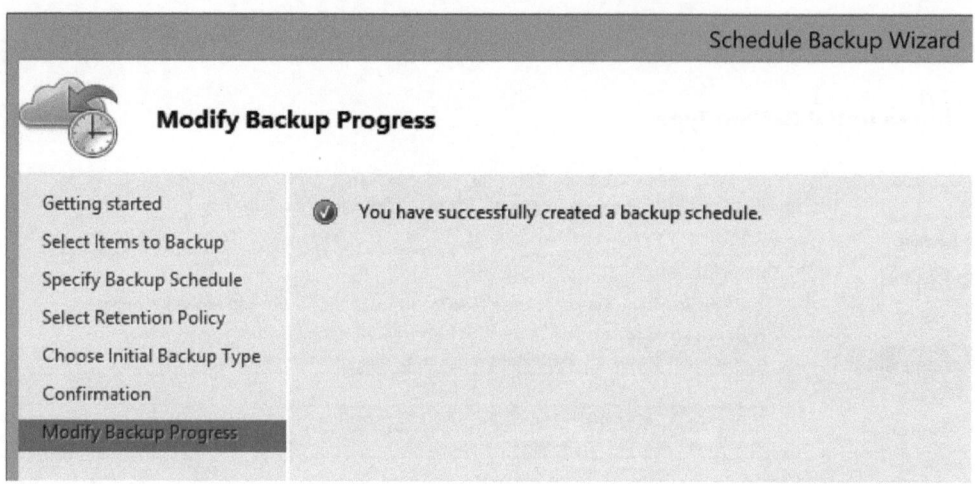

Figure 3-20. Configuration has completed successfully

10. Depending on what time you configured the backup job and when it is scheduled to start, it might take some time before you see the backup in action and can monitor it. To speed up the lab a bit, select Backup Now from the actions pane on the Azure Backup console (see Figure 3-21).

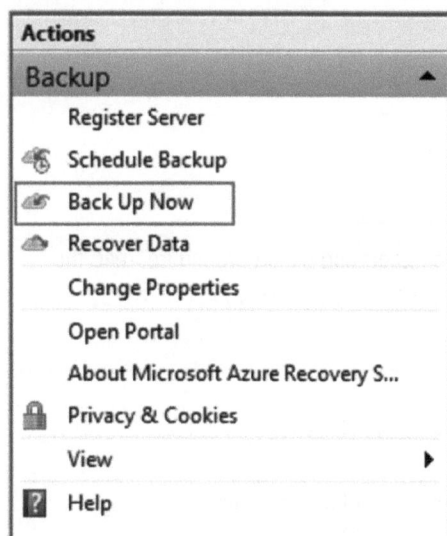

Figure 3-21. Manually start the scheduled backup job now

11. Confirm the start of the manual backup job and wait until the job runs. Follow the progress from the popup window shown in Figure 3-22.

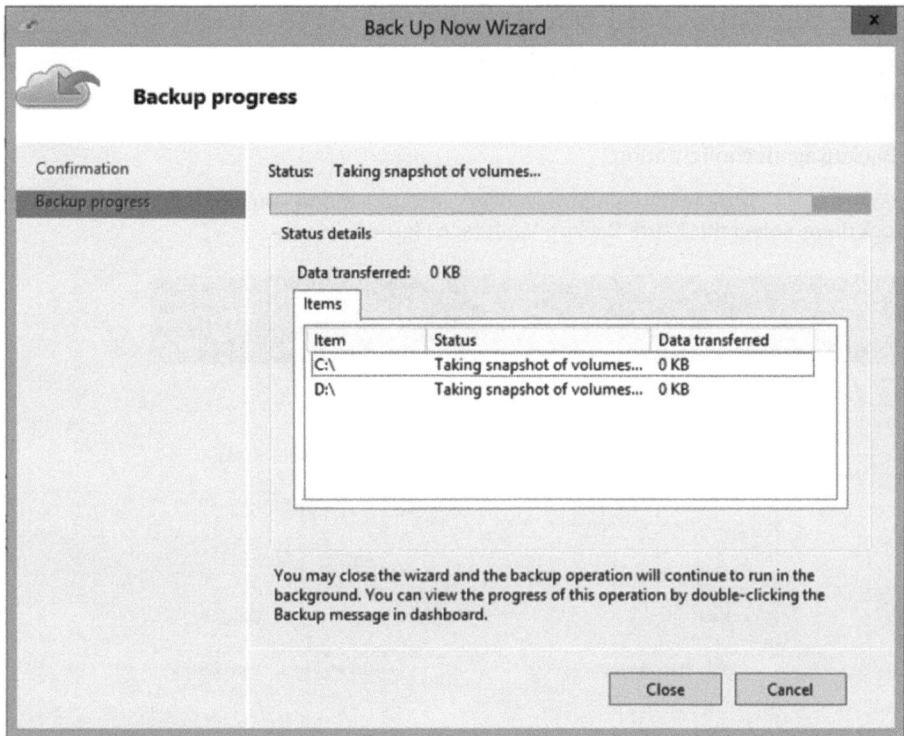

Figure 3-22. Backup is in progress

12. Close the popup window, which brings you back to the Azure Backup console. From there, you can get more details regarding the backup jobs. Information includes the status of the last backup, when the next backup task is scheduled, and how many recovery points there are. For most items, more detailed views are available. See Figure 3-23.

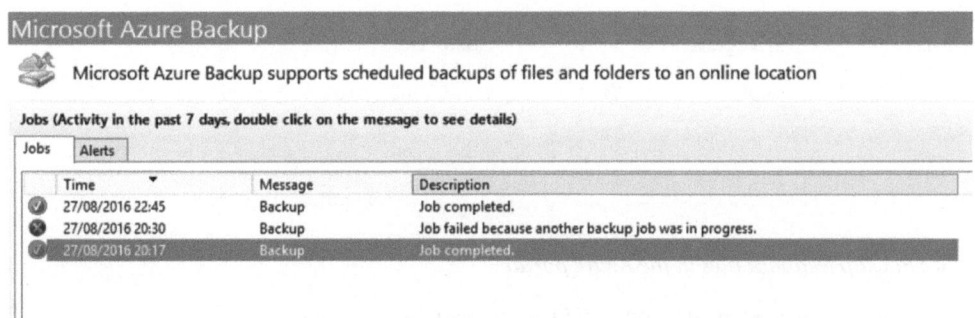

Figure 3-23. Backup jobs status window

Monitoring Azure Backup Agent Setup from the Azure Portal

In the previous section, you successfully configured an Azure Backup job on a Windows machine, which has the Azure Backup agent installed.

In this section, we head back over to the Azure portal and see what information can be viewed there regarding your Azure Backup agent configuration.

1. From the Azure portal, browse to the Azure recovery resource group you created before. From there, select the Azure Backup Vault (see Figure 3-24).

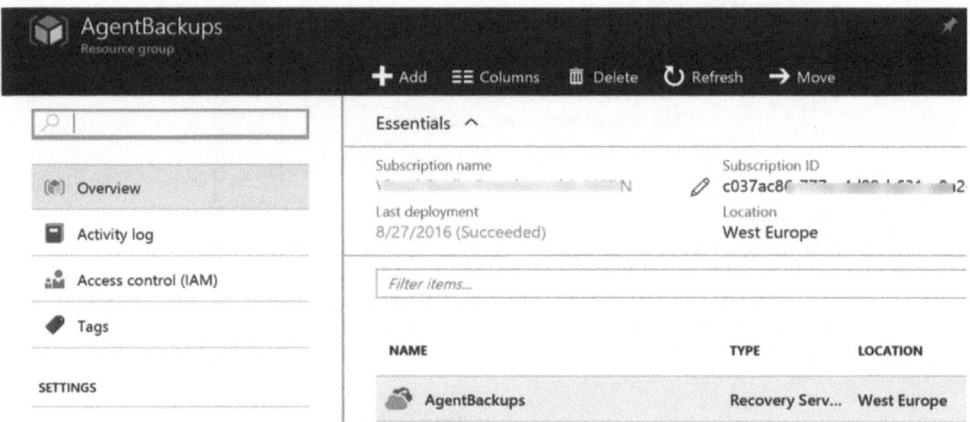

Figure 3-24. *Azure backup resource group and Azure Backup Vault*

2. When you select the Azure Backup Vault, the Settings blade displays some informational tiles with feedback regarding the backup vault configuration (see Figure 3-25).

Backup		Add tiles ⊕
Backup Items	**Backup Jobs**	**Backup Usage**
Azure Virtual Mac... 0	In progress 0	Cloud - LRS 0 B
File-Folders 2	Failed ⊗ 1	Cloud - GRS 0 B

Figure 3-25. *Azure Backup feedback tiles in the Azure portal*

3. From these tiles, click the Backup/File-Folders tile. This routes you to a more detailed view regarding this kind of backup job. You get input on the backup item, which is the source drive per server. It shows the protected server, which points to the machine(s) having the Azure Backup agent installed and a job configured; it shows the state of the last backup and the timestamp of the last recovery point (see Figure 3-26).

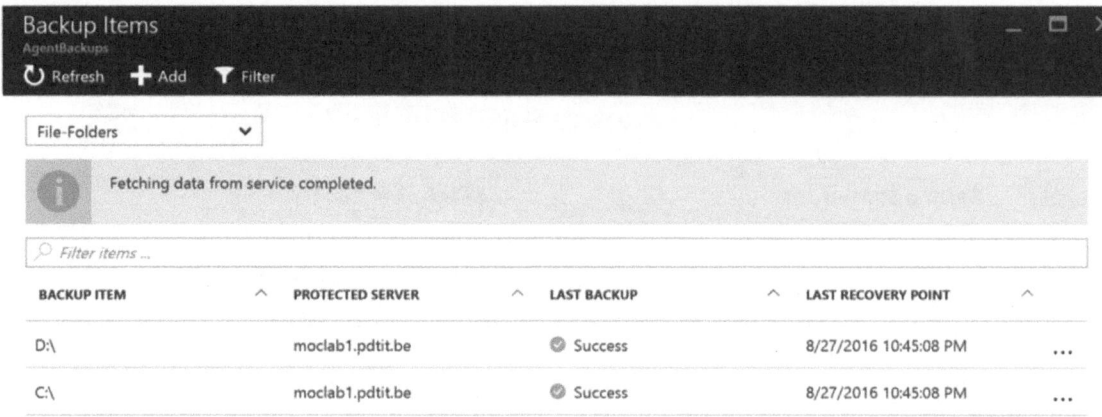

Figure 3-26. More Azure Backup feedback kdetails in the Azure portal

Performing an Azure Backup Agent Folder Restore

Taking backups is fine, but the main intention of taking backups is not just having a copy aside, but also being able to actually restore the backed-up data, which is exactly what we are going to do here.

1. Connect to a source backup server that has at least one single successful backup. Open the Azure Backup console.

2. From the Azure Backup console, go to the Actions pane and click Recover Data, as shown in Figure 3-27.

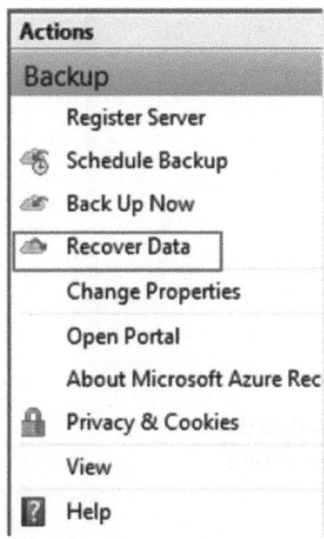

Figure 3-27. Recover data using Azure Backup

3. This launches the Recover Data Wizard. Make sure This Server is selected as the first option (see Figure 3-28). Click Next to continue.

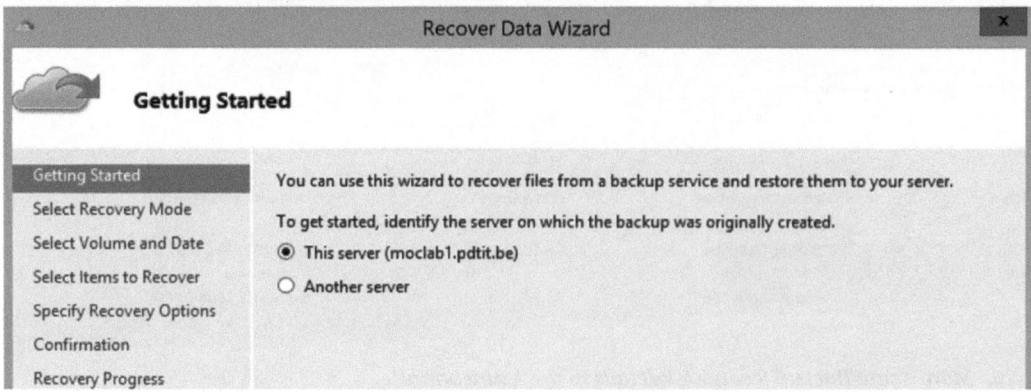

Figure 3-28. *Choose a server to recover data from*

4. In the next step, you can choose between selecting files and searching for files. When you choose Selecting Files, a scan of the backup catalog will occur, after which you can select the volume and the folders and files as needed (see Figure 3-29).

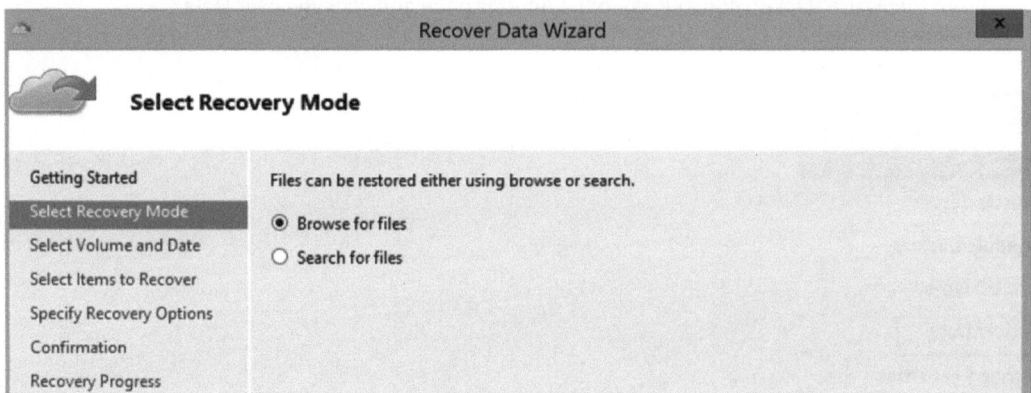

Figure 3-29. *Browse for files to recover*

5. The restore selection is based on backup date and timestamp. Based on the number of backups or retention settings you have, you can make about any point-in-time restore happen (see Figure 3-30).

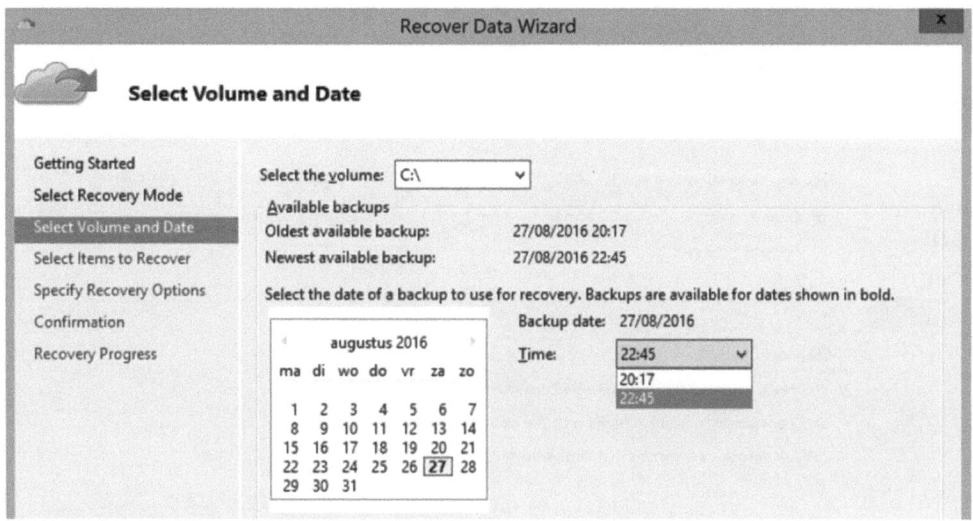

Figure 3-30. *Select a volume and data to restore*

6. In the next step, you can browse through the list of folders and files at the moment when the backup was made. You can select multiple folders and files or make individual file selections (see Figure 3-31). Clicking the Next button takes you to the next step.

Figure 3-31. *Select items to recover*

7. In the Specify Recovery Options step, you define whether to restore the selected files and/or folders to the original location or to another location that you specify. You also can choose what needs to happen if the restored items are still present in the source location, and whether the ACL permissions also must be restored (see Figure 3-32).

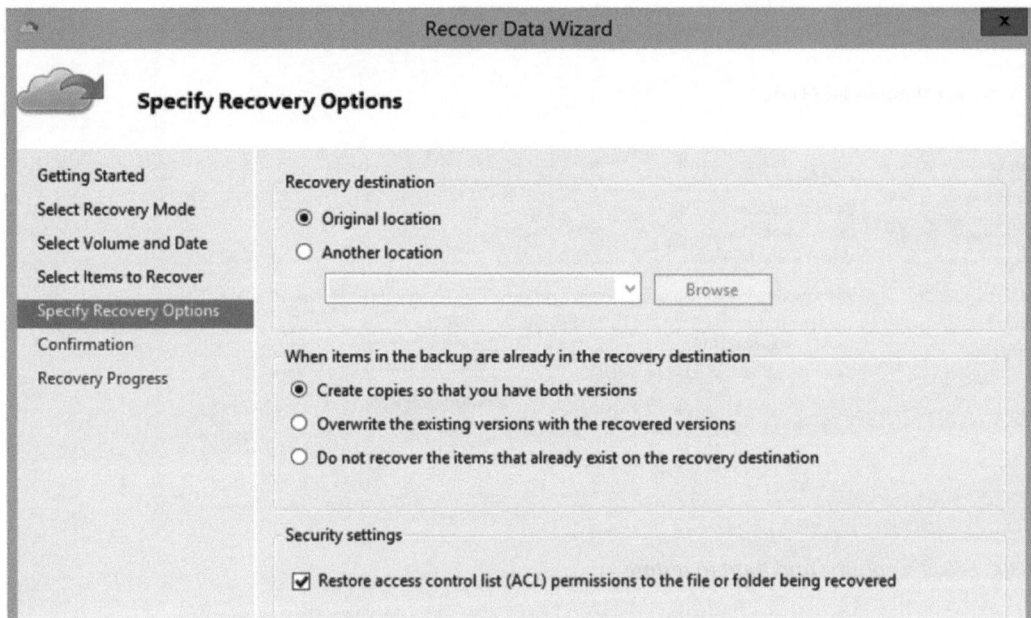

Figure 3-32. *Specify the recovery options*

    8.   Click the Restore button to start the restore process and job. Figure 3-33 shows the recovery process in action.

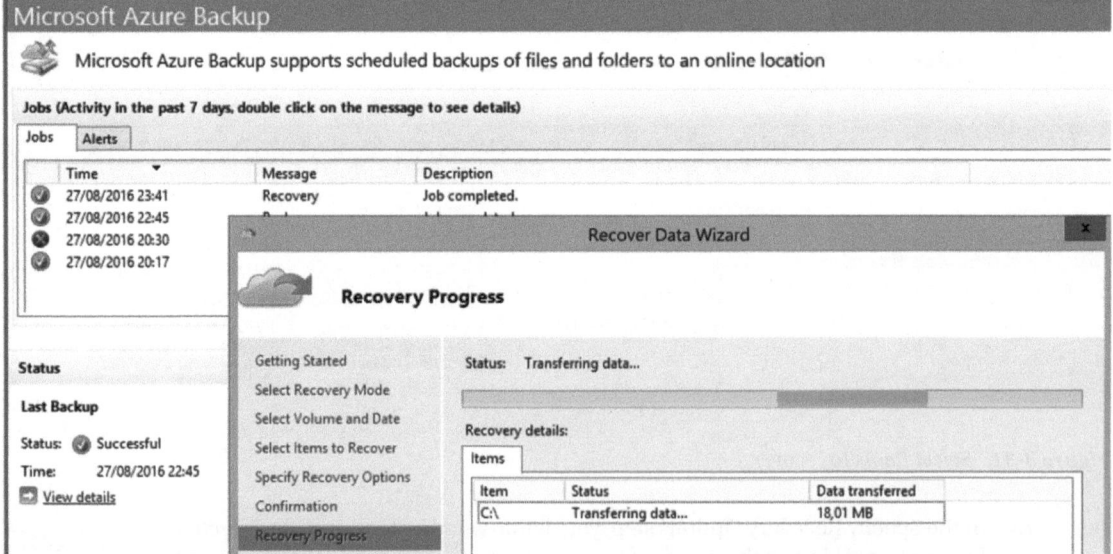

Figure 3-33. *The Recovery progress in action*

9.   Wait for the restore job to complete.

■ **Note**   It's important to keep in mind that—when restoring to an alternative location—shared network locations and external media like USB drives are not supported. If the alternative location is a machine without the Azure Backup agent installed and thus does not have the Azure Backup Vault credentials, you are asked for the vault passphrase during restore, in order to decrypt the backup files (see Figure 3-34).

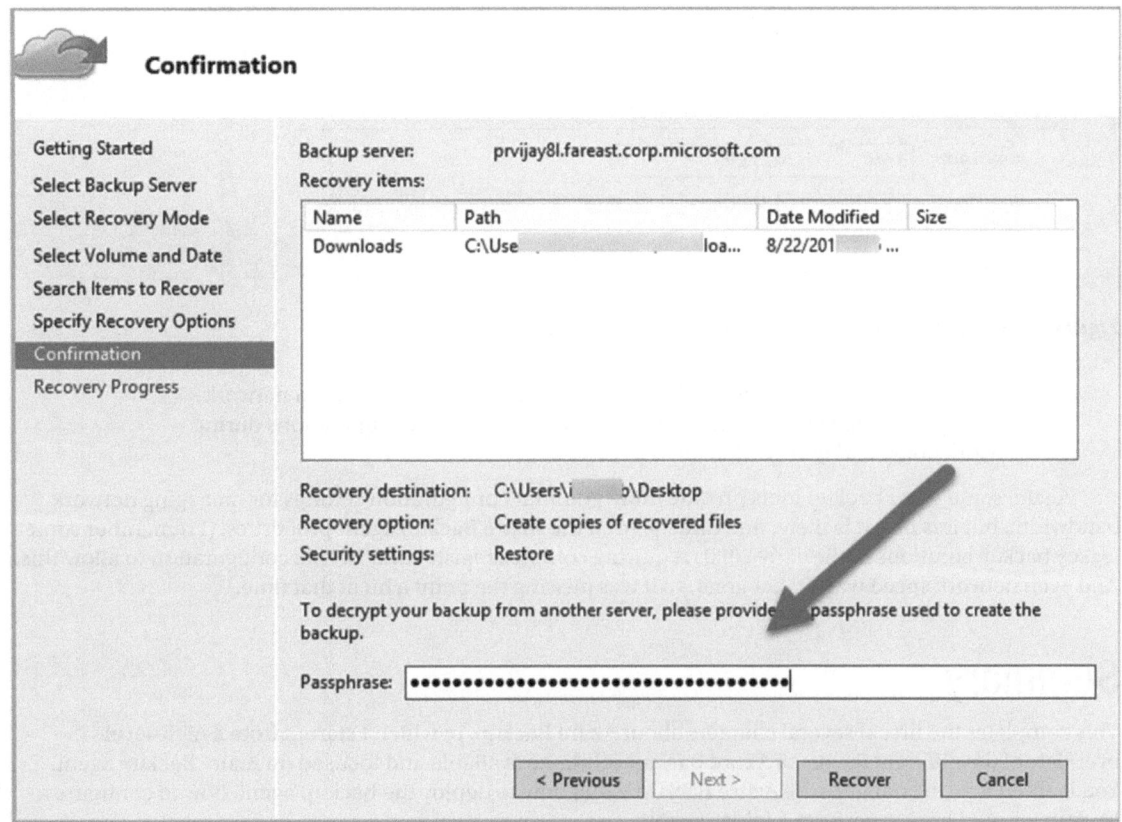

Figure 3-34. *The passphrase is required when restoring to an alternative server*

Optimizing Restore Speed—Network Bandwidth Throttling

In an Enterprise environment, many administrators are configuring dedicated backup network subnets. Partly for security reasons, management restrictions, and bandwidth control. While I haven't determined how to limit or configure Azure Backup agent traffic to pass through a specific NIC out of the Azure Backup agent configuration—you could build something close to this by directing traffic through a proxy server that's supported and configurable—the Azure Backup agent allows for (minimal) bandwidth throttling configuration.

1. Open the Azure Backup agent console, navigate to the action pane, and select Change Properties.

2. Click the Throttling tab (see Figure 3-35).

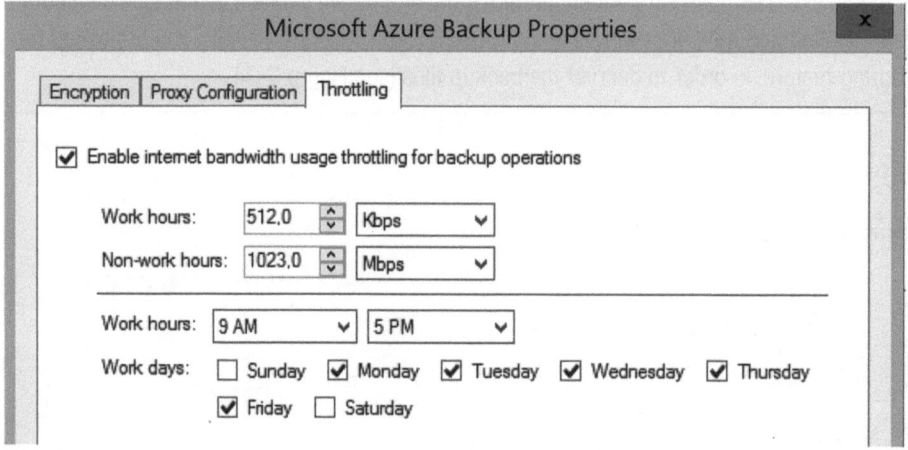

Figure 3-35. *Azure Backup agent—throttling configuration*

3. Here you can enable bandwidth throttling by defining the maximum network bandwidth capacity that can be used for backup and restore operations during work hours and non-work hours.

Again, some other backup tools provide more granular configuration settings for managing network bandwidth, but it is nice it is there, and directly from the Azure Backup agent properties. (I remember some legacy backup solutions in the early 2000s requiring complex registry and INI file configuration to allow this. And even network speed wasn't that great, so it was missing the point a bit at that time.)

Summary

This completes the first of several chapters about Azure Backup, in which I started from a high-level overview of the different flavors of Azure Backup solutions available and focused on Azure Backup agent. You learned how to configure the Azure Backup Vault, how to deploy the backup agent, how to configure a backup job, and how to perform a folder restore.

In the next chapter, you will learn about Azure Backup Server in a similar structure used in this chapter.

CHAPTER 4

■ ■ ■

Deploying and Configuring Azure Backup Server

Welcome to the second chapter about Azure Backup, dedicated to Azure Backup Server.

In this chapter, I assume you went through the basics of the Azure Backup in Chapter 3, which will give you enough information to know the difference between the different Azure Backup flavors. Maybe you went through the exercises too, which will make it easy to understand and complete the exercises in this chapter, since there are a lot of similarities and overlap between both solutions. After all, they belong to the same Azure Backup family.

Supported Environments

Before going through a step-by-step deployment and configuration exercise, it's important to remember that Azure Backup supports the Windows Server 2012 and 2012 R2 operating systems for backup.

■ **Note**   Windows Server 2008 R2 SP1 is *not* supported for running Azure Backup Server, and the Windows 2012 or 2012 R2 server on which you want to install Azure Backup Sever solution cannot be a domain controller.

Now you know what platforms are supported, let's jump back into the technology. I walk you through the different solutions and configurations step-by-step.

Deploying and Configuring Azure Backup Server

As you learned in Chapter 3, in addition to Azure Backup agent, there is a second Azure Backup flavor available. It is this version I will tackle in this chapter, called Azure Backup Server.

The biggest differences compared to the Azure Backup agent are these additional features:

- Enterprise workload support (Hyper-V VMs, Exchange, SQL, and SharePoint)

- Feature-complete Azure Backup Server console, providing you with a rich set of configuration options to create backup and restore jobs, monitoring your backups, and more

If you are familiar with System Center Data Protection Manager (SCDPM), you will find there is a lot of overlap and similarities between both products. But there are also some serious differences:

- Azure Backup Server does not integrate with System Center.

- Azure Backup Server does not support tape drives as a backup target.

- Azure Backup Server does not require a specific license, although you need an Azure subscription and must have created an Azure Backup Vault. (The Windows Server 2012 R2 to which you install the backup tool must also be licensed.)

■ **Note** While Azure Backup Server could be configured as an on-premises only backup solution, therefore not using Azure storage as the backup target, it is still required to have the server registered in Azure Backup Vault.

Azure Backup Server can be set up in two ways:

- Deploy it as a backup server on-premises; the backup target can be on-premises disks or Azure storage. Backup clients can be any machine having an Azure Backup Server client agent installed, running on-premises or in a public Cloud.

- Deploy it as a backup server within an Azure VM; backup target can be Azure storage. Backup clients can be any machine having an Azure Backup Server client agent installed, running on-premises or in a public Cloud.

The exercise you will go through in this section looks like this:

- Deploy two Azure Virtual Machines running Windows 2012 R2.

- Configure one of these VMs as domain controller, since this is required by MABS.

- Configure the other VM as Azure Backup Server; add a data disk to this server.

- Deploy a third VM using the SQL Server 2016 gallery image.

- Configure a backup job and take a SQL Server database backup.

■ **Note** In the next section of this chapter, I cover Azure Backup for Azure Virtual Machines, which is different from running Azure Backup Server in this scenario. If you have the capacity available in your on-premises infrastructure, you could also build an on-premises backup server, from where you store another machine's backup to Azure.

Exercise Prerequisites

Follow these steps to set up your system to be ready for the exercise:

1. From the Azure portal, create a new resource group called MABSLab or any other name you want. This is just to separate it from the resource group in the previous exercise.

2. In this new resource group, deploy three virtual machines running Windows 2012 R2 and having 4GB of memory as a minimum (I used a DS2_V2 T-shirt size). See Figure 4-1.

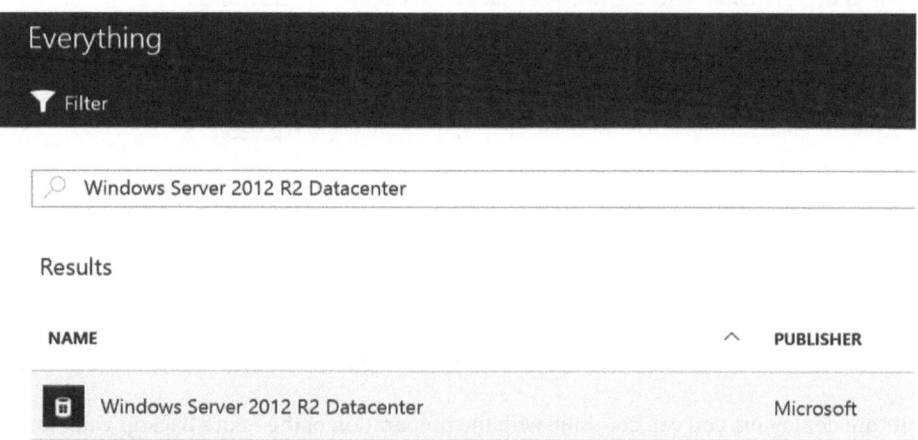

Figure 4-1. *Selecting Windows Server 2012 R2 Datacenter from the image gallery*

- The MABSDC machine is based on the Windows Server 2012 R2 Enterprise image from the Azure gallery.

- This server will become the Active Directory domain controller (assuming you know how to configure a Windows Server 2012 R2 as domain controller).

- The MABSServer machine is also based on this image from the Azure gallery.

- This server will become the Azure Backup Server. This machine should be Active Directory domain joined.

  - Add another data disk to this VM, which will be used by MABS later.

  - The MABSSQL machine is based on the Microsoft SQL Server 2016 RTM Enterprise image from the Azure gallery. Optionally, this machine can be Active Directory domain joined, which will ease the exercise, but remember non-domain joined machines can also be backed up using MABS, as long as it can authenticate to this machine. See Figure 4-2.

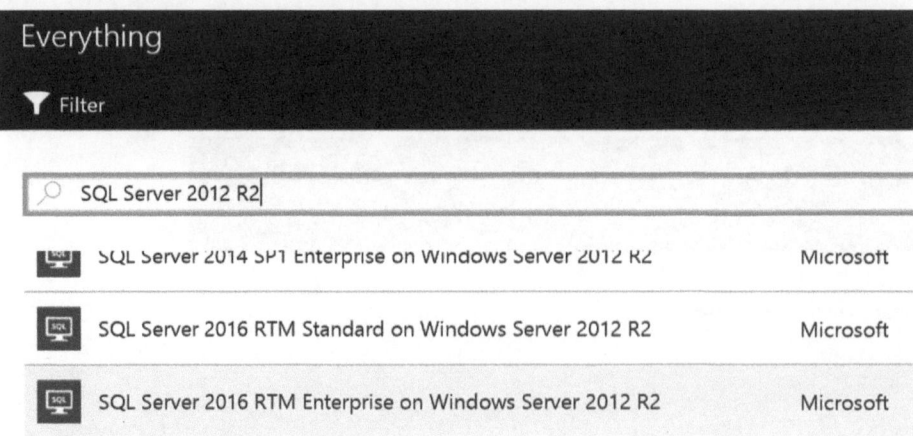

Figure 4-2. *Selecting SQL Server 2016 RTM Enterprise from the image gallery*

While the servers are deploying, you can continue with the preparation of the Azure Backup Vault for this exercise.

Configuring an Azure Backup Server Backup Vault

Follow these steps to configure an Azure Backup Server backup vault:

1. From the Azure portal, click +New and type recovery in the Search field.

2. From the list of results, select Backup and Site Recovery (OMS). Once selected, click Create. See Figure 4-3.

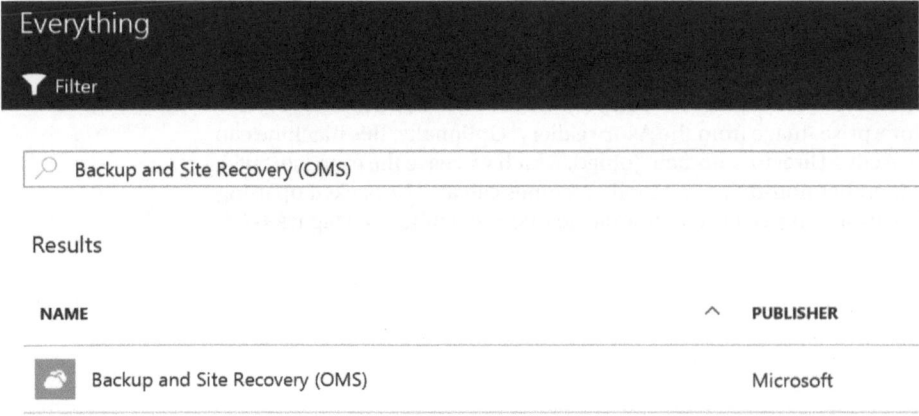

Figure 4-3. *Backup and Site Recovery (OMS) from the Azure gallery*

3. This will open the Create Recovery Vault blade, where you should enter some parameters to get the vault created (see Figure 4-4):

- Enter a descriptive name for the recovery vault, for example MABSBackup

- Select the resource group you created in the previous step (MABSLab in my example)

- Select your Azure subscription and closest Azure region

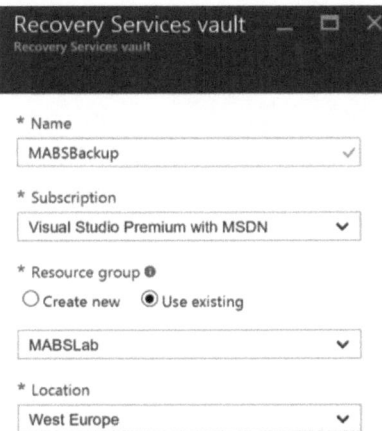

Figure 4-4. *Create Recovery Services Vault*

4. Once the recovery vault is created, select it from the Azure portal. Go to the Settings blade and navigate to Getting Started/Backup (see Figure 4-5).

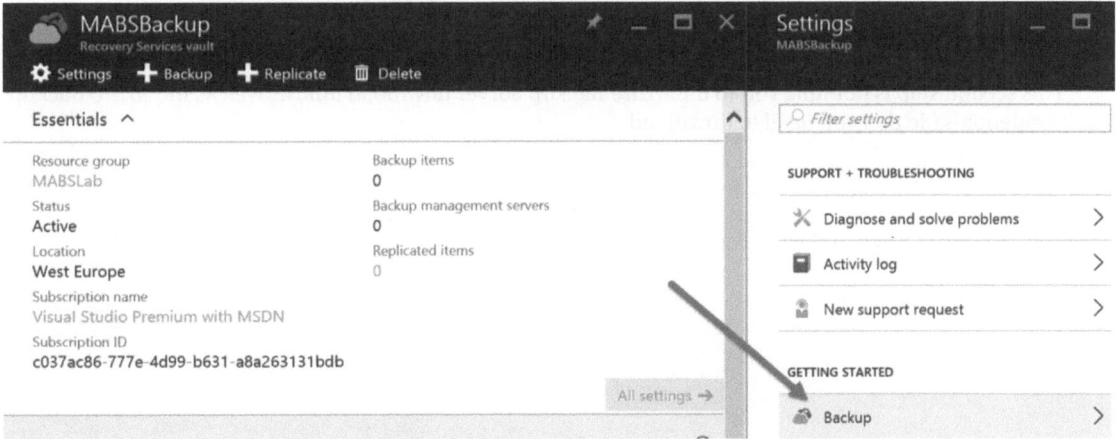

Figure 4-5. *Configuring backup for the Azure Backup Server*

5. This opens the Backup configuration blade. The configuration is a three-step scenario, starting with defining the backup goal. Almost like configuring this step for the Azure Backup agent, you select On-Premises as your source, but instead of selecting Files and Folders, select SQL Server (see Figure 4-6). Click OK to confirm.

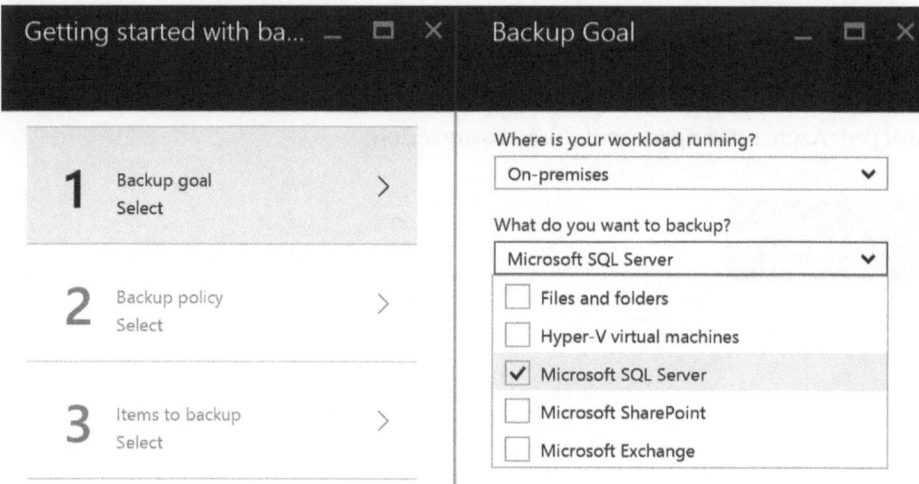

Figure 4-6. *Setting parameters for the backup goal*

■ **Note**   Pay attention to the fact that we select On-Premises, even if you want to back up Azure VMs by using Azure Backup Server. The key difference is that you are using the MABS client agent and MABS server, whereas in the third flavor, by selecting Azure as the source, you use the Azure VM extension for backup (which is covered hereafter).

---

6.   As you can see, the three-step scenario falls back to a two-step one, removing the Backup Policy step. This is because when using the Azure Backup Server, backup policies are defined in the server, and not stored in Azure.

This second step is pointing you to the Azure Backup Server download link, as well as the Azure Backup Vault credentials file that you need to download
(see Figure 4-7).

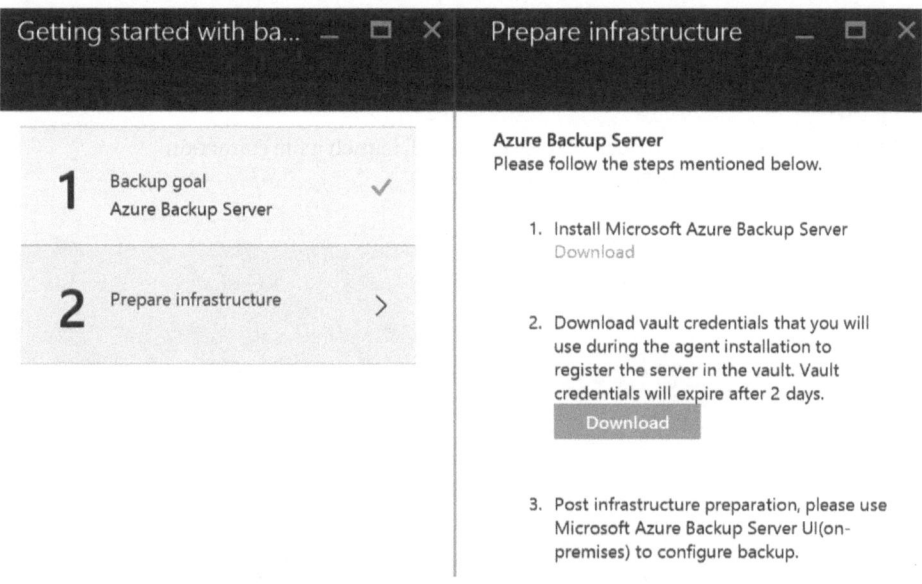

Figure 4-7. *Azure Backup Vault—prepare Infrastructure*

    7.   Click the Download link, which will redirect you to a public Microsoft web site (see Figure 4-8):

        https://www.microsoft.com/en-us/download/confirmation.aspx?id=49170

Choose the download you want

File Name	Size
MicrosoftAzureBackupInstaller.exe	682 KB
MicrosoftAzureBackupInstaller-1.bin	701.3 MB
MicrosoftAzureBackupInstaller-2.bin	701.9 MB
MicrosoftAzureBackupInstaller-3.bin	701.9 MB
MicrosoftAzureBackupInstaller-4.bin	701.9 MB
MicrosoftAzureBackupInstaller-5.bin	446.7 MB

Figure 4-8. *Azure Backup Server—download the installation files*

    From there, you can start the download of the application. Note that this download is split into separate files, since the full download is 3.2GB.

■ **Tip**   Specifically for this lab setup, I recommend you log on to the Azure Virtual Machine (that will be the Azure Backup Server) you deployed earlier and download the files directly from there.

Installing and Configuring the Azure Backup Server Application

In this section, you will learn how to install the Azure Backup Server application, as well as how to create a backup job for the SQL Server machine.

1. Start the `MicrosoftAzureBackupInstaller.exe`; this will launch a file extraction wizard, followed by the actual `setup.exe`. See Figure 4-9.

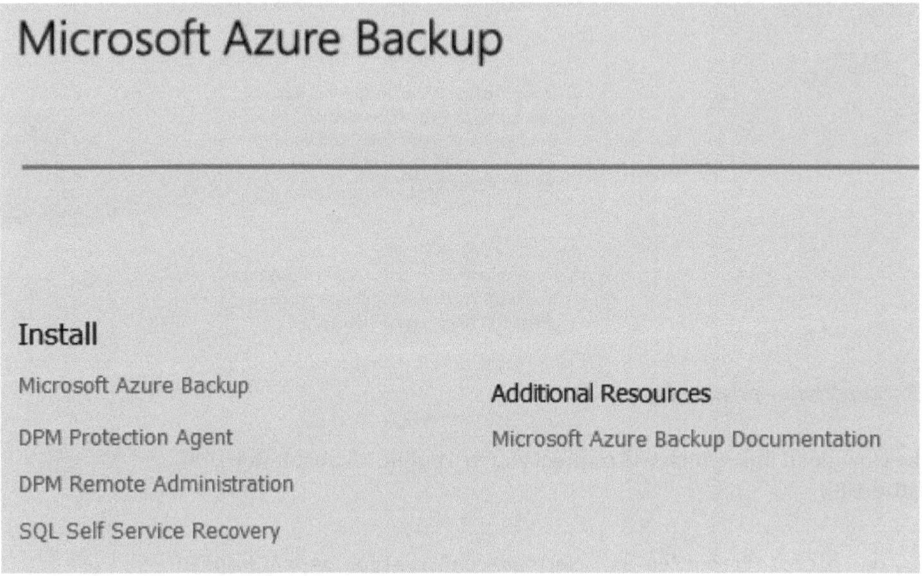

Microsoft Azure Backup

Install

Microsoft Azure Backup

DPM Protection Agent

DPM Remote Administration

SQL Self Service Recovery

Additional Resources

Microsoft Azure Backup Documentation

Figure 4-9. *Microsoft Azure Backup installation*

2. Click Microsoft Azure Backup to start the installation wizard.

3. At the welcome step, click Next to continue.

4. At the Prerequisite Check step, click the Check button. If all goes fine, the machine should meet all the requirements to continue the installation.

5. This brings us to the SQL Settings step. Choose Install New Instance of SQL Server with This Setup and click the Check and Install button to continue. See Figure 4-10.

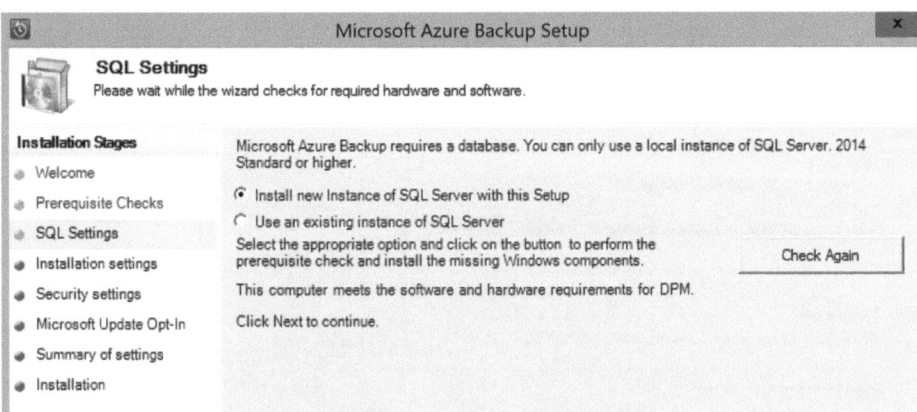

Figure 4-10. *Microsoft Azure Backup installation—SQL settings*

■ **Note**   While Azure Backup Server uses Microsoft SQL Server, there is no additional SQL Server license required. However, the SQL Server instance can only be used for Azure Backup Server in this scenario.

■ **Tip**   If you are prompted that .NET Framework 3.5 SP1 is missing, close this wizard and run the following command from an administrative command prompt:

```
DISM /Online /Enable-Feature /FeatureName:NetFx3 /All
```

Doing so installs the server feature using the online WSUS image.

6. In the installation settings step, accept the defaults as they are shown (in a live production environment, these settings should probably be changed). See Figure 4-11.

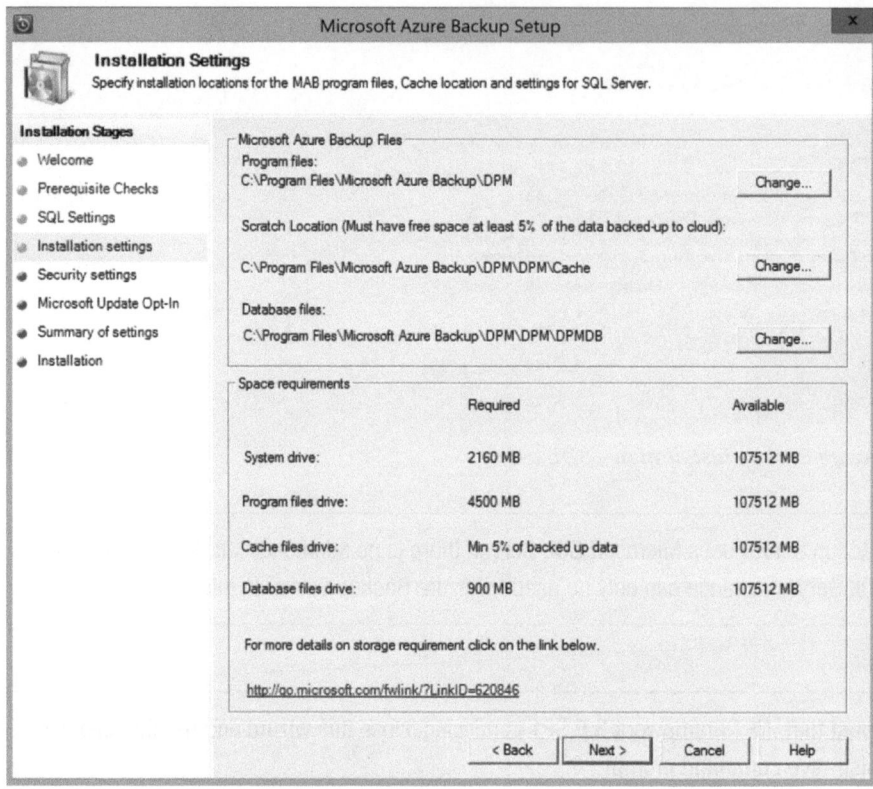

Figure 4-11. Microsoft Azure Backup installation—installation settings

7. This brings you to the Security Settings step. Here you have to create a complex password that will be used by the Azure Backup Server system account you will create, as shown in Figure 4-12.

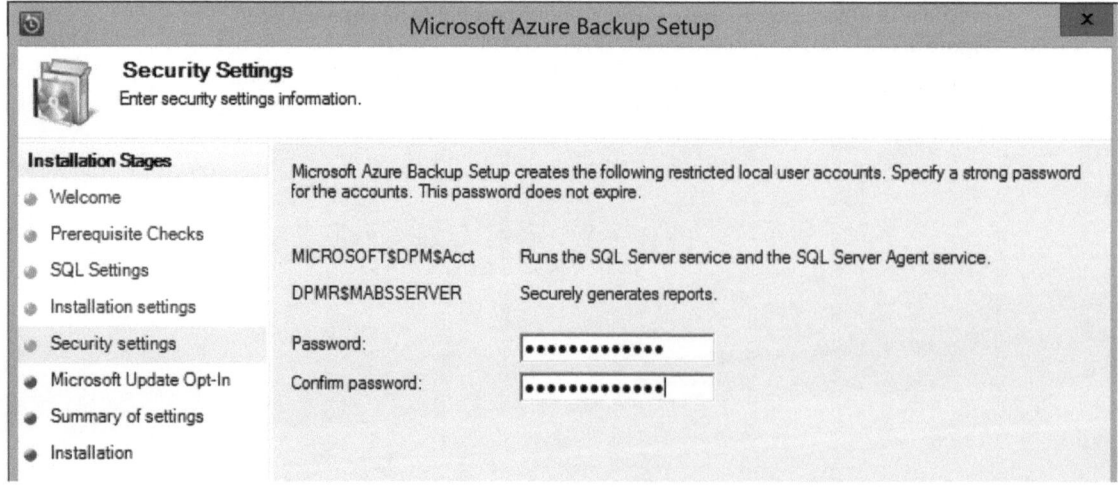

Figure 4-12. Microsoft Azure Backup installation—security settings

■ **Note**   The reference to DPM is clearly visible here: `Microsoft$DPM$Acct`.

8. The remaining steps in the wizard is whether to allow a Windows update for this application or not (I recommend you allow this) and a summary of all settings and parameters. Click Install to continue.

9. This kicks in the installation of the Azure Recovery Services Agent first, during which you are asked to import the Azure Vault credentials file. This is needed to be able to register the server in the Azure Backup Vault. See Figure 4-13.

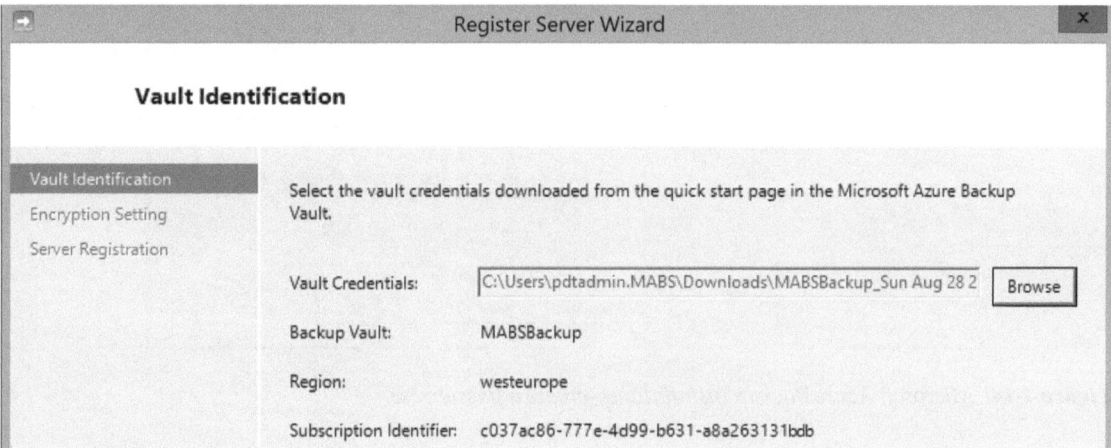

Figure 4-13. Microsoft Azure Backup installation—Register Server Wizard

10. The Azure Backup Server encrypts backups in the same way as the Azure Backup agent does. Therefore, you are asked to create a (complex and long) passphrase and export it to a text file, so you can retrieve it later (for example, during a restore to an alternative server other than the original source machine). See Figure 4-14.

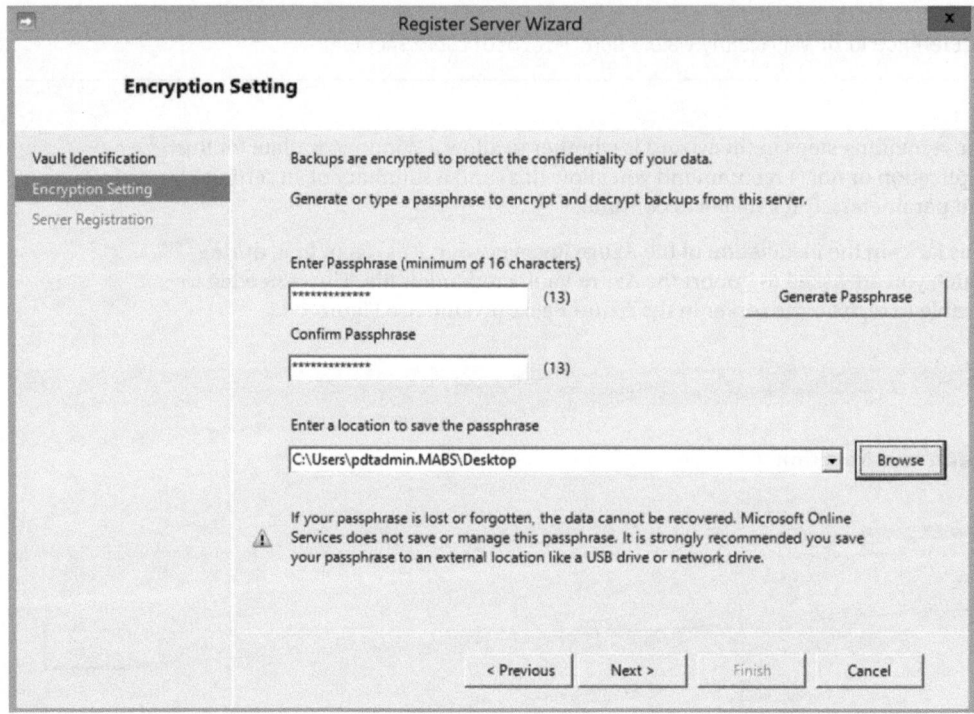

Figure 4-14. *Microsoft Azure Backup installation—create a passphrase*

11. Once the Azure Recovery Service agent configuration is completed, the Azure
Backup agent installation process continues, by installing and configuring a SQL
Server 2014 instance. See Figure 4-15.

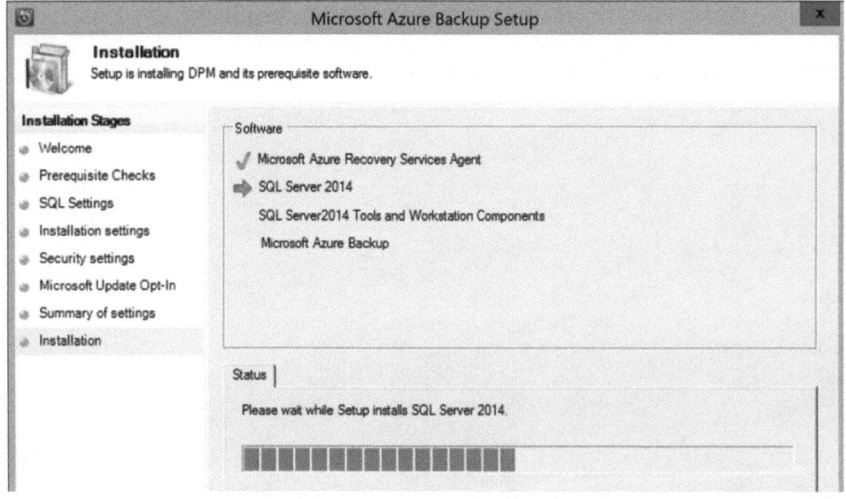

Figure 4-15. *Microsoft Azure Backup installation—SQL Server 2014 setup*

■ **Note**   This setup will take about 15-20 minutes, so now might be a good time to get a cup of coffee.

12. Wait for the installation to complete successfully. Figure 4-16 shows the end result.

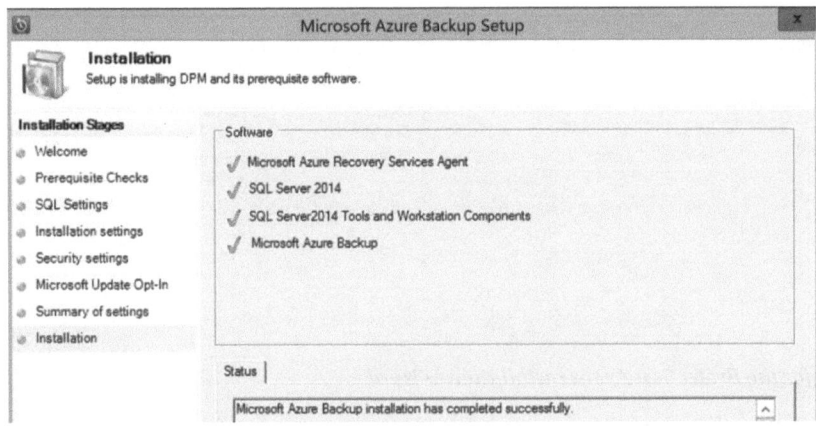

Figure 4-16. *Microsoft Azure Backup installation has completed successfully*

13. Start the Microsoft Azure Backup Server from the shortcut that is available on the desktop or from the Start menu.

14. From within the application console, select Management and click the Install button from the top menu. This launches the Protection Agent Installation wizard. Select Install Agents and then click Next to continue as shown in Figure 4-17.

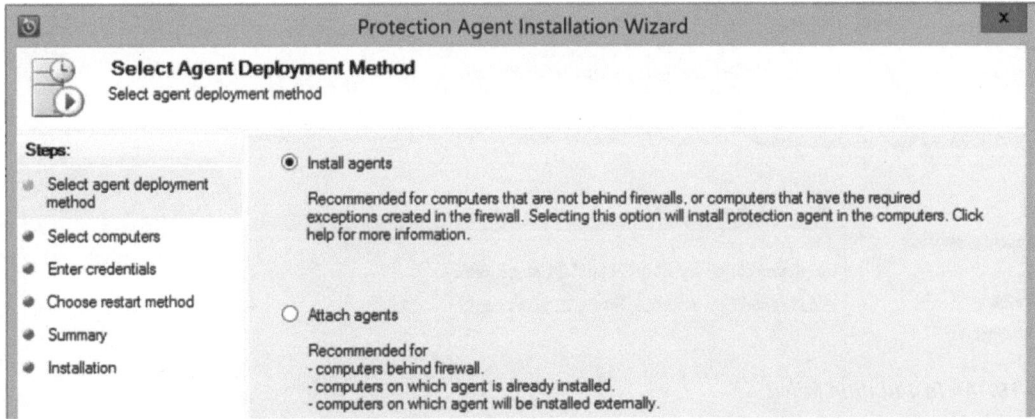

Figure 4-17. *The Protection Agent Installation Wizard*

15. In the next step, your domain joined servers should be listed. Since we have only two in our lab environment, select both of them. See Figure 4-18.

Figure 4-18. *Select the servers for the Protection Agent Installation Wizard*

16. After selecting the computers and clicking Next, you are asked to provide the credentials to authenticate these machines. A domain administrator account is required here.

17. The remaining steps of this wizard ask you to define if you want these computers to restart automatically after getting the protection agent installed, and that's all you need to do to complete this wizard. At the end of the wizard, the remote agent installation will start.

18. As you can see in Figure 4-19, the remote agent push install failed for server MABSDC. Select the Errors tab to get more details about the cause of this failure as shown in Figure 4-20.

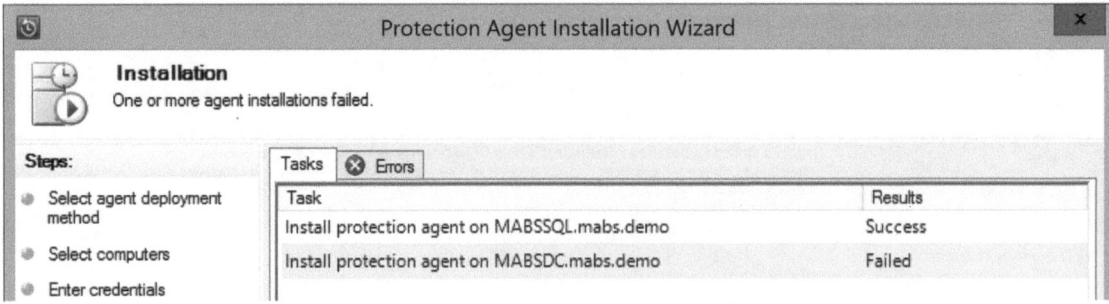

Figure 4-19. *An installation failed*

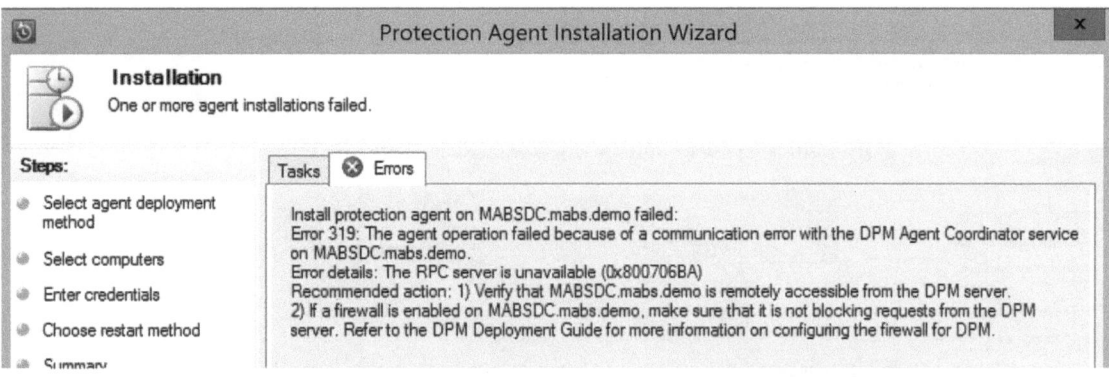

Figure 4-20. View the errors to determine why it failed

19. Fix the error on the MABSDC (disabling the firewall or creating a firewall exception rule to allow the traffic) and restart the installation process. The agent is installed successfully this time as shown in Figure 4-21.

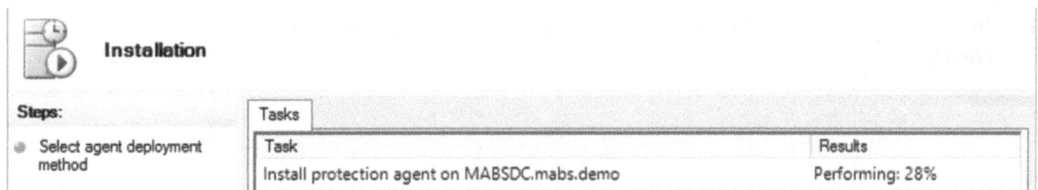

Figure 4-21. The protection agent installation has been fixed

20. Since both machines have the agent installed now, you can continue configuring the protection group and defining a backup job (see Figure 4-22). From the Azure Backup Server console, select the Protecting pane and click New from the top menu.

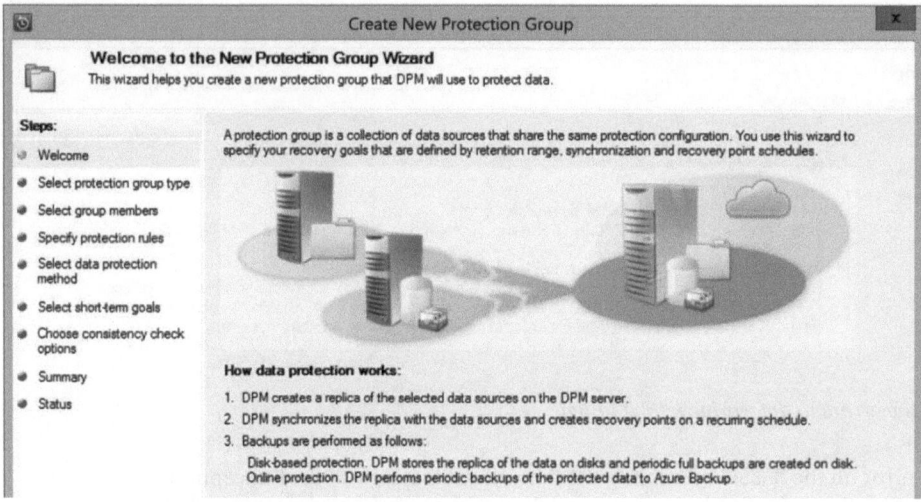

Figure 4-22. *Create a new protection group*

21. In the Select Protection Group type step, select Servers (see Figure 4-23).; click Next to continue.

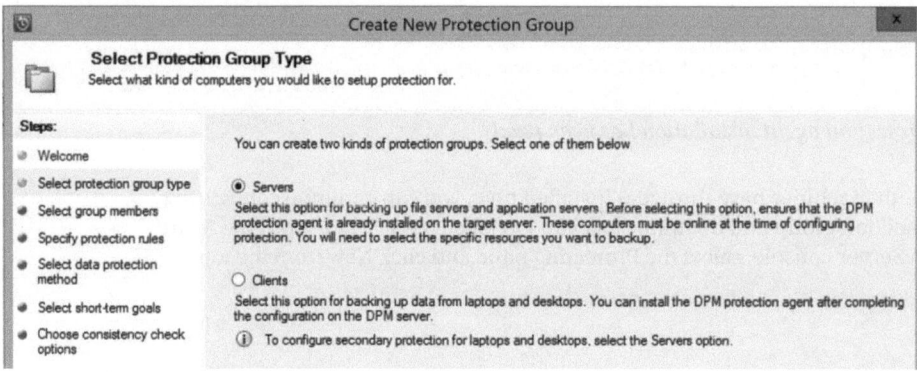

Figure 4-23. *Select the protection group type*

22. In the Select Group Members step, you select which servers you want to enable backup, as well as which shares, volumes, and system states (see Figure 4-24). Since having shares is not what we want—that would basically be a "folders and files-only" backup—select volumes. Confirm the popup about also selecting the system state and mark it for backup. Click Next to continue to the next step.

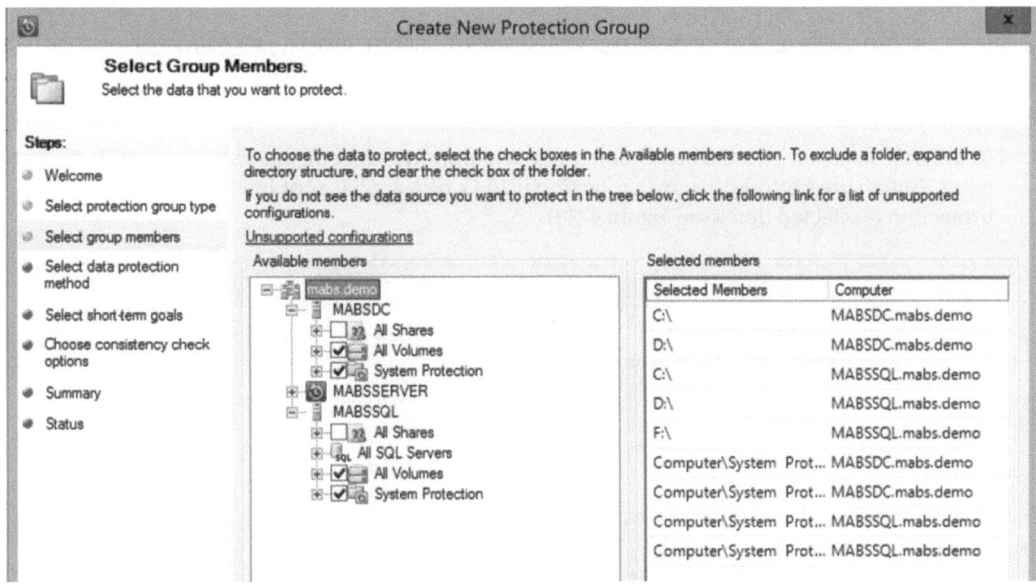

Figure 4-24. *Select the group members*

■ **Note**   Notice the All SQL Servers within the SQL Server machine; this allows you to take granular backups of SQL Server databases. These can be configured in a separate protection group, and can be configured on the SQL instance level or per SQL database individually.

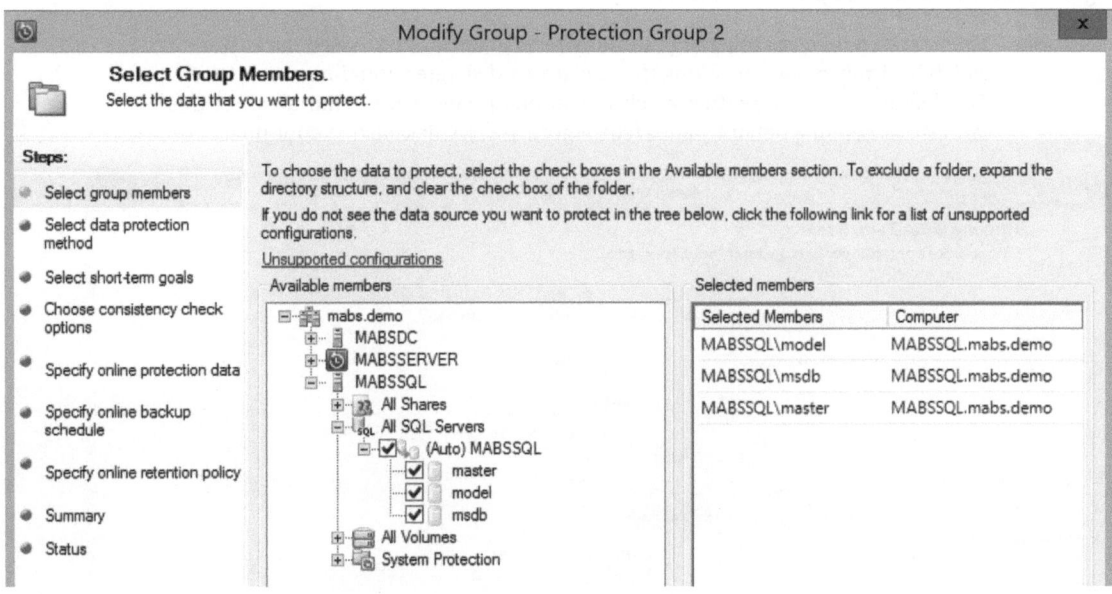

Figure 4-25. *Select the SQL Server backup options*

■ **Note** The same view exists for Exchange Server and SharePoint Server, allowing for individual mailbox database or SharePoint data restores.

23. In the next step, you give the protection group a name and select the backup target. Make sure both short-term protection using a disk as well as online protection is selected here (see Figure 4-26).

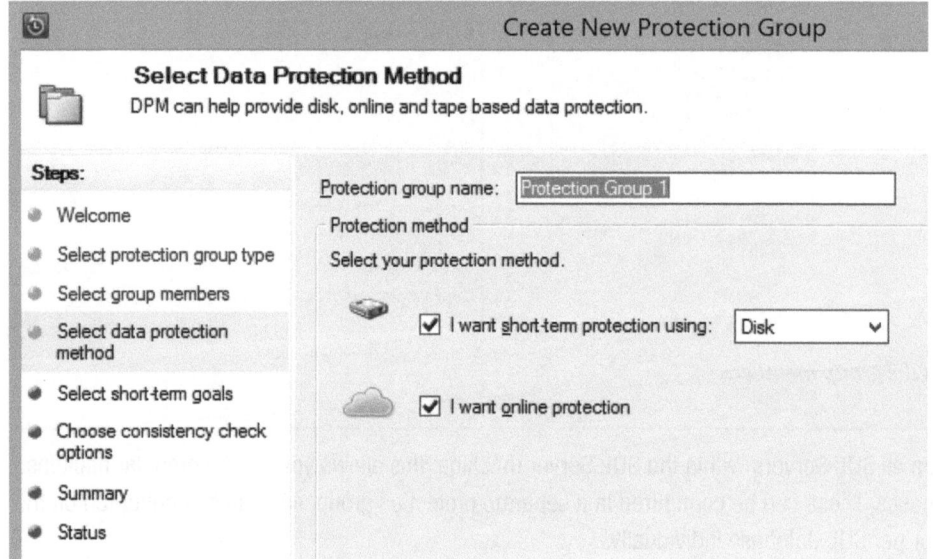

Figure 4-26. *Select the data protection method*

24. The next step involves selecting the short-term goals for disk-based backup, which basically means how long the backup-to-disk retention time needs to be. The default is five days, with a synchronization update every 15 minutes. For this exercise, accept the default values (see Figure 4-27). Click Next to continue.

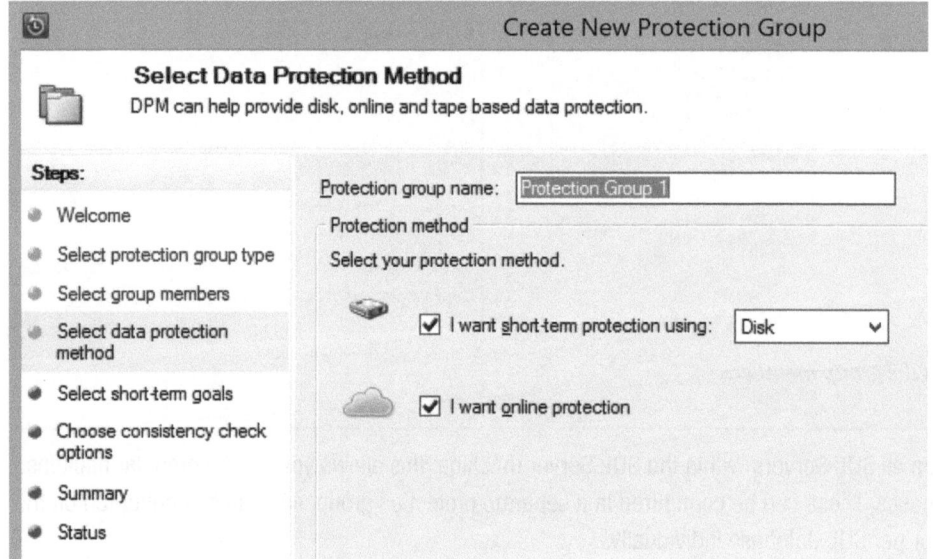

Figure 4-27. *Specify the short-term goals*

25. Disk allocation shows you how much disk space is estimated to be in use by Azure Backup Server, for protecting the selected items in the protection group. In most cases, it is OK to accept the default settings (see Figure 4-28). Click Next to continue.

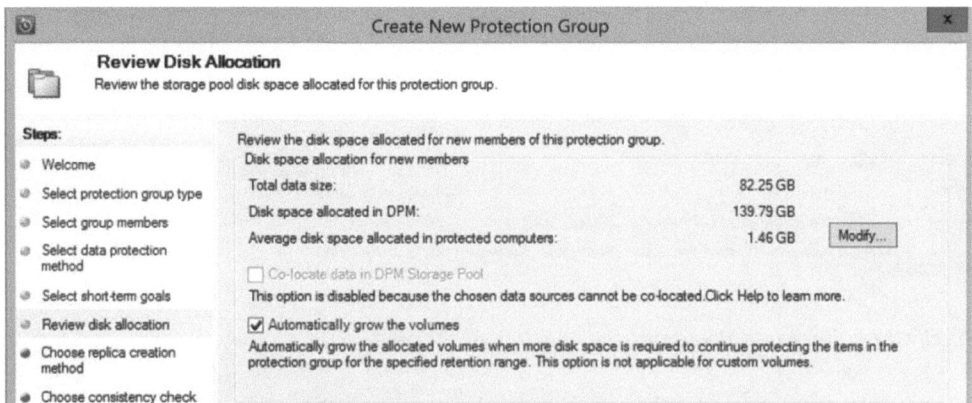

Figure 4-28. *Review the disk allocation*

26. You now see Choose Replica Creation Method, where you specify how the initial replica (the backup) should be created (see Figure 4-29). This can be done over the network, immediately, or at a later scheduled moment, or you can also choose to manually copy existing images using removable media. This could be interesting when migrating backups from an older on-premises DPM server to MABS, or when centralizing backups from a remote site.

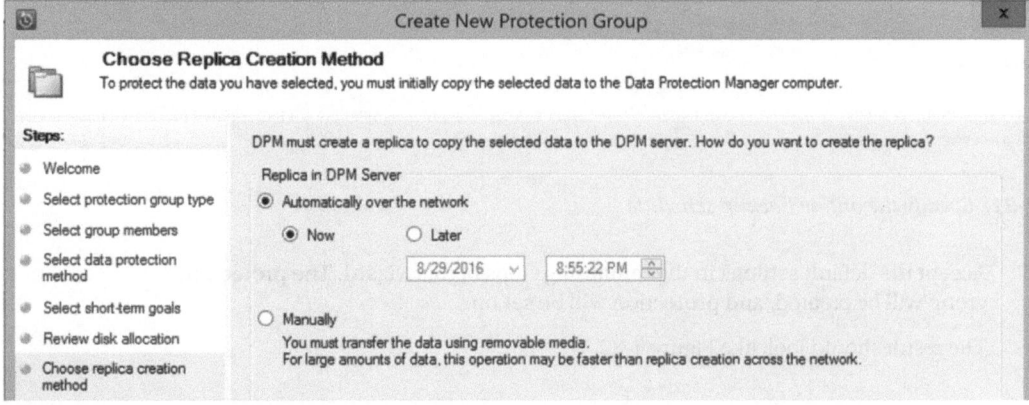

Figure 4-29. *Choose the replica creation method*

27. In the next step, you specify which of the items within the protection group should be synchronized to Azure as online protection data (see Figure 4-30). This is a really interesting feature, since you can decide to have full machine backups available on-premises from the MABS disk backup, and only specify certain volumes as online backup (which will be a second copy).

93

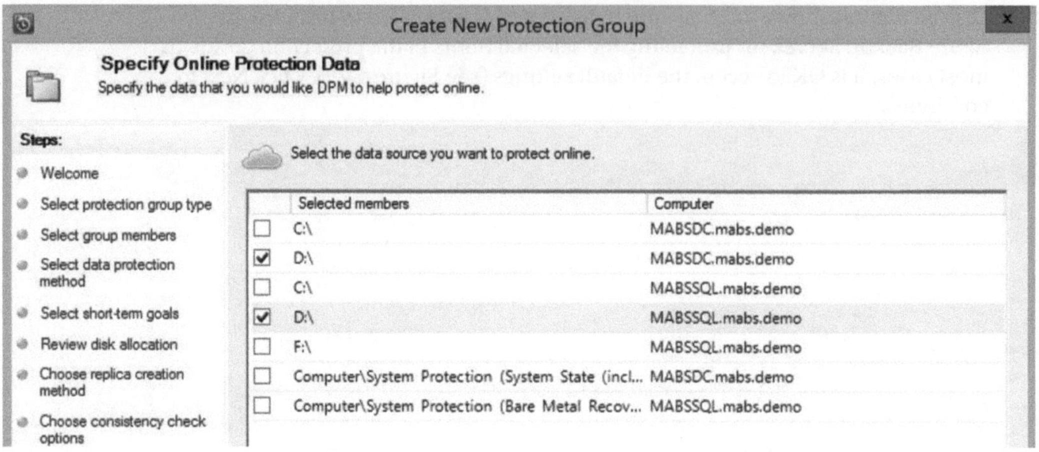

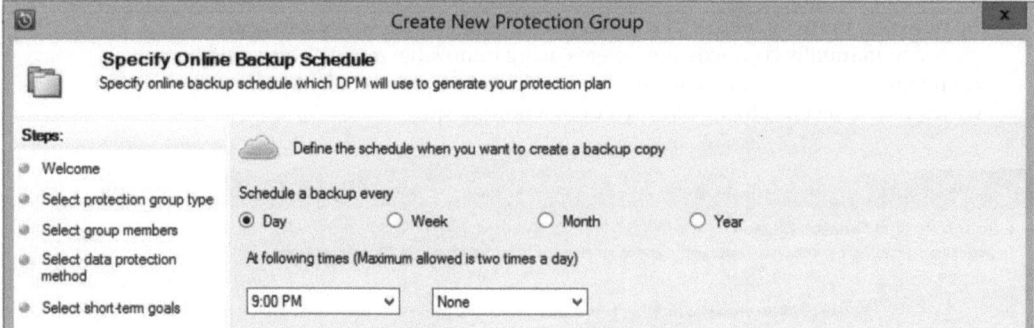

Figure 4-30. Specify the online protection data

28. Once the online protection data has been selected, you can create a corresponding schedule for this in the next step (see Figure 4-31). It is possible to have two synchronization times per instance (day, week, month, or year). Once the schedule is defined, you can also specify the retention settings.

Figure 4-31. Specify the online backup schedule

29. Accept the default settings in the remaining steps of this wizard. The protection group will be created, and protection will be set up.

The result should look like Figure 4-32.

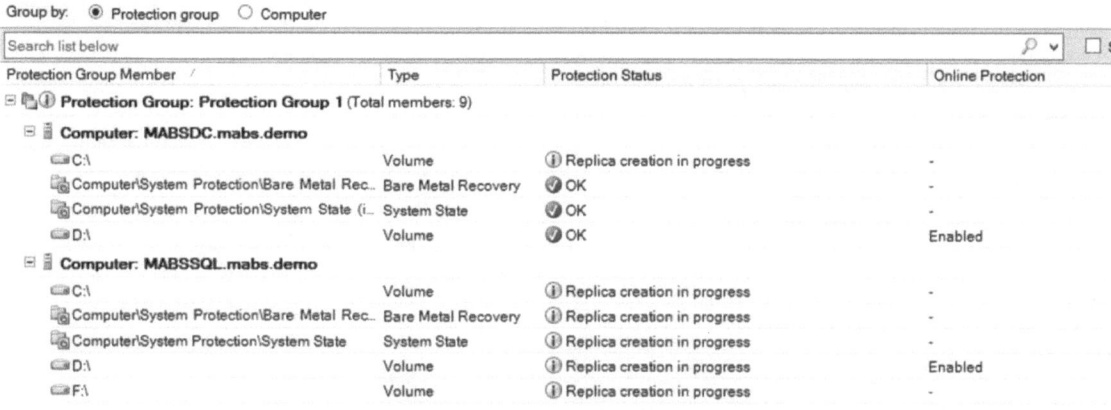

Figure 4-32. Microsoft Azure Backup—protection group protection status

Wait for the replica creation to be completed for each item. Depending on the backup schedule timings you defined, it might take some time (hours) before you can continue to the next section, restoring data out of MABS backups.

Performing a Restore from Azure Backup Server Application

What's the purpose of having a backup solution if you cannot restore, right? Using Azure Backup Server, this process is pretty straightforward in any way, and I quickly want to walk you through the key concept and steps involved.

1. From within the Azure Backup Server console, select Recovery (see Figure 4-33).

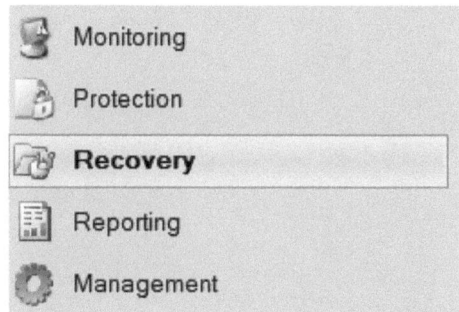

Figure 4-33. Microsoft Azure Backup—Recovery menu

2. In the same pane, a list of all protected items is listed, allowing you to browse to the volume from where you want to restore data (see Figure 4-34). This data can be the full volume, individual folders and files, or in case of a specific workload like SQL Server, allowing you to restore up to the SQL database level.

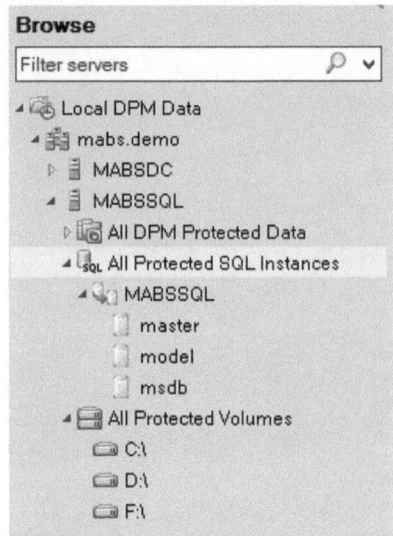

Figure 4-34. *Browse protected items to recover*

3. In this example, select the C drive under All Protected Items of the MABSSQL machine and browse to any of the subfolders. Notice that the recovery points are visible at the top, showing you the view per day and per recovery time window, as shown in Figure 4-35.

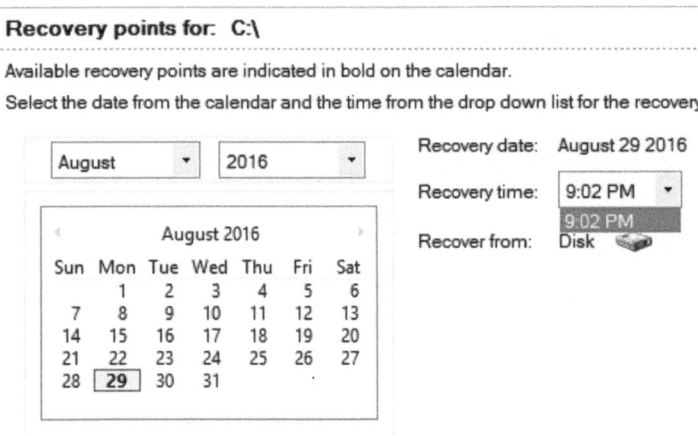

Figure 4-35. *Select a recovery point*

4. From the data selection window, select the folder you want to restore, and then right-click and select Recover... from the context menu (see Figure 4-36). This will start the Recovery Wizard.

Path: C:\Program Files\

Search list below

Recoverable Item /	Last Modified
Common Files	8/22/2013 3:39:31 PM
desktop.ini	8/22/2013 3:38:18 PM
Internet Explorer	8/5/2016 11:45:20 PM
Java	8/5/2016 10:48:05 PM
Microsoft Analysis Services	8/5/2016 10:11:23 PM
Microsoft Data Protection M	⏱ Show all recovery points	28/2016 10:43:11 PM
Microsoft Help Viewer	⏲ Recover...	5/2016 10:09:40 PM
Microsoft MPI	8/5/2016 10:38:21 PM

Figure 4-36. *Select the data to be restored*

5. From the Recovery Wizard, find the folder you selected before being shown for review (see Figure 4-37). Click Next to continue.

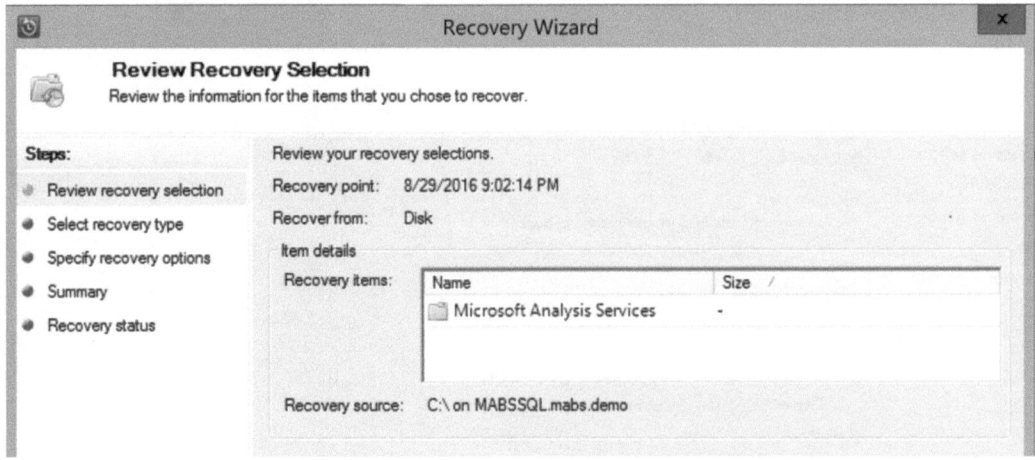

Figure 4-37. *Microsoft Azure Backup—review recovery selection*

6. Now you define the recovery location to be used (see Figure 4-38). Accept the default to recover to the original location. Click Next to continue.

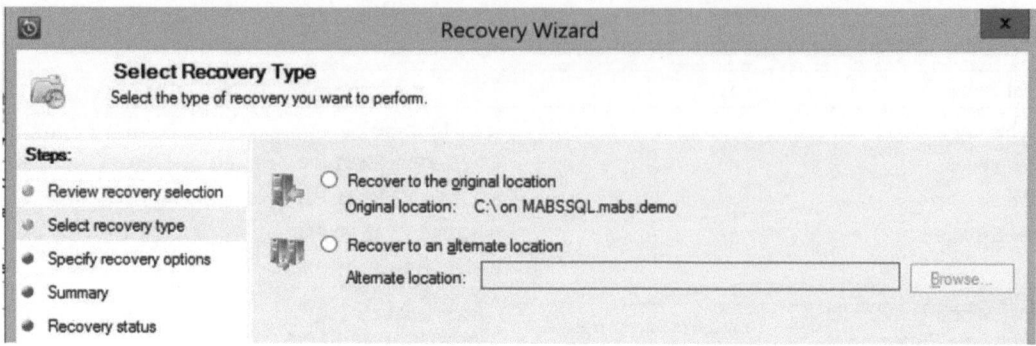

Figure 4-38. *Microsoft Azure Backup—select the recovery type*

7. In the Recovery Options window, you can define how to manage existing versions, determine if folder NTFS ACL security should be restored too, and configure any notifications if needed (see Figure 4-39). Accept the default values for now and click Next to continue.

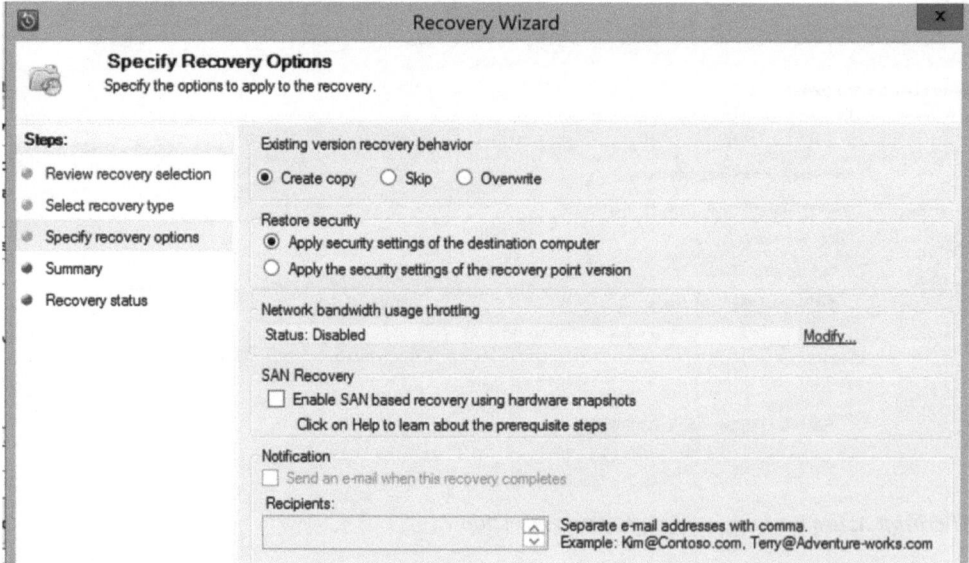

Figure 4-39. *Specify the recovery options*

8. Wait for the recovery to happen and complete successfully, after which you can close the wizard.

    Feel free to try another restore of a SQL Server database if you are interested in playing with it. The overall concept and ease of the tool is the same as when restoring a folder, which you just did.

Summary

This chapter focused on the deployment and configuration of Azure Backup Server, which I like to describe as a "Cloud-integrated version of System Center Data Protection Manager". As you experienced by going through the exercise, only a few pointers within the application point to Azure Backup Server, where most references to SCDPM are retained. I walked you through the installation of the solution and showed you how to configure a protection group and related backup job. In the last section, you learned how to restore a folder.

If you are interested in learning the last flavor of Azure Backup, Azure VM Backup using VM extensions, I welcome you back in the next chapter.

CHAPTER 5

■ ■ ■

Deploying and Configuring Azure Virtual Machine Backup

This is the third and last chapter of the Azure Backup story, in which I describe how to take "in-Azure" backups (I don't know if that actually is an official or existing term) of Azure Virtual Machines.

While using Azure Backup Server from the previous chapter is also a valid option for taking Azure VM backups, it acts more like a "server-based" application, where this Azure VM Backup feels more like a true Platform as a Service (PaaS) Cloud solution. Everything you need is available as a Cloud service. You define the backup configuration and create backup policies, and then the backup agent extension is deployed and backup jobs are scheduled to run automatically. So there is no need to install and configure any specific backup applications (like in the previous chapter).

To guide you through the subject, you will work on another exercise that is again a step-by-step scenario. It shows you the technical deployment and configuration of a Windows Server operating system VM backup, as well as how to do this for a Linux operating system VM backup, which is a little bit trickier.

Supported Environments

Before walking you through a step-by-step deployment and configuration exercise, I want to remind you of the different supported environments for Azure VM Backup, which were listed in Chapter 3.

Supported Operating Systems for Azure VM Backup

The following operating systems are supported by Azure VM Backup, leveraging on the virtual machine agent and backup extensions:

- Windows Server 2012 and 2012 R2

- Windows Server 2008 SP2 and 2008 R2 SP1

- Linux operating systems:

    - CentOS 6.3+ and 7.0+

    - Debian 7.9+ and 8.2+

    - Oracle Linux 6.4+ and 7.0+

    - Red Hat Enterprise Linux 6.7+ and 7.1+

    - SUSE Linux Enterprise 11 SP4, 12+, and 11.3+ (SAP specific)

    - Ubuntu 12.04 LTS, 14.04 LTS, and 16.04 LTS

© Peter De Tender 2016

P. De Tender, *Implementing Operations Management Suite*, DOI 10.1007/978-1-4842-1979-9_5

That's not to say that it won't work on other versions of these platforms, but these are the supported ones. For Windows Server, it is obvious, as those are the only Windows Server versions running on Azure (not taking Server 2016 Technical Preview into account). As there are many different custom flavors of Linux, it could be that it is not working, although this would be more the exception in my opinion.

Now you know what platforms are supported, I jump back into the technology and walk you through the different solutions and configurations step-by-step.

Deploying and Configuring Azure VM Backup

In this exercise, you learn how to:

- Configure Azure Backup Vault for Azure VM Backup

- Configure an Azure VM Backup policy

- Perform a full Azure VM Backup (one Windows OS VM, one Linux OS VM)

- Restore an Azure VM from a backup

Exercise Prerequisites

Two Azure VMs are required for this exercise, so make sure you deploy one new Azure resource group called AzureVMBackup or similar. It should contain one Windows 2012 R2 VM, based on the gallery image, as well as one Linux Server VM. (I use the Ubuntu Server 14.04 gallery image, since you need a subscription without a spending limit for Red Hat Enterprise.)

Configuring Azure Backup Vault for Azure VM Backup

The first thing you need to do is configure another Azure Backup Vault, as follows:

1. From the Azure portal, click +New and search for Recovery.

2. From the list of solutions that appears, select Backup and Recovery (OMS) (see Figure 5-1).

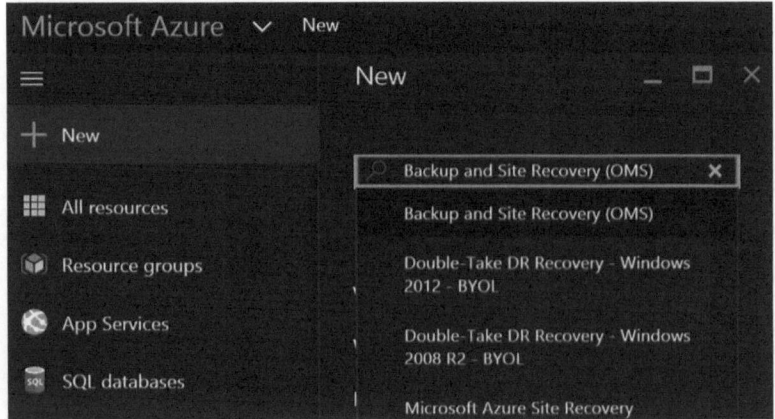

Figure 5-1. *Selecting Backup and Site Recovery (OMS) from the portal*

3. Confirm the creation in the next step.

4. This opens the Recovery Services Vault setup blade, where you have to enter some parameters (see Figure 5-2):

   • Enter a descriptive name for the vault

   • Create a new resource group or select an existing one

   • Select the Azure region closest to your location

Click the Create button to set up the Azure Backup Vault.

Figure 5-2. *Selecting Backup and Site Recovery (OMS) from the portal*

5. Wait for the Azure Backup Vault to be created. Once this is done, select it from the portal. This will open its settings, where you can find the Backup option under Getting Started (see Figure 5-3).

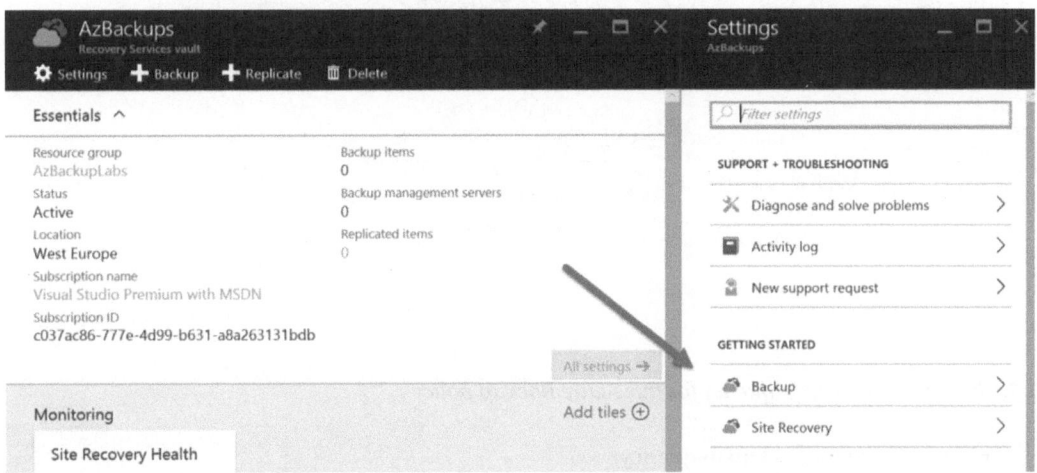

Figure 5-3. *Selecting the Backup and Site Recovery (OMS) from the portal*

6. This opens up the configuration blade, where you walk through a three-step scenario in getting the Azure VM Backup protection configured.

    In the first step, the Backup Goal, you specify Azure as the workload and the virtual machine as to where you want to back up, as shown in Figure 5-4.

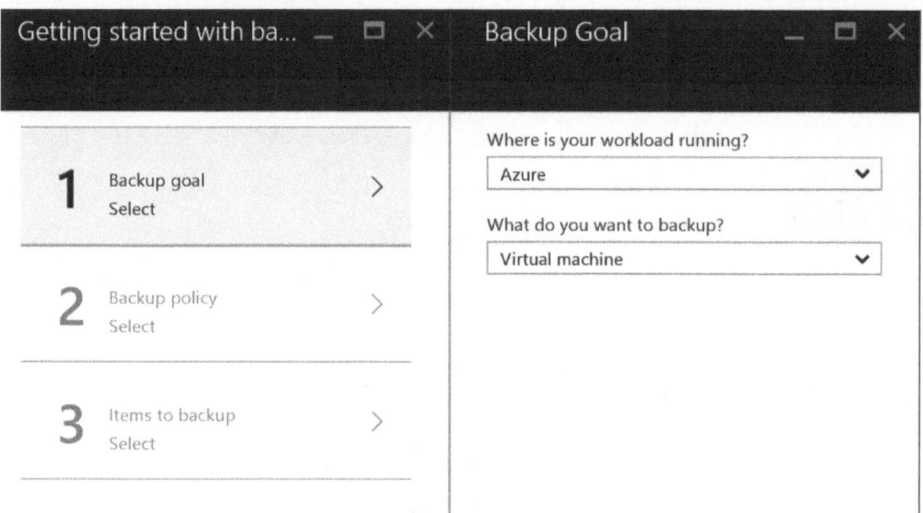

Figure 5-4. *Specify the backup goal for this Azure Backup Vault*

7. This brings you to Step 2, where you create a backup policy (see Figure 5-5). This is similar to the backup policy and retention settings policy you created earlier in the Azure Backup Agent or Azure Backup Server scenarios.

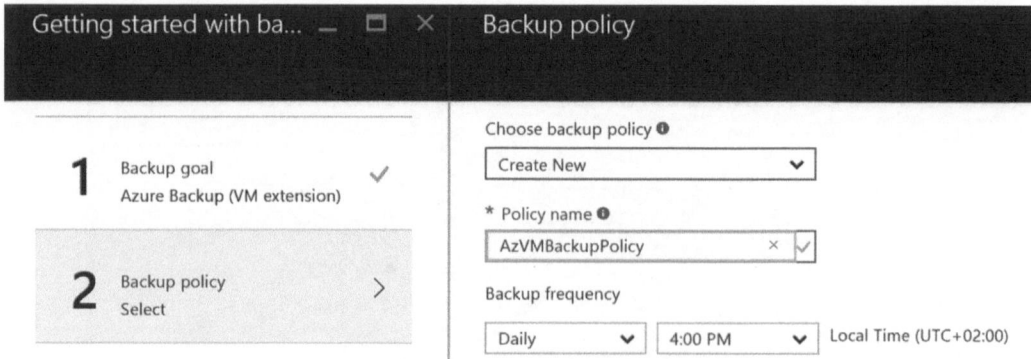

Figure 5-5. *Specify the backup frequency for this Azure Backup policy*

- Configure the backup frequency.
- Specify a retention setting for daily/weekly/monthly and yearly backup points (see Figure 5-6).

Retention range

☑ Retention of daily backup point.

* At   For

| 4:00 PM ▾ | 180 ✓ | Day(s) |

☑ Retention of weekly backup point.

* On   * At   For

| Sunday ▾ | 4:00 PM ▾ | 104 ✓ | Week(s) |

☑ Retention of monthly backup point.

| Week Based | Day Based |

* On   * Day   * At   For

| First ▾ | Sunday ▾ | 4:00 PM ▾ | 60 ✓ | Month(s) |

☑ Retention of yearly backup point.

| Week Based | Day Based |

***Figure 5-6.** Specify the backup retention settings for this Azure Backup policy*

> 8. In the third and last step, select the Azure Virtual Machines you want to include in this backup protection (see Figure 5-7).

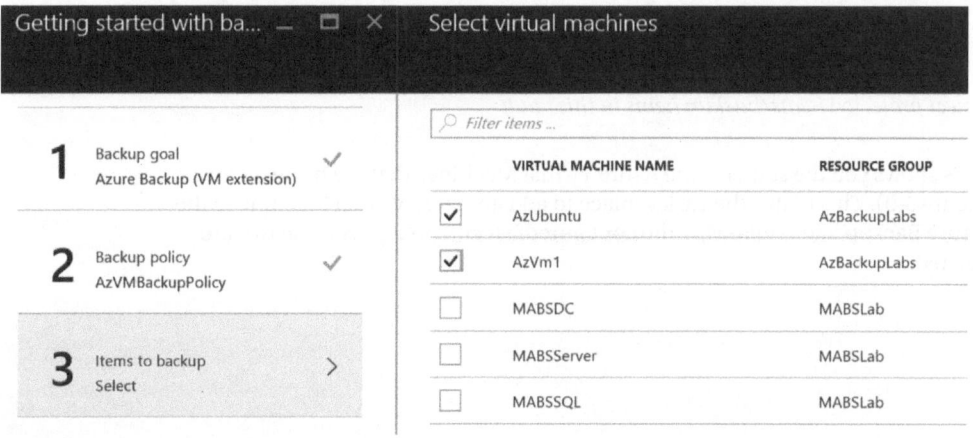

***Figure 5-7.** Select the virtual machines you want to protect in this vault*

■ **Note** Notice that the Azure Virtual Machines we used in the previous chapter on Azure Backup Server are also visible here. This makes sense, since they are Azure Virtual Machines. It would be nice though if they could be excluded from this list, since they are part of another backup solution, which might cause confusion in larger enterprises running a large number of Azure VMs.

Monitoring Azure VM Backup Jobs and Alerts

Now you will learn how to monitor Azure VM Backup jobs and alerts:

1. Wait for the backup configuration to be finished (see the notification area). Once it's done, go back to the Azure Backup Vault and browse to Protected Items/Backup Items (see Figure 5-8).

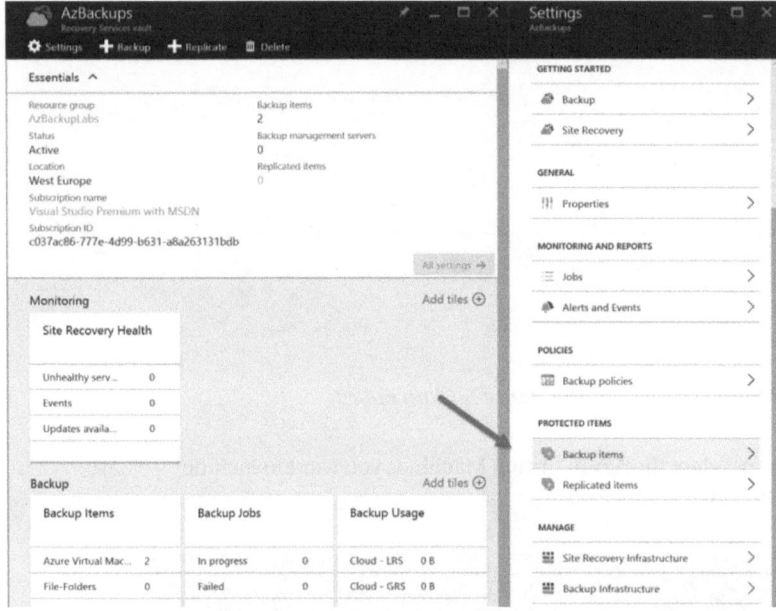

Figure 5-8. *Select protected items/backup items in this vault*

2. This shows you the status of the Azure Virtual Machines that are protected (see Figure 5-9). This is also the easiest place to add an Azure Virtual Machine to the Azure Backup Vault, following the configured backup policy, as these two are related.

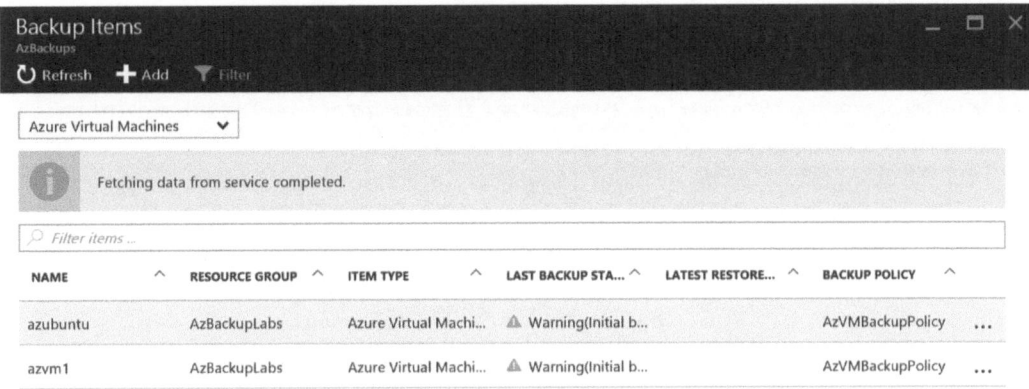

Figure 5-9. Backup items in this vault with their latest status

3. Notice the last backup state is currently in the Warning state, since the initial backup has not yet run. This is normal. To fix this warning state, select each VM, which will bring up the Azure VM backup details. Click the Backup Now button from the top menu to manually initiate the first backup (see Figure 5-10).

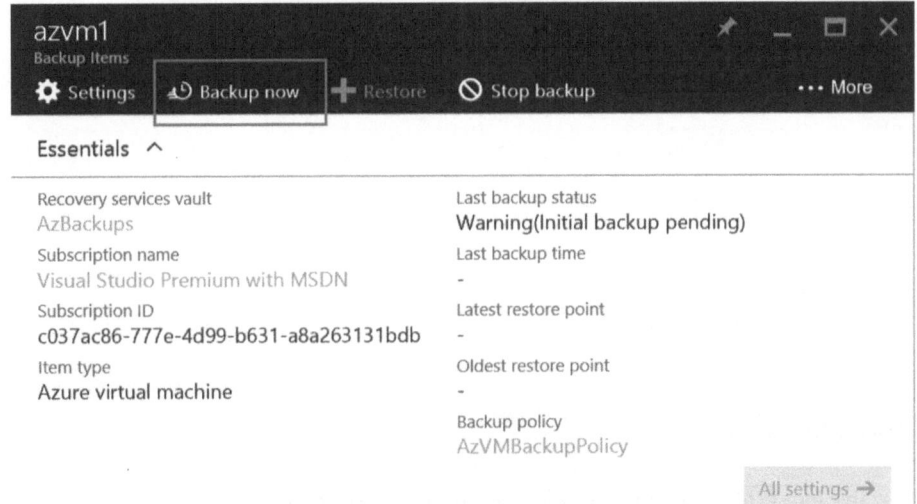

Figure 5-10. Click the Backup Now button to initiate the first backup

4. Wait for the backup triggering notification, after which you can monitor the job from the Azure Backup job pane (see Figure 5-11). To get there, select the Azure Backup Vault/Monitoring and Reports/Jobs/Backup Jobs.

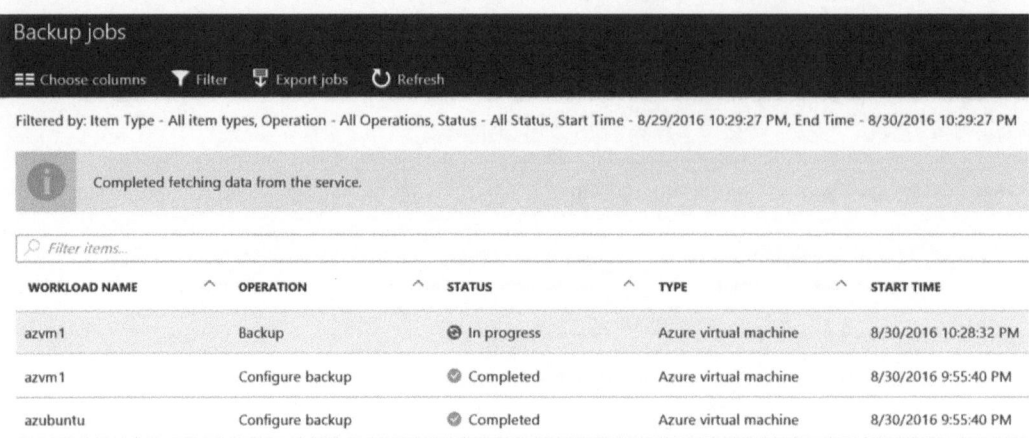

Figure 5-11. *Backup Jobs*

5. Select the active job (backup/in progress) to get a more detailed view of the different actions in this job, as shown in Figure 5-12.

Figure 5-12. *Detailed view of the backup jobss*

6. Seeing the active jobs is okay, but most system admins are not watching the portal all day long to see the active backup job giving issues and failing. Also, most backup jobs run after business hours. So some kind of additional monitoring or notification would be beneficial.

While I will talk about a (at the time of writing) preview monitoring integration of Azure Backup with OMS, there is some basic monitoring and alerting built into the backup vault. It even supports sending out notifications by e-mail.

To configure this feature, go back to the Azure Backup Vault Settings, select the Monitoring and Reports section, and then choose Alerts and Events (see Figure 5-13).

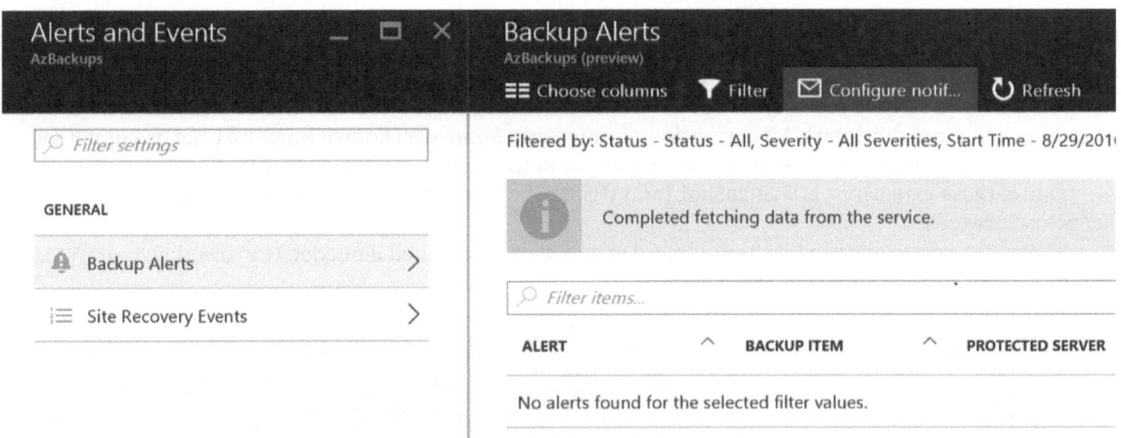

Figure 5-13. *Backup Vault—backup alerts configuration*

7. Click Configure Notification from the top menu and complete the parameters (see Figure 5-14).

    •   Enter the recipients' e-mail addresses. This can be individual addresses or distribution lists aliases.

    •   Specify whether a notification should be sent out per alert or on an hourly basis.

    •   Select the severity category(ies) you want to receive notifications for.

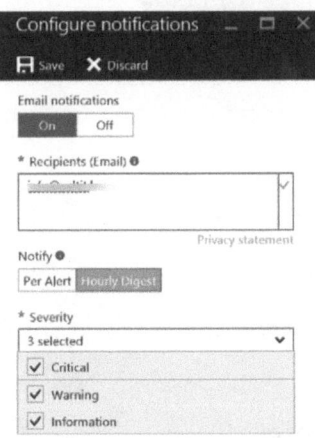

Figure 5-14. *Backup Vault—configuring the backup alerts*

Azure VM Extensions for Backup

From the introduction of Azure Backup in Chapter 3, you learned about the three different "flavors" of Azure Backup. The two flavors we already covered are recognized by deploying a specific Azure Backup agent to the machines we want to protect. This third flavor is a bit different, as you don't need to install anything... or do you?

Well, yes and no. The action "behind the curtains" is pretty cool and is driven by the Azure Virtual Machine extensions.

Azure VM extensions make many of the core features between Azure and the virtual machine possible. Think of an RDP connection or PowerShell DSC integration. Next to basic extensions, there are also more and more third-party VM extensions coming out. Some well known ones are Chef or Puppet for configuration management, McAfee and Symantec for antivirus features, and a lot more.

One of these extensions is VMSnapShot (and VMSnapShotLinux), also known as Microsoft.Azure. RecoveryServices.

These VM extensions can be checked (and installed or uninstalled if needed) by selecting Azure VM/ Settings/Extensions, as shown in Figure 5-15.

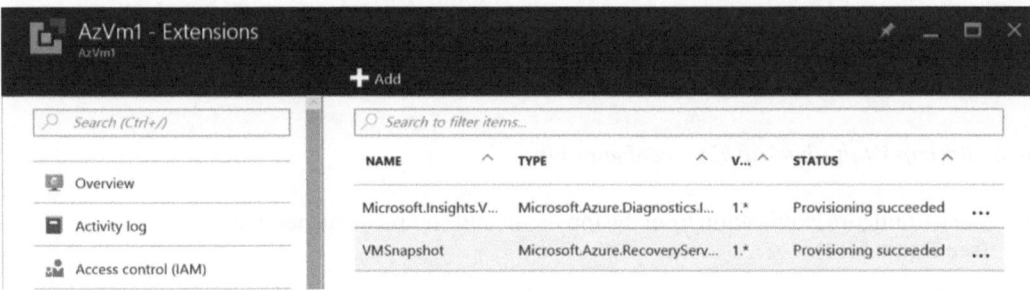

Figure 5-15. *Azure VM extensions—Microsoft.Azure.RecoveryServices.VMSnapShot*

The process is similar if it is a Linux operating system, as shown in Figure 5-16.

NAME	TYPE	V...	STATUS	
LinuxAsm	Microsoft.Azure.Extensions.Li...	2.*	Provisioning succeeded	...
Microsoft.Insights.V...	Microsoft.OSTCExtensions.Lin...	2.*	Provisioning succeeded	...
VMSnapshotLinux	Microsoft.Azure.RecoveryServ...	1.*	Provisioning succeeded	...

Figure 5-16. *Azure VM extensions—Microsoft.Azure.RecoveryServices.VMSnapShot*

■ **Note**   The LinuxASM VM extension is the alternative to the Windows VM agent.

While I said there is nothing magically happening, actually up to some point there is. If you browse to another Azure VM that is not being backed up by Azure Backup in this scenario, and you try to manually install the RecoveryServices VM extension, it is not in the list of available extensions. That's because it gets installed automatically when trying to start the backup job.

The reason this works is because it relies on the Azure VM agent, which is provisioned automatically when deploying an Azure VM from the image gallery. But what happens if you deploy Azure VMs from a custom image, or you upload a custom VM VHD to Azure that does not have the Azure VM agent installed, or it is outdated?

The solution here is to manually install the Azure VM agent to this machine. While this works for both Windows and Linux operating systems, the procedure for installing this VM agent is a bit different.

Manually Installing the Azure VM Agent to Azure VMs Running Windows OS

Here is the Windows OS process:

1. Download the package for the Azure VM agent from the following location:

   http://go.microsoft.com/fwlink/?LinkID=394789&clcid=0x409

2. Run the installer with administrative credentials.

3. You basically just click Next to continue, wait for the agent to be installed, and then close the installer by clicking Finish at the end.

4. You can verify that the VM agent installed successfully in two ways:

   a. From the File Explorer VM agent log file. During the installation of the VM agent, the MonitoringAgent log file is created. This file can be found under <systemdrive>\Windows Azure\Logs (see Figure 5-17).

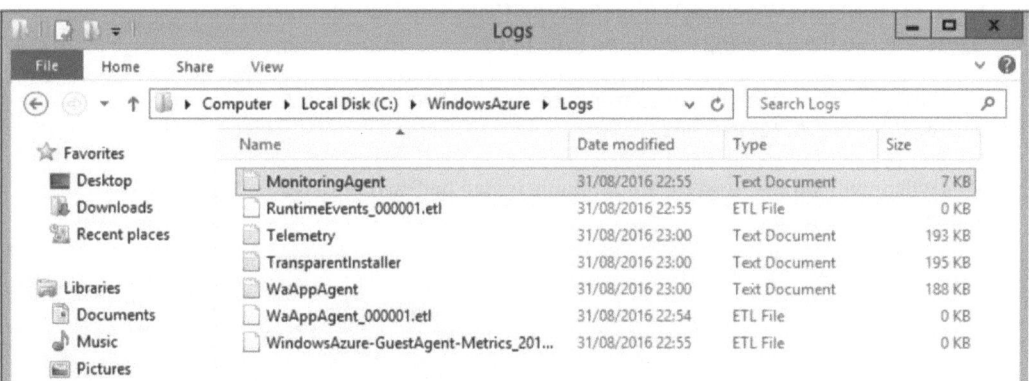

Figure 5-17. *Azure VM agent installation log file*

5. After installing the VM agent, you must also use Azure PowerShell to update the ProvisionGuestAgent property so that Azure knows the VM has the agent installed.

   The script that I used is shown in Figure 5-18.

```
1   Login-AzureRmAccount
2   Get-AzureRmSubscription
3   Select-AzureRmSubscription -SubscriptionName "|                                  n"
4   Get-AzureRmVM
5
6   $vm = Get-AzureRMVM -resourcegroupname "redhat" -name "rh68vm2"
7   $vm.ProvisioningState = $true
8   Update-AzureRMVM -resourcegroupname "redhat" -VM $vm
9   |
```

Figure 5-18. *Azure VM agent ProvisioningState update*

■ **Tip**   Updating the `ProvisionGuestAgent` property is necessary only if the VM is already running in Azure and the agent was not provisioned when the VM was created. When creating a VM from an image (including from custom image), the VM agent is installed by default and that property is updated automatically.

Manually Installing the Azure VM Agent to Azure VMs Running Linux Server OS

The process to install the VM agent on Linux is overall similar to the installation on a Windows OS VM, but it is different. If you are fairly new to the Linux world, it can be tricky. I will guide you through it.

1. Log on to the Linux VM console from Putty/SSH session with administrative rights and run the following command (one line):

   ```
   wget https://raw.githubusercontent.com/Azure/WALinuxAgent/
   WALinuxAgent-2.0.12/waagent
   ```

   This will download the most recent available install package from the GitHub, as shown in Figure 5-19.

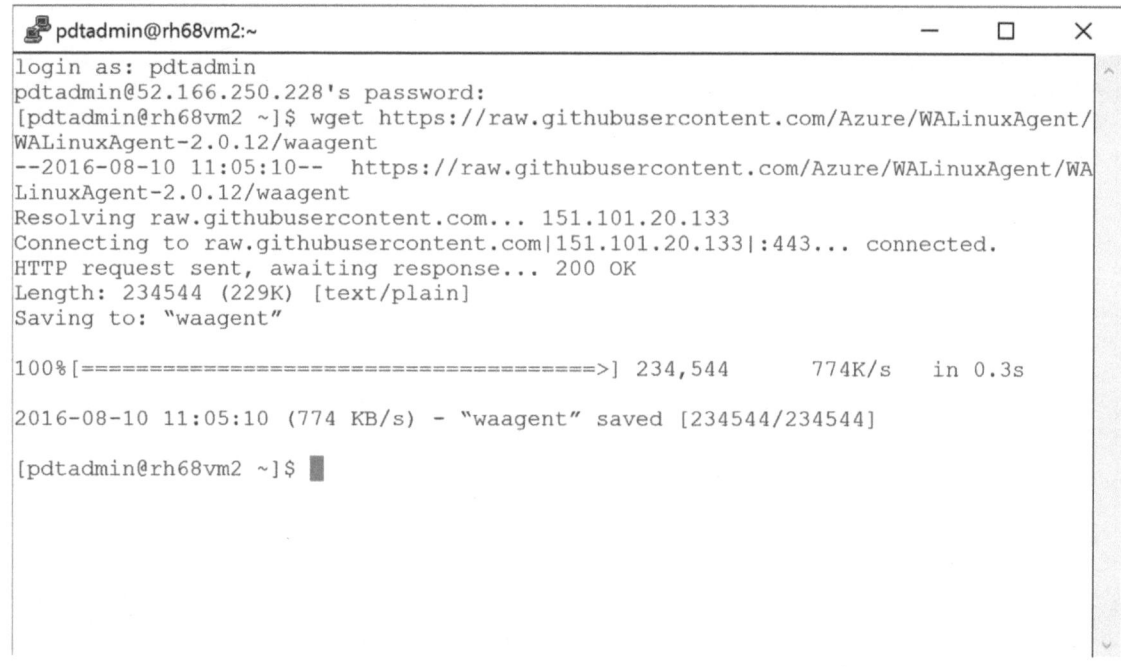

Figure 5-19. Linux VM Agent package download from GitHub repository

    2.   Then run the following commands in the Linux shell (see Figure 5-20):

```
chmod +x waagent
sudo cp waagent /usr/sbin
sudo /usr/sbin/waagent -install -verbose
sudo service waagent restart
```

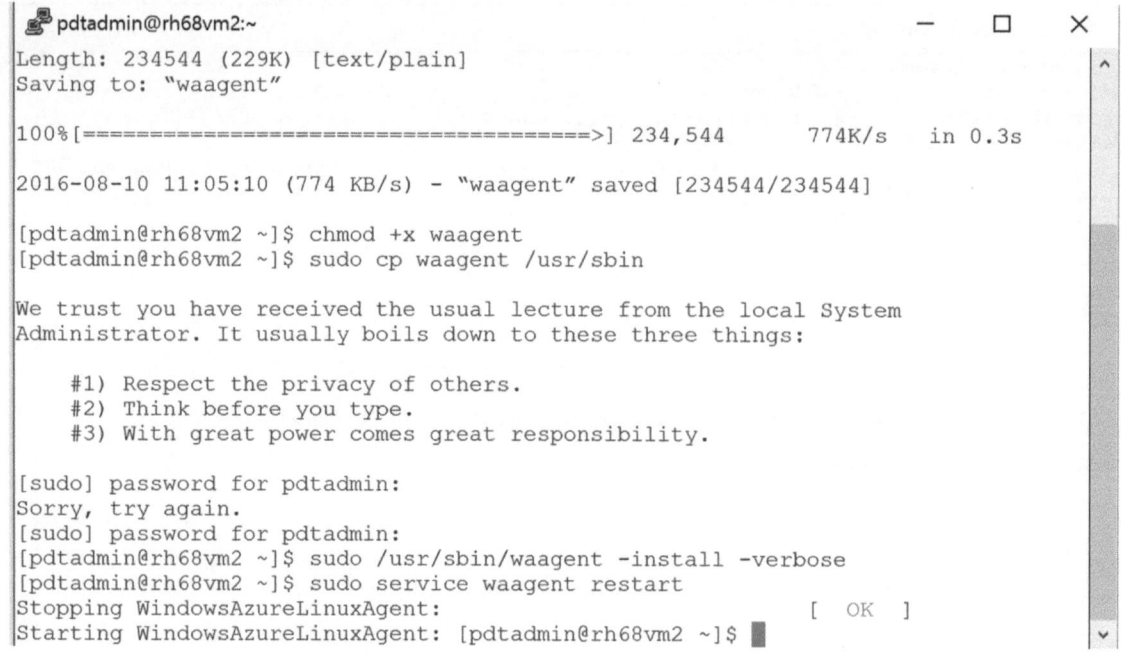

Figure 5-20. *Linux VM agent package install*

■ **Note** For a more official documentation on the Linux VM agent, see https://azure.microsoft.com/en-us/documentation/articles/virtual-machines-linux-update-agent/.

---

3. Next to that, run the following Azure PowerShell cmdlet to update the ProvisioningState parameter of the Azure Linux VM.

Followed by this PowerShell script, tell Azure the VM has been provisioned with the agent shown in Figure 5-21.

```
1    Login-AzureRmAccount
2    Get-AzureRmSubscription
3    Select-AzureRmSubscription -SubscriptionName "Microsoft Azure Internal Consumption"
4    Get-AzureRmVM
5
6    $vm = Get-AzureRMVM -resourcegroupname "redhat" -name "rh68vm2"
7    $vm.ProvisioningState = $true
8    Update-AzureRMVM -resourcegroupname "redhat" -VM $vm
9
```

Figure 5-21. *Linux VM updating the ProvisioningState parameter using PowerShell*

■ **Note** Updating the `ProvisionGuestAgent` property is necessary only if the VM is already running in Azure and the agent was not provisioned when the VM was created. When creating a VM from an image (including from custom image), the VM agent is installed by default and that property is updated automatically.

4. After some time, WAAGent is in failed state, as shown in Figure 5-22.

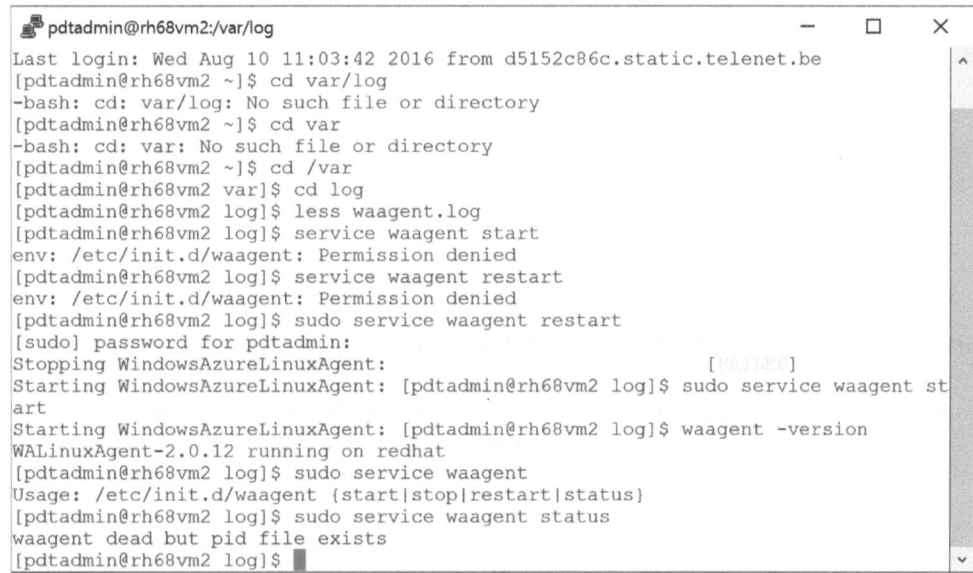

Figure 5-22. *Linux VM agent is in a failed state*

5. Rebooting the Linux VM will fix that issue immediately, as after the reboot the WAAgent has a running status, as shown in Figure 5-23.

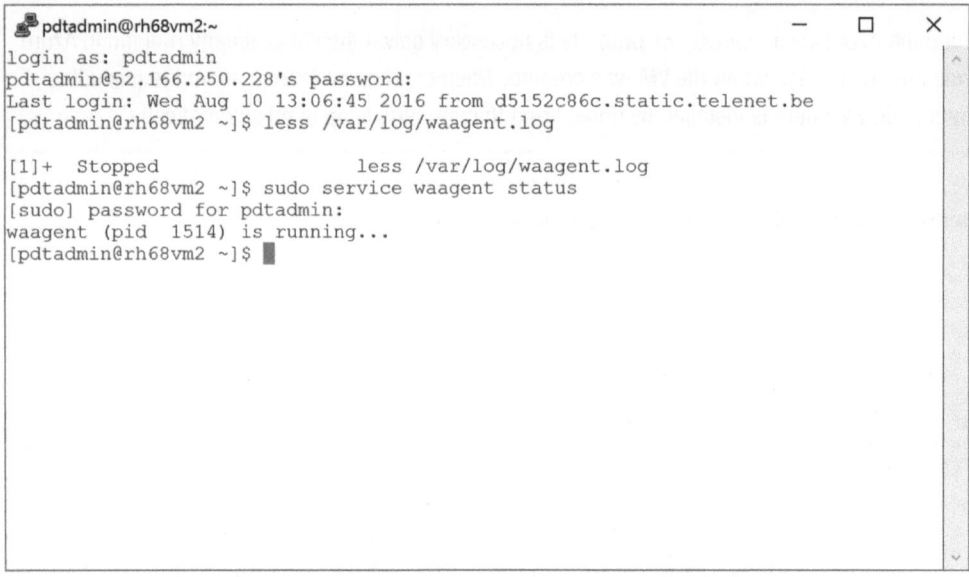

Figure 5-23. *Linux VM agent is running again after rebooting the VM*

This in turn will allow for a successful backup of this Azure VM. In the same way as it works on a Windows VM, the Azure.RecoveryServices.VMSnapShotLinux is configured because of the initial backup of the Azure VM (see Figure 5-24).

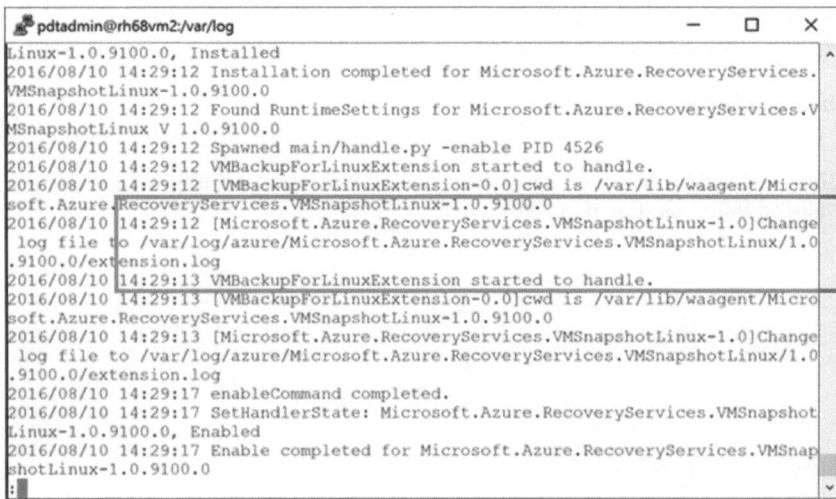

Figure 5-24. *Linux VM Agent Azure.RecoveryServices.VMSnapshotLinux is installed*

Restoring an Azure VM from a Backup

Azure VM Backups are basically snapshots, also known as *recovery points*. Based on the backup policy configured and corresponding retention settings, you can always revert a backup to the state of the Azure VM at the time the recovery point was created. This process is known as a *restore* in typical backup solutions.

What typically happens in this restore process is the following:

- The administrative user selects the recovery point.

- The recovery point is mounted from the Azure Recovery Vault.

- The Azure VM is recreated in its own Azure resource group, named after the hostname of the Azure VM; the disks are restored and linked to the recovered Azure VM.

- The recovered Azure VM can be started and used from there. It might be used to, for example, restore individual files and folders, or to keep the fully recovered Azure VM machine image, such as in a "bare-metal" restore operation you would do on-premises.

From within the portal, go through the following steps:

1. Browse to the Azure resource group in which the Azure Recovery Vault is configured. After selecting the Azure Recovery Vault, browse to the Backup Items tile in the middle section.

2. From the Backup Items, select the Azure VM you want to restore (see Figure 5-25).

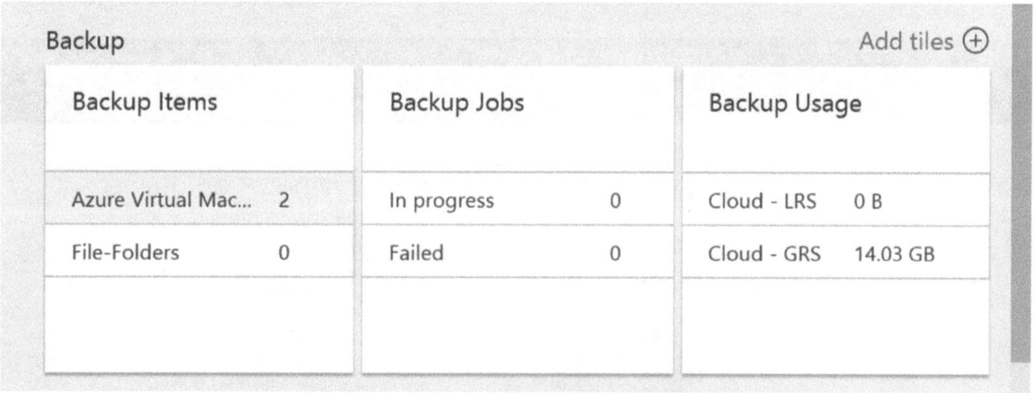

Backup		Add tiles ⊕
Backup Items	**Backup Jobs**	**Backup Usage**
Azure Virtual Mac... 2	In progress 0	Cloud - LRS 0 B
File-Folders 0	Failed 0	Cloud - GRS 14.03 GB

Figure 5-25. Backup items within the Azure Recovery Vault

3. Once the VM is selected, it will show the details in the next blade. Click the Restore button from the top menu, as shown in Figure 5-26.

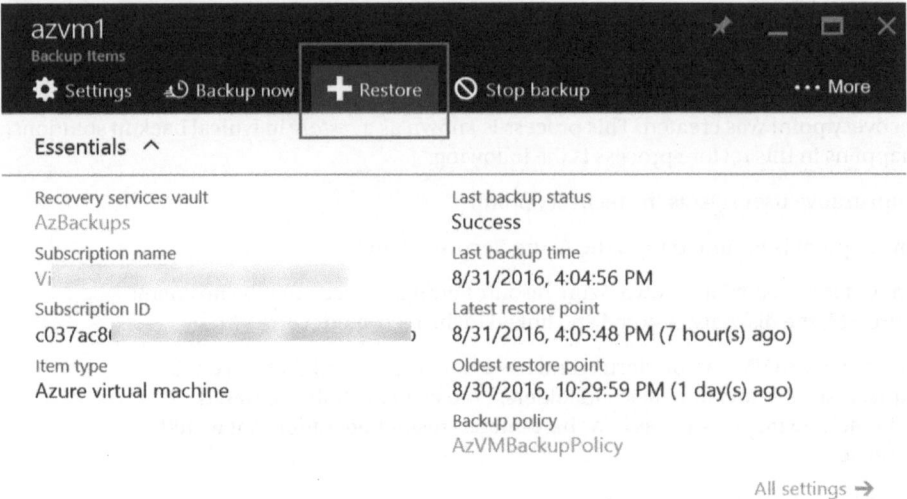

Figure 5-26. Restoring an Azure VM

4. This opens the Restore blade. From there, you can browse through the several
    recovery points that are available for that specific Azure VM. Select any of the
    recovery points you want to use (see Figure 5-27).

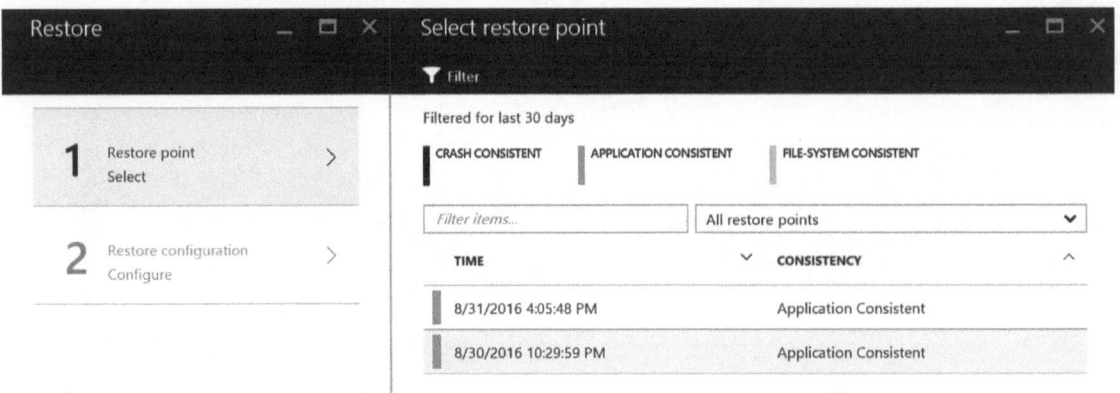

Figure 5-27. Restoring an Azure VM by selecting a recovery point

5. Click OK to continue to Step 2. Provide some parameters that are required to
    create the RestoredVM, such as a machine name, in which Azure resource group
    this should be created, and which network and storage account should be used
    (see Figure 5-28).

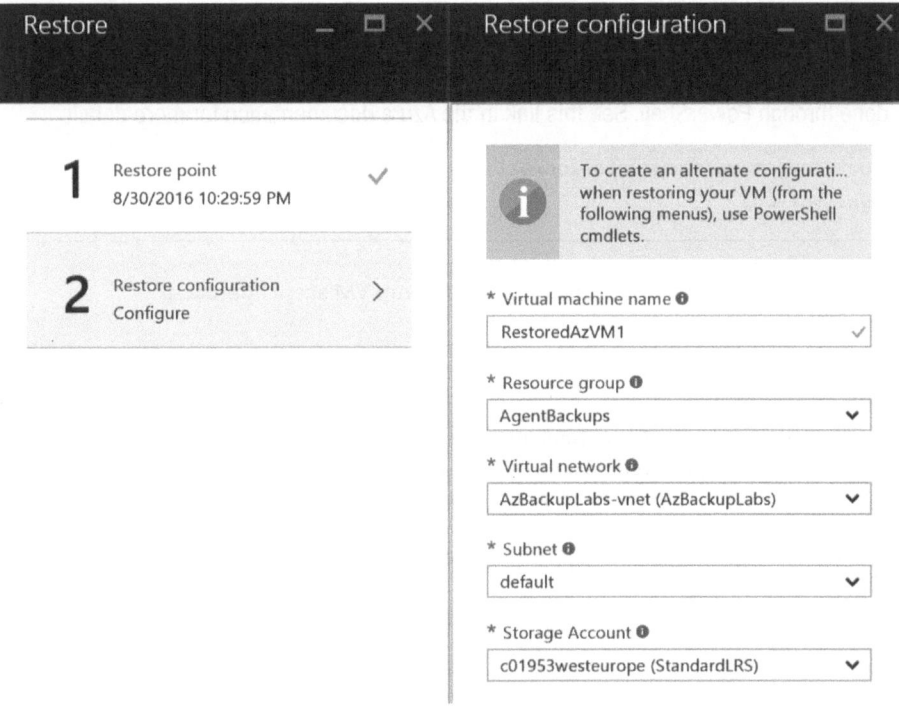

Figure 5-28. *Entering parameters for restoring an Azure VM*

6. Browse to the settings of the Azure Recovery Vault/Monitoring/Backup Jobs to see the restore job running (see Figure 5-29).

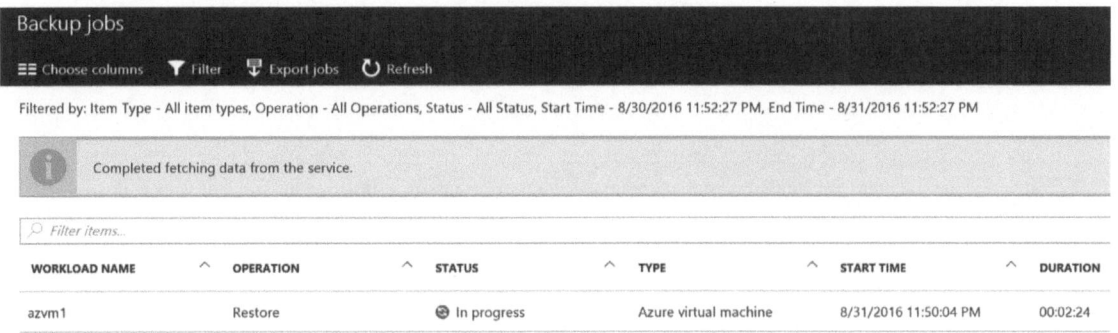

Figure 5-29. *Azure VM restore job in progress*

7. Wait for the restore job to complete.

8. Once restored, the RestoredVM is created under the Azure resource group you picked, and it will have network access and can be started just like a normal Azure VM.

■ **Note**   If your original Azure VM has a rather "complex" architecture, like having multiple NICs, fixed IP-addresses, part of a load balancer and alike, the restore won't be possible from within the Azure Portal. Instead, it needs to be done through PowerShell. See this link in the Azure documentation for more details:

https://azure.microsoft.com/en-us/documentation/articles/backup-azure-vms-automation/#restore-an-azure-vm

---

This completes the restore of an Azure VM, using the Azure Backup VM agent approach.

Summary

In this chapter, you learned the details about Azure Backup, by using the Azure VM agent extension approach. You configured a resource group, created a new Azure Recovery Vault, and configured the Azure Backup configuration. You learned how to install the Azure VM agent and extension manually for both Windows and Linux operating systems. In the last section, you performed a full Azure VM restore (recovery).

This is the third chapter covering Azure Backup. The remaining chapters will cover the ins and outs of Azure Site Recovery (ASR).

CHAPTER 6

■ ■ ■

Understanding Azure Site Recovery

Just like Azure Backup discussed in the previous chapters, Azure Site Recovery (ASR) is part of the "business continuity" features of OMS. And that is exactly what it does; it provides a solution to make sure businesses can run their applications in case of a disaster. This is made possible by replicating on-premises servers to Azure Virtual Machines. Or by replicating machines between two datacenters, and using ASR as the control and failover/failback management solution, without replicating data to the Azure Cloud itself.

ASR allows you to replicate from an on-premises infrastructure running on physical servers, VMware vSphere ESX VMs, Microsoft Hyper-V, or System Center Virtual Machine Manager VMs, whether running Windows or Linux.

■ **Note**   Source physical servers need to run Windows Server 2012 or R2 operating systems, where the virtual machines need to run an Azure VM supported operating system to make ASR work.

In this chapter, I mainly focus on the overall features and possibilities, as well as describing the architectural topology of Azure Site Recovery, where the following three chapters will guide you through the exact technical configuration and deployment steps:

> Chapter 7: Configuring ASR between an on-premises Hyper-V site and Azure
>
> Chapter 8: Managing and deploying protection groups and recovery plans in Azure ASR
>
> Chapter 9: Using ASR for non-hyper-V workloads disaster recovery

So depending on the source environment you are running, it might be you that don't have to go through all chapters, and instead you should picking the one that is most relevant.

Introduction to Disaster Recovery

Before jumping into the Azure technology itself, let's spend a few minutes discussing disaster recovery. While I'm pretty sure you know what disaster recovery means, I found out that customers sometimes have a different view on this than I do. Sometimes it is just a misconception and sometimes it leads to a major discussion.

© Peter De Tender 2016
P. De Tender, *Implementing Operations Management Suite*, DOI 10.1007/978-1-4842-1979-9_6

Definitions and Terminology

This first section starts with some common definitions and terminology to set the scene (see Figure 6-1).

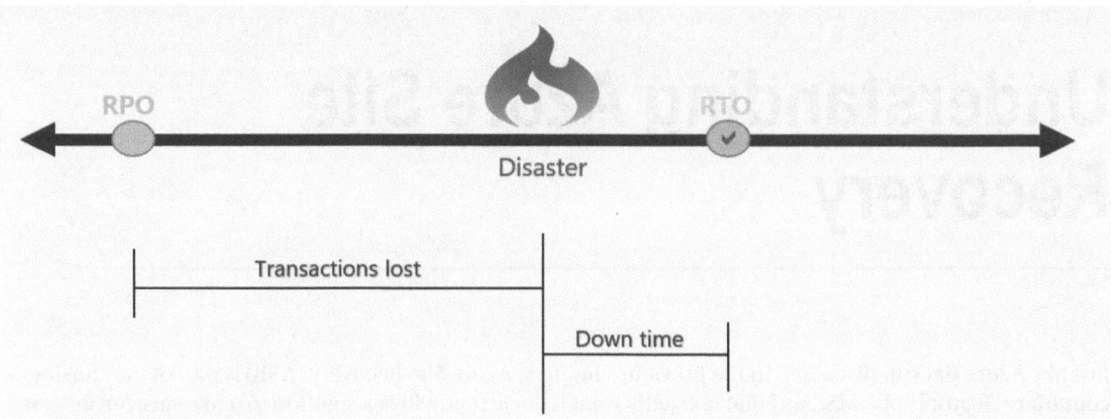

Figure 6-1. *RPO-RTO-DR-BC explained*

Disaster Recovery (DR)

Disaster Recovery enables the recovery or continuation of critical IT infrastructure and systems, following a human or natural disaster like system downtime, system crashes, fire, earthquake, and the like.

Business Continuity (BC)

Business Continuity or Business Continuity Plan is the concept and guidelines that guarantee a business can continue operating or recovering quickly despite any incident occurring to their IT systems. In a lot of situations, this could be understood as High Availability (HA), as no downtime is involved here.

Recovery Point Objective (RPO)

Recovery Point Objective refers to the maximum amount of data loss that is acceptable or allowed in case of system downtime or system unavailability. This basically refers to the point in time an application can be restored. For example, if an application is being secured by a nightly backup at 22:00 pm every day, the RPO would be "previous day, 22.00 pm: for any issue occurring. In case of a database, this could be extended by restoring in-between log files, if there are any and if it's possible.

Recovery Time Objective (RTO)

Recovery Time Objective refers to the amount of time (in minutes, hours, days, and so on) it takes to get an application or system up and running again to a fully operational state. This could include delivery time for spare parts, time to wait for backups to become available and restored, system testing before go-live after disaster, and the like.

Figure 6-1 shows a diagram that explains it a bit more how RPO and RTO relate.

Why Disaster Recovery Is Important

When I started investigating ASR Manager early in 2013, the initial version of the current ASR, I gave several presentations at community events around the topic. To illustrate why disaster recovery is important for an IT environment, I studied and searched some reputable sources like Gartner, Markets and Markets, and the like for arguments and statements. Here are some numbers I used in these original presentations. I'm pretty sure they are still valid today:

- Enterprise organizations face more than three datacenter outages per year

- Any IT systems outage results in an average downtime of 1,45 hours

- Average cost per datacenter outage is USD $650.000

- Cost for building a fully redundant datacenter is estimated at $20 million

- Three out of four enterprise companies are at risk, failing in preparing for disaster recovery

- 50% of downtime is due to hardware and software failure and human interaction

- 80% of critical business applications are not capable of meeting the expected RPO/RTO

Why Use Azure Site Recovery for Your DR Solution?

First of all, I don't want to do any flat commercial marketing for the product, honestly. But since I'm writing on the subject, it should not be a surprise that I am a true fan of the technology. I used it in numerous implementations at different sized organizations. At some, because it was an affordable solution compared to third-party software. At others, because it was so easy to implement, because it worked cross-technology and cross-platform, and because it just gets the job done. Now I know my experience doesn't count in all situations, and I have had some issues too. But overall, I'm super happy with the product so far, especially its features and its promising roadmap.

If you don't trust my opinion (maybe I just want to sell my book, right?), let me head back to a more formal source again, Gartner. They position ASR and Azure Backup in their leaders quadrant (see Figure 6-2).

Figure 6-2. *Gartner's magic quadrant for disaster recovery as a service (2016) (https://info.microsoft. com/OMS-DRaaS-MQ-2016.html?ls=Website)*

I know some of you may not put a lot of trust in Gartner's quadrants. But even if you don't, know that a lot of CxO's at companies decide their next technology partners on this.

Consider another source (see Figure 6-3), Markets and Markets, who recently published a report on Cloud-based disaster recovery solutions. Although I don't have access to the report itself (it's rather expensive to get an account there), the headline uncovers enough for me.

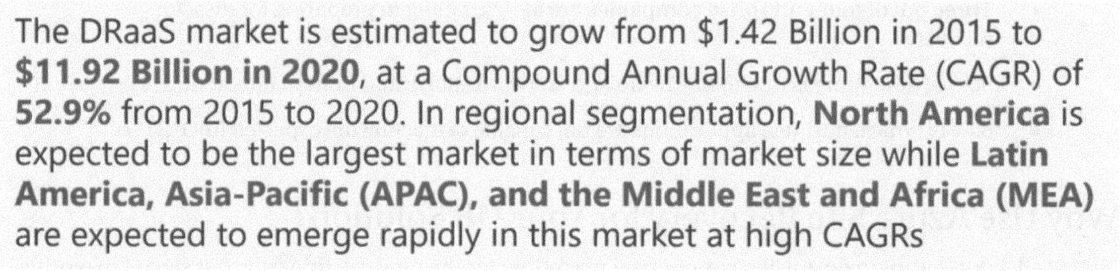

The DRaaS market is estimated to grow from $1.42 Billion in 2015 to **$11.92 Billion in 2020**, at a Compound Annual Growth Rate (CAGR) of **52.9%** from 2015 to 2020. In regional segmentation, **North America** is expected to be the largest market in terms of market size while **Latin America, Asia-Pacific (APAC), and the Middle East and Africa (MEA)** are expected to emerge rapidly in this market at high CAGRs

Figure 6-3. *Markets and Markets DRaaS report (2016) (http://www.marketsandmarkets.com/Market-Reports/recovery-as-a-service-market-962.html)*

If you are still not convinced about the interest and use case for ASR, you might not be the reader for this book. But since you are reading it already, I think now is a good time to introduce ASR to you.

Introduction to Azure Site Recovery

Organizations have been deploying high availability and disaster recovery solutions since the early days of using technology. Depending on how critical the applications and workloads were, the complexity and several other factors, organizations were investing huge amounts of money to make sure applications didn't "go down". Now, let me emphasize that a little bit. Disaster recovery is not the same as high availability.

High availability refers to a system or component that continuously runs without interrupting services. Typical examples are redundant power supplies in physical servers and storage components, uninterruptible power supply (UPS) systems guaranteeing power uptime in case the electricity is not available, Microsoft clustering for file services, SQL database server, Exchange Server, and the like. All or most components in the architecture are redundant, guaranteeing the application or system keeps running. Along the years, IT organizations and solution vendors have been incorporating high availability in many of their solutions. Some of these solutions could even provide high availability between different locations, replicating data blocks between two storage components for example, or having data replication occurring on software level or directly out of the application itself. SQL Server AlwaysOn is a good example here.

Disaster recovery refers to a process that allows you to quickly restore the operation of a system or application in case of a disaster. Think of a crashed server, a malfunction in the hardware in the datacenter, a natural disaster like an earthquake happening in your area or fire happening in your server room or building. While the first solution for disaster recovery has always been backing up, more and more organizations wanted quicker and easier ways to recovery their data in case of a disaster.

Ultimately, an organization relied on an IT architecture that could provide both high availability and disaster recovery at the same time. Think of storage replication between two redundantly configured SAN storage boxes in the same datacenter (high availability), as well as replicating to an off-site datacenter's storage solution (disaster recovery), whether replicating with a defined delay.

Even by going over these topics quickly and describing some examples of topologies and solutions that have been available, it should be clear now it has always been complex and costly to implement the necessary high availability and disaster recovery. In most cases, it also meant vendor-locking, meaning it was not always easy, and even sometimes just technically not possible to build out such a high available architecture when mixing different vendor solutions.

Luckily, by using public Cloud solutions available nowadays, several of the listed concerns and painpoints are not valid anymore. That is exactly where ASR comes in to play, and it is a valid solution for providing disaster recovery in any organization's IT environment.

In a nutshell, ASR provides the following features:

- Automated protection and replication of VMs

- Remote health monitoring

- Customizable recovery plans

- No-impact recovery plan testing

- Orchestrated recovery

- Replicate to—and recover in—Azure

ASR was initially known as Hyper-V Recovery Manager, which then was renamed to Windows Azure Hyper-V Recovery Manager. An interesting point here is although there was a reference to Azure in the product, it was not linked to Azure Virtual Machines, since it only provided replication of source virtual machines in one Hyper-V environment to a second Hyper-V based datacenter. (Replication between two Hyper-V hosts in the same datacenter was made possible by Hyper-V Replica itself.)

This was early 2013, so it was a rather interesting component of the early Windows Azure days at that time.

Somewhere around summer later that same year, Microsoft acquired Inmage, a company that provided Cloud-based business continuity solutions. One of their products, Inmage Scout, was an agent-based replication solution. All changes occurring on-disk or in memory on the source system running the Inmage Scout agent were replicated to a second machine. Inmage Scout provided integration with VMware-based infrastructures and physical servers, supporting both Windows and Linux operating systems. Where a customer initially rolling out ASR at that time could see it was a combination of different technologies being used, Inmage Scout has been fully incorporated in the ASR we are talking about today.

When I first heard about ASR in early 2014, I immediately was interested by its simplicity, ease of use, and affordability. And since I'm now writing about this subject, it should be clear to you that it is one of my favorite Azure features.

This immediately also answers the obviously interesting question as to why customers should consider integrating ASR in their own IT environments.

Simplicity

Simplicity is the first key reason why I love ASR so much. By going through a five-to-seven-step configuration wizard, it is possible to have ASR up-and-running in just a few hours (depending on the complexity of the workloads, of course). Leveraging on the replication technology of Hyper-V or Inmage in the background, almost any workload can be replicated between the source and target, whether Azure or a second datacenter. Given the fact that it supports both topologies, as well as supporting different source platforms and the Windows and Linux operating systems, it's a valid solution.

Ease of Use

This aspect mainly points to the comfort of configuration, as well as the flexibility to go through a test failover, planned or unplanned failover approach. Configuration is possible from the Azure classic portal (Service Manager), Azure Resource Manager (ARM) portal or by using PowerShell scripts. On the other hand, by running a test failover, ASR will go through a simulated virtual machine failover, verifying if the source and target environments can talk to each other, data can be replicated between both environments, a dummy virtual machine is being created, and so on, without actually touching your production environment on-premises and in the Cloud or the second datacenter. Running a planned or unplanned failover is another easy-to-use approach to execute the effective failover. The main difference between them is that in case of an unplanned failover, ASR is not validating if the virtual machine is in a fully-replicated and synced state. It starts from the last successful replication state it has. (Which is very interesting if the source environment is indeed not at all reachable due to a severe disaster.)

Affordability

While I'm covering some of the costs and pricing aspects of Azure, and more specifically related to the described components of OMS in this book, I can already say ASR is surely affordable in any type of organization. In most cases, you can eliminate the need of having a second datacenter and can rely on Azure datacenter solutions for the remote machines. These machines can start costing money when they are running in Azure and generating Azure consumption (next to a fixed cost per month for using the ASR service).

What Can Be Replicated with Azure Site Recovery

As I already highlighted at the beginning of this chapter, ASR supports two main replication streams—between two on-premises private Clouds and between on-premises and Azure.

Let me zoom in a bit more on each of these streams and discuss what is supported.

On-Premises to On-Premises Replication

In this first setup, a replication occurs between two Hyper-V hosts or System Center Virtual Machine Manager Cloud environments. Replication occurs on Hyper-V level. (See Table 6-1.)

Table 6-1. *Hyper-V to Hyper-V (On-Premises) Replication*

Overview	Source	Target (Second Datacenter)
	Hyper-V host	Hyper-V host
	System Center Virtual Machine Manager Cloud (Hyper-V hosts)	System Center Virtual Machine Manager Cloud (Hyper-V hosts)

Another possible design is similar to the previous one, with the main difference being that the replication of the virtual machines is not run by the Hyper-V replication, but occurs instead on a SAN storage level. See Table 6-2.

Table 6-2. *Hyper-V to Hyper-V (On-Premises) SAN Replication*

Overview	Source	Target (Second Datacenter)
Hyper-V to Hyper-V (on-premises)	Hyper-V host System Center Virtual Machine Manager Cloud (Hyper-V hosts)	Hyper-V host System Center Virtual Machine Manager Cloud (Hyper-V hosts)

A third solution (as shown in Table 6-3) exists in a similar setup as the first one, with the major difference being that the source environment can be a VMware ESX/ESXi platform or physical servers.

Table 6-3. *VMware or Physical Servers to VMware (On-Premises)*

Overview	Source	Target (Second Datacenter)
VMware or Physical to VMware (on-premises)	VMware Virtual Machines Physical servers (Windows Server 2012 R2)	VMware Virtual Machines

On-Premises to Azure Replication

In this topology design, outlined in Table 6-4, the main difference is the fact it now uses Azure as a target environment in the solution.

Table 6-4. *Hyper-V to Microsoft Azure VMs*

Overview	Source	Target (Second Datacenter)
	Hyper-V host	Azure Virtual Machines
	System Center Virtual Machine Manager Cloud (Hyper-V hosts)	

Similar to the previous one, but from VMware and/or physical source servers to Azure, results in the overview shown in Table 6-5.

Table 6-5. *VMware/Physical Servers to Azure*

Overview	Source	Target (Second Datacenter)
	VMware hosts	Azure Virtual Machines
	Physical servers	

■ **Note**   Technically, the solution shown in Table 6-5 could also include a migration from Amazon Web Services virtual machines (AMIs) to Azure Virtual Machines, as described in Chapter 7.

Azure Site Recovery Supported Workloads

Now that you have a good understanding of how the source and target environments can look, let's look at which applications ASR replication can support.

Source/Target Operating Systems

The following operating systems are supported as the source platform for ASR:

- Windows Server 2008 R2 with SP1 or higher

- Windows Server 2012

- Windows Server 2012 R2

- Windows Server 2016 TP5 (it works, but it's not supported yet)

- Red Hat Enterprise Linux 6.7 or higher

- CentOS 6.5-6.6-6.7

- Oracle Enterprise Linux 6.6-6.5

- SUSE Linux Enterprise Server 11 SP3

Source/Target Applications

The following workload applications are currently listed as supported for ASR. In general, ASR supports about any application running on the listed operating systems. Since it is replicating all changes occurring on-disk or in memory, no changes are lost.

Taking the core list of Microsoft Server applications, the following are listed on the Microsoft Azure documentation web site (`https://azure.microsoft.com/en-us/documentation/articles/site-recovery-workload/`):

- Web Application Server (IIS)

- SharePoint Server 2013

- Exchange Server 2010, 2013 (if not using DAG replication)

- Microsoft Dynamix AX

- Windows File Server

This list will certainly continue to grow during the coming weeks and months.

■ **Note** An interesting non-Microsoft application on that list is SAP, for which Azure support was announced mid-2014.

Azure Site Recovery Capacity Planning

As discussed, the main difference between high availability (HA) and disaster recovery (DR) is downtime. A disaster recovery solution allows for downtime, whereas a high availability solution is just the opposite. The business should be prepared for both and have a good understanding of the differences between both.

That said, in case of any disaster, there will always be the question, "How long until my applications are up and running again?".

In the next chapters, you learn how efficient ASR handles replication in both failover and fallback scenario, yet there are always additional factors in the overall topology that can make your replication go terribly slow, and sometimes even failing completely. To avoid such scenarios whenever disaster strikes, you can run the Azure Site Recovery Capacity Planning tool before actually approving the GO in production. Even during the configuration steps of ASR, the final step in the wizard is confirming that you have run this tool successfully. (Luckily it doesn't block you from completing the wizard by saying you did, even if you didn't.) See Figure 6-4.

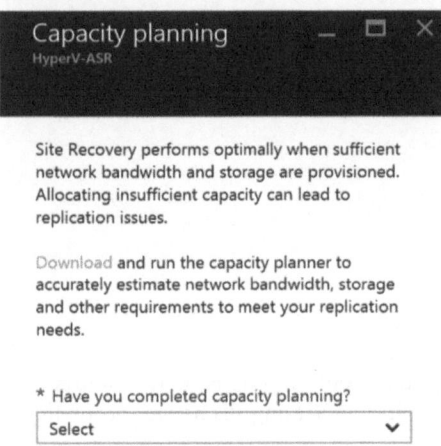

Site Recovery performs optimally when sufficient network bandwidth and storage are provisioned. Allocating insufficient capacity can lead to replication issues.

Download and run the capacity planner to accurately estimate network bandwidth, storage and other requirements to meet your replication needs.

* Have you completed capacity planning?

Select ⌄

Figure 6-4. *Capacity planning as part of the ASR configuration steps*

Running the Azure Site Recovery Capacity Planning Tool

If you are going through the configuration steps of ASR, this question will come up in Step 5 of the initial configuration wizard. If you did not run the Capacity Planning tool, you can download it from the link in the message body.

If you want to run this tool before going through the actual ASR configuration steps, head over to the following download link:

```
https://gallery.technet.microsoft.com/Azure-Recovery-Capacity-d01dc40e
```

In contrast to what you might think, this tool does not have to be installed in your environment to gather information. It is nothing more than an Excel workbook, in which you enter as many details about your source physical or virtual machine environment as possible. Actually, now that I think about it, it would actually be an interesting feature to integrate it with the other assessment tool we have available from Microsoft—Microsoft Assessment and Planning Toolkit (MAPT). MAPT basically maps out an inventory of your servers, server applications, and corresponding machine requirements. It can integrate with Hyper-V hosts and VMware and recognizes SQL, Exchange and SharePoint as well as Linux and Oracle workloads.

For more information about MAPT, visit:

```
https://www.microsoft.com/en-us/download/details.aspx?id=7826
```

Back to the ASR Capacity Planning tool now. This tool helps you plan disaster recovery resources. Use the planner to evaluate sizing requirements in your source deployment (Hyper-V and VMware/physical) and to understand the resources you need for seamless disaster recovery.

You can use this planner in two ways, for quick planning and for detailed planning.

Quick Planning

Use this to get a quick estimation of your source environment. Using this approach, you'll need to provide an overall average of your source environment resources, including the total number of VMs, total number of disks, average disk size, compression, retention, and so on. This is okay if the environment you are assessing is not that large, or you already have a good view of the environment you want to migrate/ASR replicate to Azure.

Upon opening the XLS sheet, select Quick Planner from the listbox.

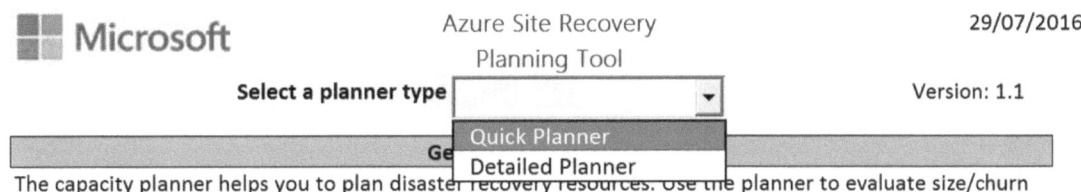

The capacity planner helps you to plan disaster recovery resources. Use the planner to evaluate size/churn

Figure 6-5. *Select a planner type from the Azure Site Recovery Planning tool*

Detailed Planning

Using this method, you can get VM-level information, validate VMs, and get recommendations. For this sizing tool to work, you need to provide information for each VM, including the number of disks attached to a VM, the total VM storage, VM capacity utilization, and daily changes. You also need to provide general information about retention, compression, etc.

Running through the detailed planner is possible by selecting the option in the listbox in the XLS sheet. For more detailed instructions, go to http://aka.ms/asr-capacity-planner-doc.

In this example, I start by going through some basics of the quick planner.

1. Complete the fields with the valid numbers and parameters from the source environment. In my example, customer is running 20VMs, each machine having three disks of 150GB in size (see Figure 6-6).

Capacity Planner					
INPUTS				**OUTPUT**	
Infra Inputs source	Manual		**Reset to Defaults**	**Network Bandwidth requirements**	
Select your scenario	Hyper-V to Azure			Bandwidth required for delta replication (in Megabits/sec)	30 Mbps
Total number of virtual machines		20		Bandwidth required for initial replication (in Megabits/sec)	359 Mbps
Average number of VHDs per virtual machine		3		Bandwidth refers to dedicated bandwidth for replication.	
Average size of VHD (in GBs)		150		**Azure requirements**	
Average utilization per disk (%)		70%		Storage required (in GBs)	6405
Total data to be replicated (in GBs)		6300		Total IOPS on standard storage accounts	478
Churn Inputs				Number of standard storage accounts required	2
Average daily data change rate (%)		5%		Number of Blob disks required	60
Amount of data changed per day (in GBs)		315		Number of premium storage accounts required	0
Compression		0%		Total IOPS on premium storage accounts	0
Amount of data Xfered per day (in GBs)		315			
Retention Inputs				**Other infra requirements**	
Number of recovery points		8		Number of Configuration Servers required	NA
Initial Replication Inputs				Number of additional Process Servers required	NA
Number of hours in which initial replication for the batch of virtual machines should complete		8		100% additional storage on the Source	9000
Number of virtual machines per initial replication batch		4			

Figure 6-6. *Quick planner view of the Azure Site Recovery Capacity tool*

The output gives you a good view as to the bandwidth requirements for replicating this source environment to Azure.

Figure 6-7 shows the advanced planner worksheet.

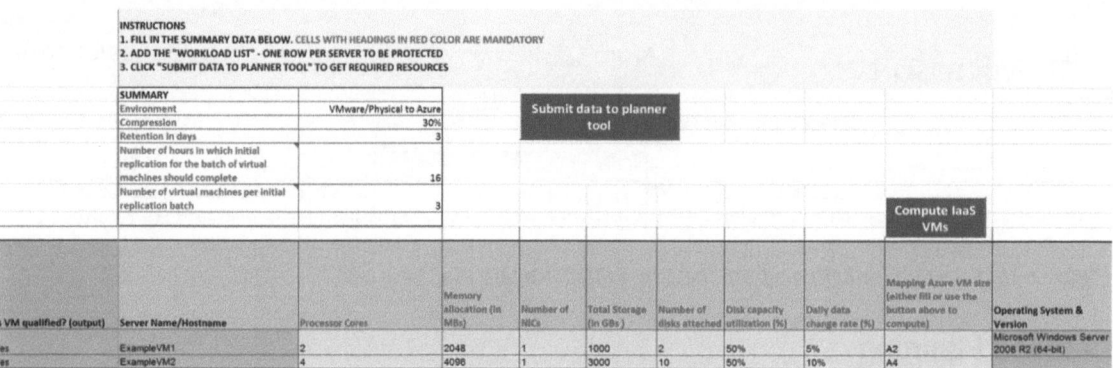

INSTRUCTIONS
1. FILL IN THE SUMMARY DATA BELOW. CELLS WITH HEADINGS IN RED COLOR ARE MANDATORY
2. ADD THE "WORKLOAD LIST" - ONE ROW PER SERVER TO BE PROTECTED
3. CLICK "SUBMIT DATA TO PLANNER TOOL" TO GET REQUIRED RESOURCES

SUMMARY	
Environment	VMware/Physical to Azure
Compression	30%
Retention in days	3
Number of hours in which initial replication for the batch of virtual machines should complete	16
Number of virtual machines per initial replication batch	3

Submit data to planner tool

Compute IaaS VMs

s VM qualified? (output)	Server Name/Hostname	Processor Cores	Memory allocation (in MBs)	Number of NICs	Total Storage (in GBs)	Number of disks attached	Disk capacity utilization (%)	Daily data change rate (%)	Mapping Azure VM size (either fill or use the button above to compute)	Operating System & Version
es	ExampleVM1	2	2048	1	1000	2	50%	5%	A2	Microsoft Windows Server 2008 R2 (64-bit)
es	ExampleVM2	4	4096	1	3000	10	50%	10%	A4	

Figure 6-7. *Advanced planner view of the Azure Site Recovery Capacity tool*

As you can see, the advanced approach needs a lot more detailed information from your servers, which by itself is sometimes hard to provide if you don't have any true assessment tool available.

Once the source tables are completed with the correct information, select either Compute IaaS VMs to get a recommended Azure VM T-shirt size for each source machine, or click Submit Data to Planner tool, which generates a summarized view like the one from the quick planner scenario.

Optimizing Azure Site Recovery Replication

The benefits of optimizing bandwidth and decreasing replication time include:

- Increasing effective network throughput. With optimization, bandwidth reduction allows you to carry more data on your existing infrastructure. This can eliminate or reduce costs associated with adding capacity and allows you to replicate more virtual machines. simultaneously. In addition, you reduce costs where bandwidth utilization is metered.

- Reducing the time it takes to implement Business Continuity Disaster Recovery (BCDR). As VMs replicate faster, time to coverage is reduced. Project duration is decreased while you realize the benefits of BCDR earlier. In addition, new VMs can be added in less time when optimized.

- Due to increased bandwidth from optimization, potentially decreasing the delay between delta updates, thereby improving the recovery point objective (RPO).

Out of the aforementioned Azure Site Recovery Capacity tool, you gets a good understanding of the bandwidth requirements needed to make sure the on-premises machines are capable of synchronizing to Azure. However, this information is still rather static and only to be used to give you a good estimate of what the possibilities are, without making them a hard statement and guaranteeing a fast replication.

Does this mean no optimization of the replication is possible? Luckily not.

There are a few mechanisms available that can integrate with ASR to provide the welcome optimization, which I would like to discuss briefly here.

Maximizing Hyper-V Replica Threads

In case of a Hyper-V/SCVMM source replication to ASR VMs, you can set a registry key, which maximizes the number of threads of the Hyper-V replica engine to 32.

This registry key was initially documented in a Microsoft Product Team blog post in relation to ExpressRoute network bandwidth and ASR optimization. However, it is not specifically related to ExpressRoute replication as such, but more to the Hyper-V core. That means it can also be used in a non-ExpressRoute topology.

Defining this registry key goes as follows:

1. On each Hyper-V host you are running on-premises, start the Registry Key editor regedit.exe from a command prompt (admin).

2. Browse to the following key:

   HKEY_LOCAL_MACHINE\SOFTWARE\Microsoft\Windows Azure Backup

3. If the Replication key does not exist yet, create it.

4. Under the Replication key, add a new DWORD (32-bit) value, named UploadThreadsPerVM (note the case sensitivity) and give it any decimal value between 1-32. 32 will give you maximum threads, although your on-premises server and Internet network infrastructure must be sized adequately to give that kind of performance boost. See Figure 6-8.

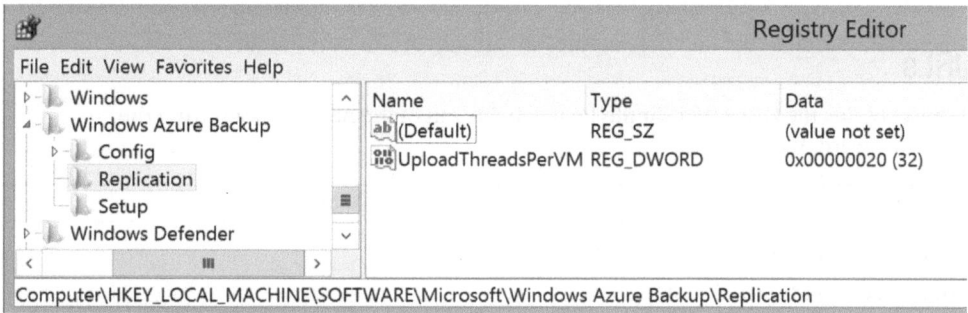

Figure 6-8. *Registry Key to maximize number of replication threads*

5. Restart the Microsoft Azure Site Recovery Service.

You should now see an improvement in replication speed from the on-premises Hyper-V host to the ASR environment.

Integrating WAN Optimizers

In whatever way you think, optimizing network speed means optimizing the time it takes to get the data through the line. In ASR terms, this means faster replication between the source and target environment. Maximizing the number of threads from the previous topic is a good starting point, but still has a rather limited impact.

While investigating ASR and learning how to optimize replication speed, I bumped into this very interesting article from the Microsoft ASR product team:

https://azure.microsoft.com/en-us/blog/azure-site-recovery-wan-optimization-with-riverbed/

They describe optimization in required time to replicate to half the time of the normal replication time needed, and data compression goes up to a whopping 70%! This solution is based on Riverbed Steelhead (http://www.riverbed.com). Riverbed is a well-known company when it comes to WAN optimizers. The idea here is to implement a Riverbed Steelhead appliance on each end of the connection (one on-premises in front of the Azure site-to-site or ExpressRoute gateway, and the other one can be configured as a virtual appliance in Azure directly), which are then exchanging data in a compressed way. This not only speeds up the replication, but also makes it cheaper for outgoing data, in case of a restore from Azure to on-premises.

I suggest you go through the mentioned blog article to get a better view on where Riverbed Steelhead can be of help.

Planning your Firewall Configuration

I already mentioned that a great benefit of ASR is that it relies on HTTPS/port 443 traffic only. So there are no complex firewall configurations and no explicit requirement for Azure site-to-site VPN or ExpressRoute (although more on that later).

That said, I have noticed some deployment difficulties at customers, where the security officer was very keen on getting a detailed list of all required external communication traffic from the on-premises network to ASR. So to give you a hand, I decided to include my notes in this section.

Required URLs

The following table contains the URLs that should be reachable out of the ASR topology, from the on-premises network toward Azure.

Required URLs
*.hypervrecoverymanager.windowsazure.com
*.accesscontrol.windows.net (HTTPS/443)
*.backup.windowsazure.com (HTTPS/443)
*.blob.core.windows.net (HTTPS/443)
*.store.core.windows.net (HTTPS/443)

Required URLs
Ntp://pool.ntp.org (default port 123)
https://cdn.mysql.com/archives/mysql-5.5/mysql-5.5.37-win32.msi
(The MySQL installer is required for the on-premises process server/management server/ configuration server); might be sufficient to allow HTTPS traffic to *.mysql.com.)

Azure Public IP Address Ranges

Although Azure resources are fully public DNS integrated, some customers want to explicitly limit traffic between their own datacenter and Azure regions, based on the Public Azure IP address range information. While I always recommend relying on public DNS to reach Azure resources (since public IP address ranges can always change), you can download an up-to-date list of Azure public IP address ranges here:

https://www.microsoft.com/download/confirmation.aspx?id=41653

This is a direct download of an XML file with all current Azure datacenter IP addresses. Depending on your security and datacenter communication requirements or restrictions, you can limit traffic to a specific Azure region, based on this list of IP addresses. This list is updated frequently, so might be a good idea to bookmark the URL. See Figure 6-9.

```
<?xml version="1.0" encoding="utf-8"?>
<AzurePublicIpAddresses
xmlns:xsd="http://www.w3.org/2001/XMLSchema"
xmlns:xsi="http://www.w3.org/2001/XMLSchema-instance">
  <Region Name="europewest">
    <IpRange Subnet="40.112.124.0/24" />
    <IpRange Subnet="65.52.128.0/19" />
    <IpRange Subnet="94.245.97.0/24" />
    <IpRange Subnet="104.47.169.0/24" />
    <IpRange Subnet="104.214.240.0/24" />
    <IpRange Subnet="137.116.192.0/19" />
    <IpRange Subnet="168.63.0.0/19" />
    <IpRange Subnet="168.63.96.0/20" />
    <IpRange Subnet="168.63.112.16/28" />
    <IpRange Subnet="168.63.112.64/26" />
    <IpRange Subnet="168.63.112.128/25" />
    <IpRange Subnet="168.63.113.0/24" />
    <IpRange Subnet="168.63.114.0/23" />
    <IpRange Subnet="168.63.116.0/22" />
    <IpRange Subnet="168.63.120.0/21" />
```

Figure 6-9. *Azure Public IP address XML file snippet for the Azure region "EuropeWest"*

■ **Note** Figure 6-9 just shows part of the list. The XML file contains all IP addresses for all current, active Azure regions.

Planning Your Network Topology

One of the common questions when discussing disaster recovery and more specifically the failover process, is how the recovered virtual machines that are running in Azure during this process will be reachable for the end users (and IT admins).

As you will learn and experience in the next chapters, ASR allows you to specify the Azure Virtual Network (VNet) that should be used for these virtual machines.

Briefly, there are two possible scenarios:

- ASR VNet is different from the on-premises source subnet of the virtual machines

- ASR VNet is similar to the on-premises source subnet

I will walk you through both scenarios here, describing the pro and cons, as well as possible impact, advantages, and disadvantages of each scenario.

Using Different Azure VNet and IP Addresses

In this scenario, the IP address range of the virtual machines in ASR is different from the source IP address range. While most applications and operating systems nowadays don't experience a lot of serious issues when seeing their IP address change, it still provides some challenges on DNS name resolution. My assumption is that you are familiar with DNS, so I don't have to explain all the details about this service. The reason why name resolution is the problem here is because DNS relies on caching, as well as requiring a flush of the DNS entries stored in cache on both sides—servers and clients.

The easiest workaround here is to configure a short Time-To-Live (TTL) for these IP addresses and machine names that are members of the ASR topology.

It also depends on how the end user will connect to the application. If the connection is made from internal sources, leveraging on the site-to-site VPN connectivity between on-premises network and Azure, DNS is mostly also controlled by the IT team, so its rather easy to manage and control. However, if the applications are to be reached from an external/Internet source, an additional routing or redirect mechanism might be required to reroute traffic from the (unavailable) on-premises infrastructure to the Azure platform. Azure Traffic Manager could be a good solution here.

A huge advantage to this approach is the fact that IP addresses will be different for only those machines that are "in failover". Machines that are still running and reachable in the source network can stay there (depending on the disaster of course). In case of keeping the IP address ranges identical between both environments, a full subnet failover is required, even when only a single or a few machines are "in failover". Otherwise, network communication won't be routed correctly and routers will go crazy. See Figure 6-10.

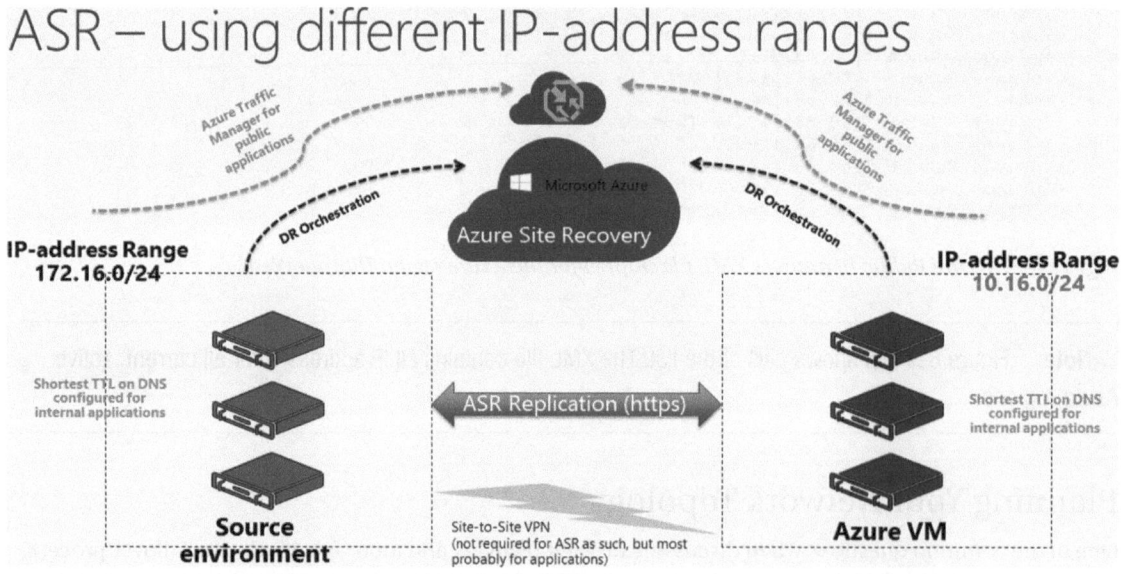

Figure 6-10. *ASR using different IP address ranges*

As you can see, there are certain advantages and reasons for using this scenario, but it all depends on the specifics of the failover process, how critical the systems are, and the overall desire and needs of the customer's environment. My personal favorite is using different IP address ranges. That's where handling DNS caching and flushing, as well as integrating Azure Traffic Manager, might be a challenge at first.

Keeping Similar IP Address Ranges

Let's have a look at the second scenario, keeping similar IP address ranges.

When positioning this scenario to customers, the first reaction is, "Let's use this one and makes live a lot easier". But does it?

From a name resolution perspective, it is indeed rather straightforward, as your internal DNS servers don't need to worry about any updates or caching and flushing. If the applications should be reachable from the external/Internet side, a solution like Azure Traffic Manager is still recommended.

What causes most of the issues, however, is the fact that your routers must be capable of handling stretched IP subnets, and if not, a full IP subnet failover must be initiated. This all sounds good in case of a major disaster where the source environment is completely unreachable. But it might not be the best approach if only a few machines need to be failed over to the Azure DR site. So the same statement as before can be stressed here—*making your final design on which approach to use mainly depends on your DR requirements and severity.*

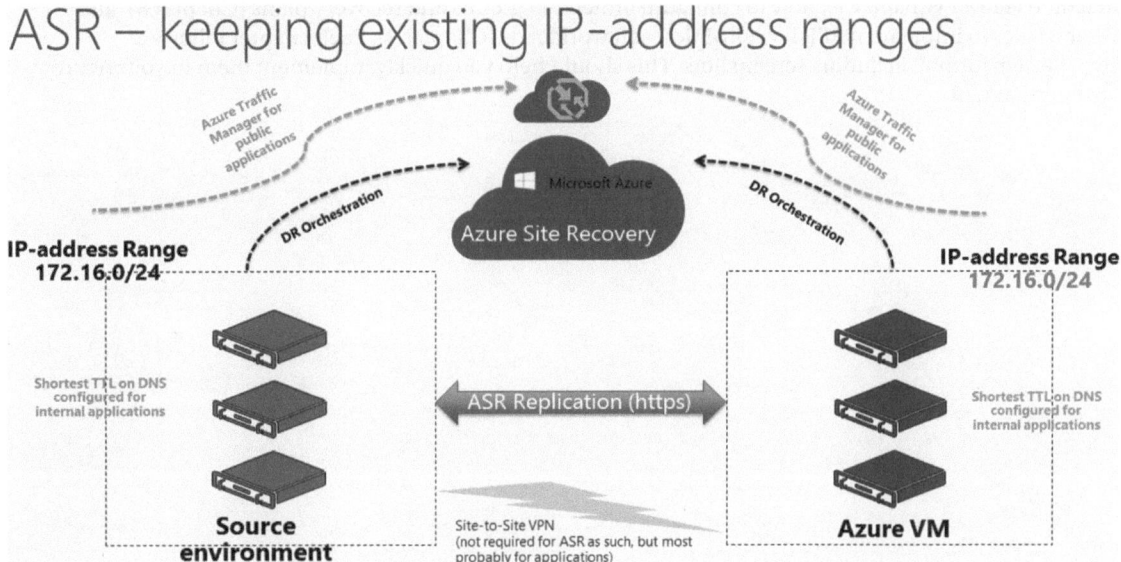

Figure 6-11. *ASR keeping existing IP address ranges*

Watch Out When Using System Center Virtual Machine Manager

While I'm not covering on-premises to on-premises datacenter failover, nor System Center Virtual Machine Manager failover to Azure in this book, something should be said when talking about IP address ranges and failover, specifically.

While the aforementioned scenarios are both valid in a Hyper-V/VMware/AWS/Physical to ASR network scenario, there is a special "watch out" when System Center Virtual Machine Manager is being used. This "watch out" is known as Network Mapping.

SCVMM Network Mapping is a configuration setting within Virtual Machine Manager, allowing you to configure a "mapping" between on-premises networks and ASR networks. For each virtual machine in a VMM Cloud, both source network and failover network are defined. In the case of a failover, SCVMM will control and define to which failover network the virtual machine in ASR will connect.

For more details on SCVMM Network Mapping, I recommend you look at the following Microsoft Azure documentation:

`https://azure.microsoft.com/en-us/documentation/articles/site-recovery-network-mapping/`

Summary

In this chapter, you learned about the concept of disaster recovery, including some key terminologies and definitions. This was followed by learning what AST is and how it can help organizations build their DR strategy. I zoomed in on the different ASR topologies that are supported today. From a more technical perspective, I walked you through the Azure Site Recovery Capacity Planning tool, which helps you size and map ASR. I also talked about some ASR optimization settings and solutions that can be of use, and ended this chapter by describing different IP address range failover solutions.

In the next following chapters, you learn how to deploy ASR and configure it for Hyper-V virtual machine failover (Chapter 7), how to configure protection groups and recovery plans (Chapter 8), and what it takes to implement ASR for non-Microsoft workloads (Chapter 9). Each chapter follows a step-by-step format, including screenshots. This should help you quickly implement them in your Azure lab environment.

CHAPTER 7

Configuring ASR for an On-Premises Hyper-V Infrastructure

I assume you read the previous chapter, in which I described what Azure Site Recovery (ASR) is, and in what different scenarios and topologies it can be deployed to provide organizations with a true disaster recovery solution, leveraging the powers of Azure and Cloud computing.

In this chapter, I guide you through a full end-to-end configuration on how to implement ASR in an on-premises Hyper-V infrastructure environment.

■ **Note** While this chapter focuses on a Hyper-V based infrastructure, note that the process is largely identical for a System Center Virtual Machine Manager (SCVMM)-based infrastructure, except that the source environment differs and the ASR provider download file is different.

By going through the detailed steps in this chapter, you will learn how to:

- Configure Azure Site Recovery Vault in Azure
- Install the Azure Site Recovery Provider
- Configure Azure Site Recovery protection for Hyper-V based virtual machines
- Perform failover/failback

At each step I provide the corresponding screenshots and some additional explanation where required to understand what you are doing.

Prerequisite Check

To make sure you can start configuring ASR services right away, here are some of the prerequisites needed to go through the exercises:

- An active Azure subscription
- A running Hyper-V host (running Windows Server 2012 R2)
- A few active virtual machines on the Hyper-V host

© Peter De Tender 2016
P. De Tender, *Implementing Operations Management Suite*, DOI 10.1007/978-1-4842-1979-9_7

- A good understanding of Azure Virtual Machines, storage, and networking

- An Internet connection (direct or proxied) from the Hyper-V host to Azure (https/443)

Create a Azure Site Recovery Vault

Although this might sound obvious, you need an active Azure subscription, as well as administrative access rights to this subscription, before being able to create the Azure Site Recovery Vault.

1. Log on to the Azure Resource Manager portal (new portal) from https:// portal.azure.com.

2. Once you're logged on, click New and type recovery in the search box. This will present you with a list of all possible Azure resources that can be deployed, all related to recovery. (See Figure 7-1.)

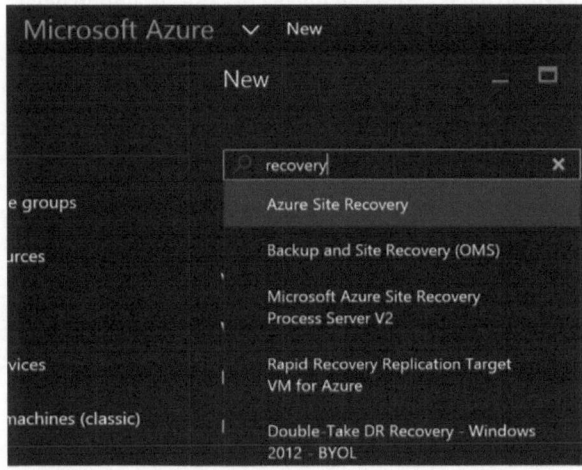

Figure 7-1. *Search for Azure Recovery resources*

3. From the results list, select Backup and Site Recovery (OMS). (See Figure 7-2.) This is the one that allows you to deploy ASR from the new portal, also known as the Azure Resource Manager.

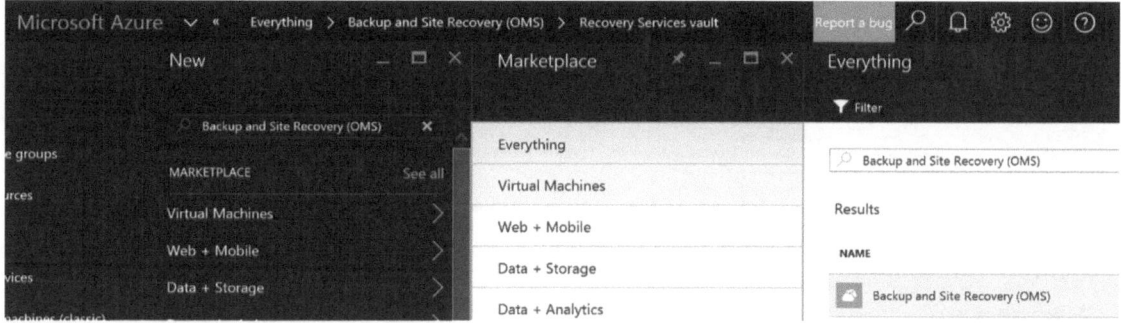

Figure 7-2. *Backup and Site Recovery (OMS) selected*

4. Select Backup and Site Recovery (OMS). This will start the configuration wizard to create the Recovery Services Vault, as shown in Figure 7-3.

    •   Provide a descriptive name, such as HyperV-ASR

    •   Select your Azure subscription

    •   Preferably, create a new resource group by giving it a name (e.g., HyperVASR)

    •   Select the Azure region closest to your location

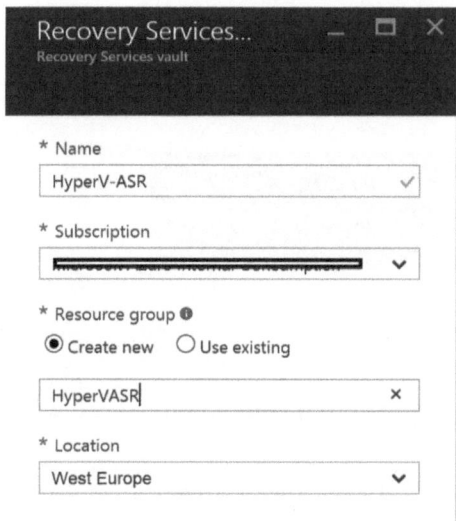

Figure 7-3. *Create the Recovery Services Vault by entering the required parameters*

5. Wait for the Recovery Services Vault to be created. Once it's finished, it will show up in the portal under the new resource group that was created (see Figure 7-4). Select this resource group.

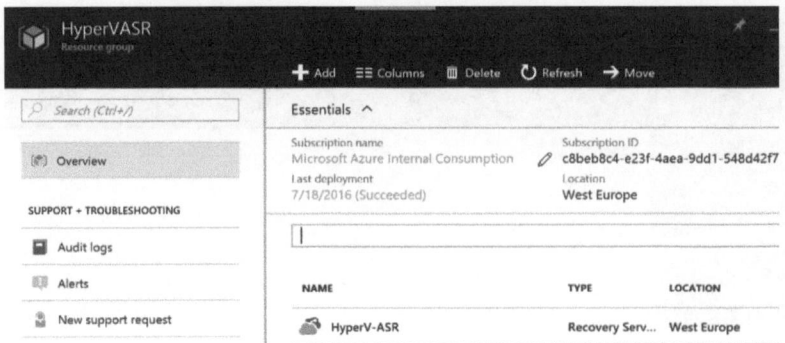

Figure 7-4. Azure Resource Group HyperVASR with recovery service HyperV-ASR

Configuring an Azure Site Recovery Vault

Use the steps in the following sections to configure an ASR Vault.

Step 1: Prepare the Infrastructure

Now that the Azure Site Recovery Vault is created, you can continue configuring it. This is a three-step scenario, where each step is split in different substeps.

1. Select the Recovery Services Vault that you created. Browse to the Getting Started option and select Site Recovery. This will launch the Site Recovery configuration blade, which is a three-step scenario, as you can see from Figure 7-5.

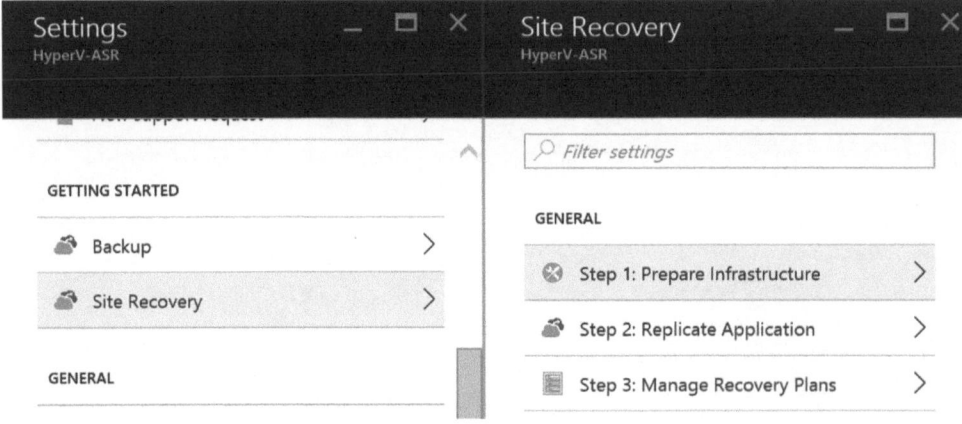

Figure 7-5. Site Recovery configuration blade

2. In Step 1—Prepare Infrastructure—you define the replication source and target parameters (see Figure 7-6).

   • Specify ToAzure as the target

   • Specify Hyper-V as the source

- Answer No to the question about whether you are using SCVMM (or Yes if you are, of course)

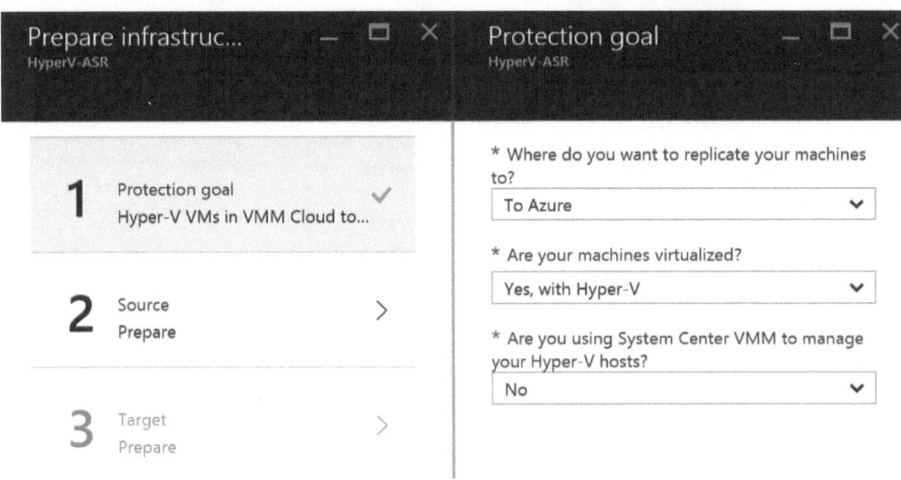

Figure 7-6. *Step 1 of the Prepare Infrastructure selection*

3. This brings you to Step 2—Prepare Source—shown in Figure 7-7. Here you start by creating a Hyper-V site, which is a logical container of Hyper-V hosts. This can have any name, such as MyHyperVSite, but could also point to a physical location like HyperV Site New York, HyperV Site Dublin, and the like.

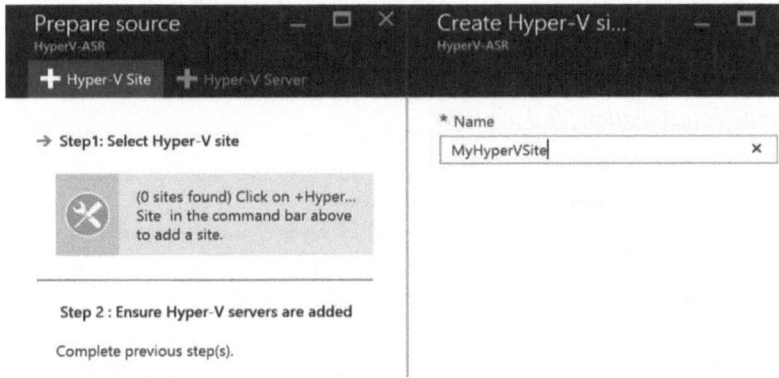

Figure 7-7. *Prepare Source—Create Hyper-V site*

4. In Step 2, you add Hyper-V servers to this configuration. This requires the installation of the Azure Site Recovery provider on the Hyper-V host machines in your on-premises network. The screen looks like Figure 7-8.

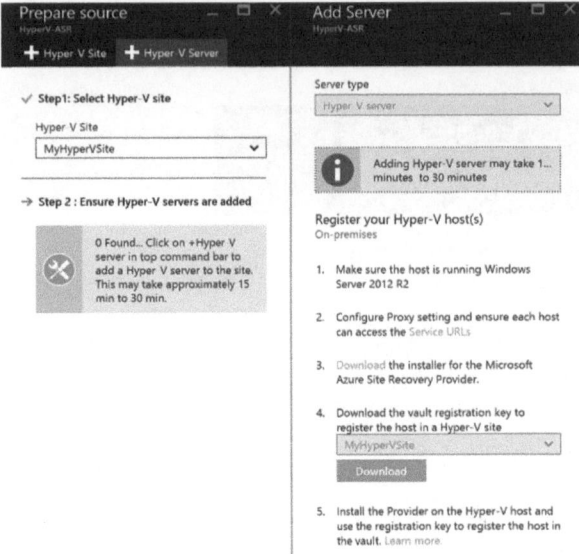

Figure 7-8. *Prepare source—add the Hyper-V servers*

5.   Download the Azure Site Recovery Provider install files (see Figures 7-9 and 7-10), as well as the vault registration key file. Copy these files to the Hyper-V host(s) to which you want to configure ASR. (Or connect to the installation files from the Hyper-V host(s) without copying them.) Filenames should be similar to Figure 7-11, from the lab environment.

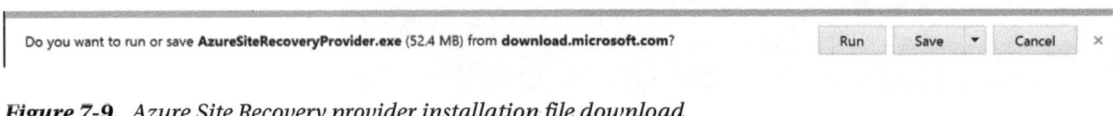

Figure 7-9. *Azure Site Recovery provider installation file download*

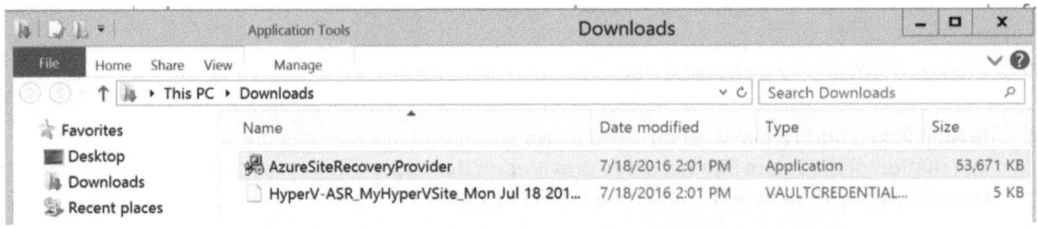

Figure 7-10. *Vault registration key download file*

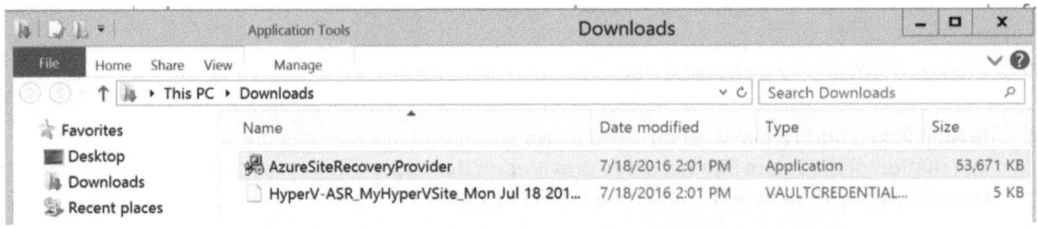

Figure 7-11. *Files have been downloaded and can be found in the Hyper-V host*

6. Log on to the Hyper-V host(s) servers and open the
   AzureSiteRecoveryProvider.msi install file. This will launch the Azure Site
   Recovery provider setup (Hyper-V server), as shown in Figure 7-12. Choose how
   you want Microsoft Update to check for updates.

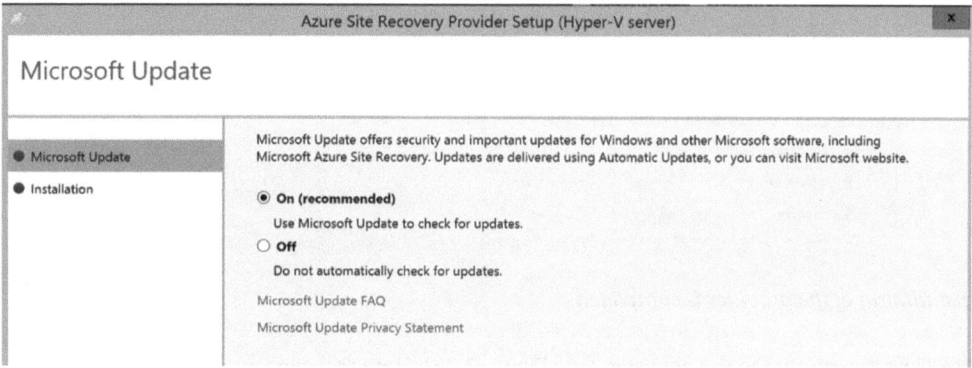

Figure 7-12. *ASR provider setup*

7. In the installation step, as shown in Figure 7-13, accept the installation location
   or choose a different folder; click Next to continue.

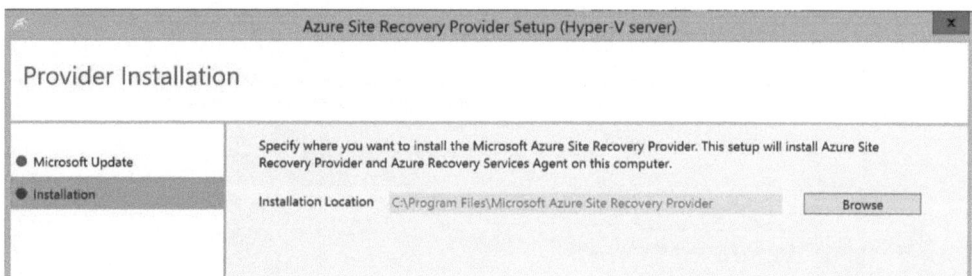

Figure 7-13. *Installation location selection*

8. The installation of the provider will continue, and it's composed of a few different
   steps (see Figure 7-14). Once you're done, you can continue with the next step.

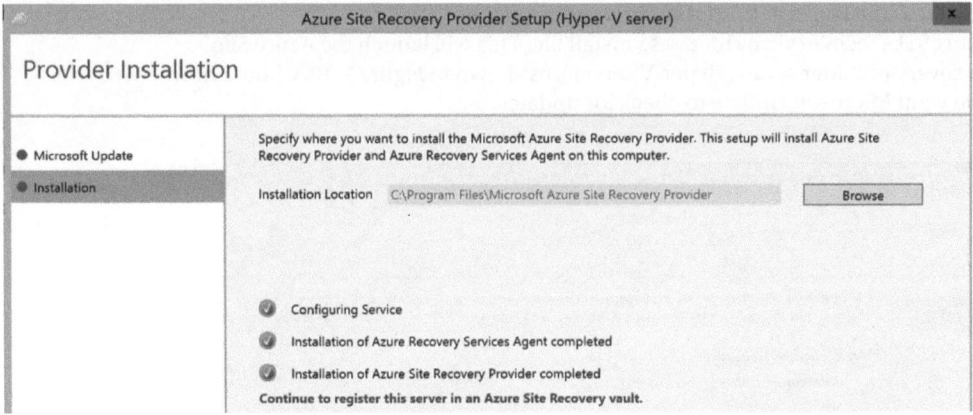

Figure 7-14. Installation of the provider is completed

9. Click Next to continue to the next step (see Figure 7-15). Here you can specify how the Hyper-V host connects to the Internet. If you are using a proxy, enter the proxy server credentials here.

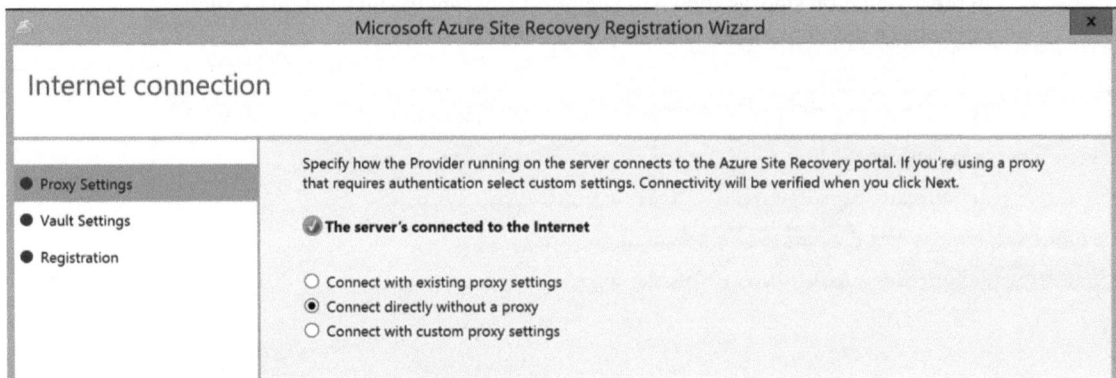

Figure 7-15. Define the Hyper-V host proxy settings to allow Internet connectivity

---

■ **Note**   Go back to Chapter 4 to learn what kind of Internet connectivity is required to complete this installation if it should fail in your environment.

---

10. In the Vault Settings step (see Figure 7-16) of the installation wizard, you define to which Hyper-V site in ASR this Hyper-V host will be registered. This secured communication is defined by importing the settings from the vault registration key you downloaded earlier. Browse to this file and ensure that the information is correct.

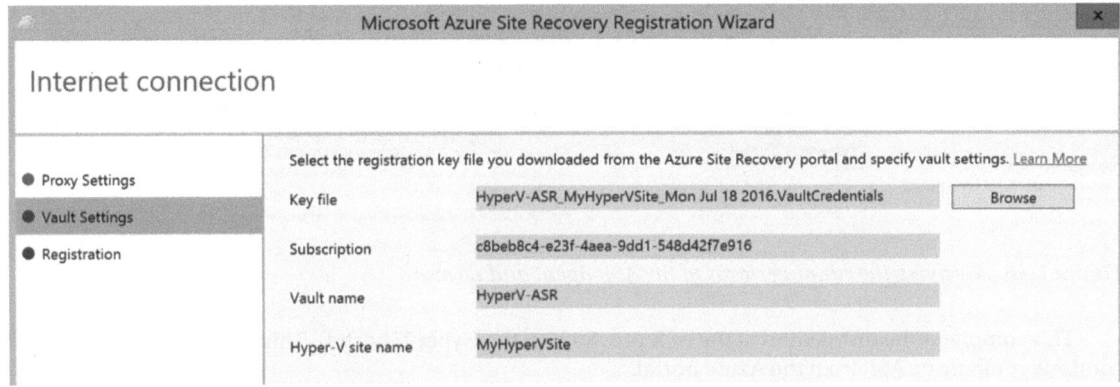

Figure 7-16. The vault registration key is being imported

11. Click Next to continue. At this time, the Hyper-V host server will try to communicate with the Azure Site Recovery Vault, and the Hyper-V host will be registered as an ASR member. The results should look similar to Figure 7-17.

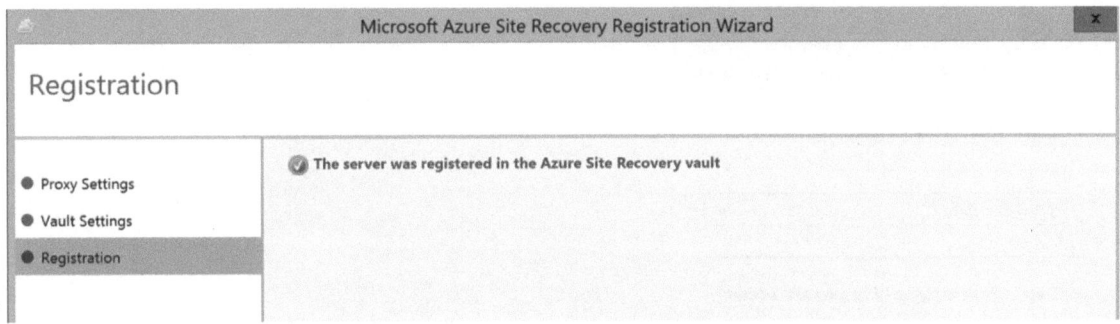

Figure 7-17. Azure Site Recovery registration setup completed successfully

12. This completes the installation of the Azure Site Recovery provider on the Hyper-V host machine, as well as the successful registration into the Azure Site Recovery Vault. The setup wizard can be closed.

Although you can assume all went fine with the installation if you got to this point, it might be a good thing to verify that the required Windows services are in a running state.

13. Go to your Services snap-in (from the Start screen or from the Administrative Tools) and verify the following:

- Microsoft Azure Recovery Services Agent

- Microsoft Azure Site Recovery Service

Both should have a status of Running, as shown in Figure 7-18.

Services (Local)				
Microsoft Azure Recovery Services Agent	Name ▲	Description	Status	Startup Type
	Link-Layer Topology Discovery Mapper	Creates a Network Map, consisting of PC and device top...		Manual
	Local Session Manager	Core Windows Service that manages local user sessions. ...	Running	Automatic
Stop the service	Microsoft Azure Recovery Services Agent	Support for scheduled backups and recovery of files and ...	Running	Manual
Restart the service	Microsoft Azure Site Recovery Service	Configures disaster recovery for virtual machines using ...	Running	Automatic
	Microsoft iSCSI Initiator Service	Manages Internet SCSI (iSCSI) sessions from this comput...		Manual
Description:	Microsoft Software Shadow Copy Provider	Manages software-based volume shadow copies taken b...		Manual
Support for scheduled backups and recovery of files and folders to an online location	Microsoft Storage Spaces SMP	Host service for the Microsoft Storage Spaces managem...		Manual
	Multimedia Class Scheduler	Enables relative prioritization of work based on system-w....		Manual

Figure 7-18. *Verifying the running status of the ASR agent and service*

This completes the installation of the ASR provider on the Hyper-V host(s). This means you can continue configuring ASR from the Azure portal.

If you didn't close the Azure portal during the installation of the provider on the Hyper-V server, you should now see that the Hyper-V server host(s) are being recognized in the Prepare Source step, as shown in Figure 7-19. (If you did close the portal, log back on to `http://portal.azure.com`, select the resource group you created, and then select the Azure Recovery Vault you configured. Then go back to Step 1—Prepare Infrastructure—in Section 1—Protection Goal.)

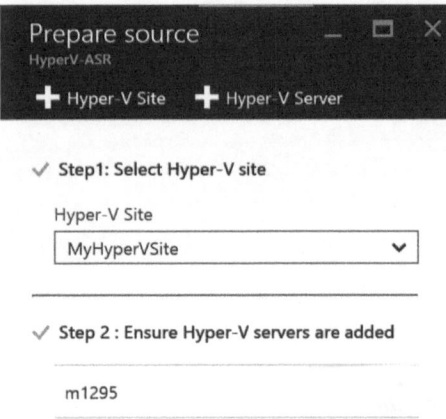

Figure 7-19. *Hyper-V server is registered under the Hyper-V site now*

14. You are now at Step 3 of the Prepare Infrastructure configuration, which looks like Figure 7-20. The goal is to configure/select an Azure Storage account as well as an Azure Virtual Network. Both will be used for the virtual machines that are being failed over to Azure during a disaster scenario. If you already have these configured, feel free to reuse them. However, in most production environments I have deployed at customers, a dedicated one will be created for each, isolating the ASR Virtual Machines. Both options work though.

- Select your Azure subscription.

- Select Resource Manager as the deployment model; this means the virtual machines and related resources will be created in the new Azure portal, not in the classic mode.

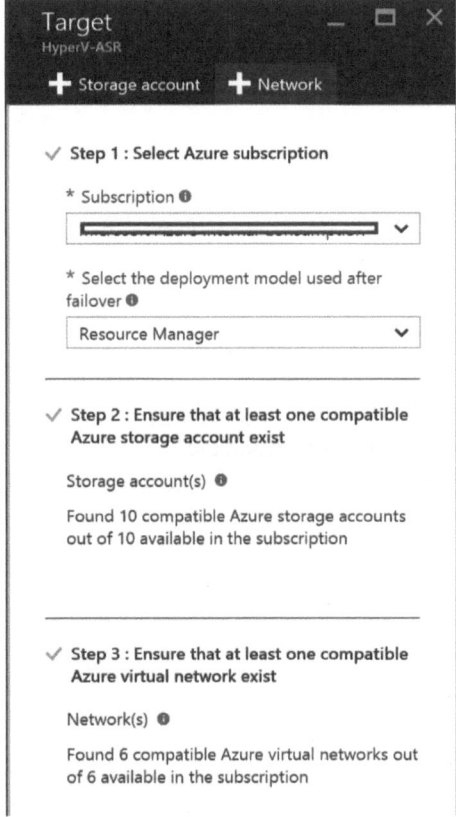

Figure 7-20. *The Hyper-V server is now registered under the Hyper-V site*

15. If you don't have a storage account, now is a good time to create one. (Use Figure 7-21 as a reference for what to choose.)

- Provide a unique name (unique among all Azure subscriptions…).

- Select Standard as the storage performance type.

- Select LRS as the replication type.

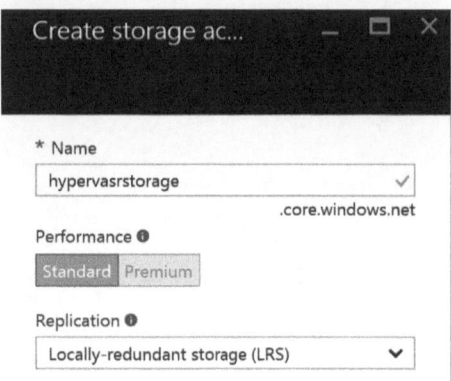

Figure 7-21. *Creating a storage account for ASR*

16. Next, fill in the options for the Azure Virtual Network, where I suggest you create a dedicated one for your ASR resources.

  • Specify a unique name for the VNet as well as the subnet.

  • Provide the address space (IP range) of addresses that can be used and the related subnet.

The result is shown in Figure 7-22.

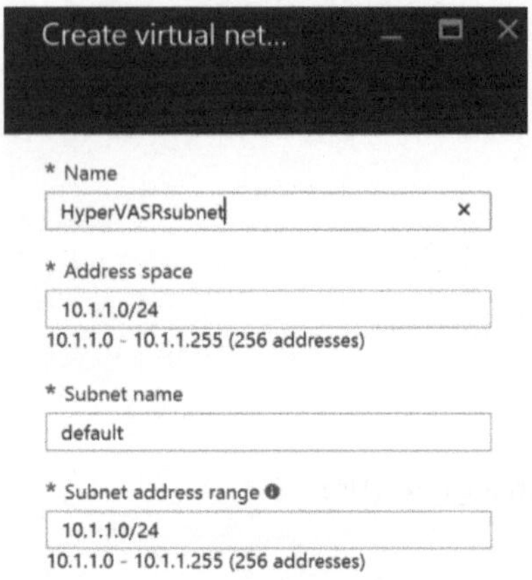

Figure 7-22. *Creating a virtual network for ASR*

This brings you to the last section in this step, creating a replication policy. A *replication policy* is a configuration that defines how the replication should be treated, the time interval for when the VM changes synchronization, and the initial replication start time.

In the real world, these settings depend on specific customer scenarios, application and operating system characteristics, and the like. In this lab environment, most of the default settings are acceptable for what you want to achieve:

- *Copy Frequency:* The default is 15 minutes, which can be lowered to 30 seconds. This points to the time interval of when changes are being synchronized from on-premises to Azure. This has no impact on the source virtual machine, as it stays active during the synchronization.

- *Recovery Point Retention:* This is the retention time for when a recovery point must be created. This allows you to restore a virtual machine in ASR from any of these recovery points, if needed.

- *App-Consistent Snapshot:* This parameter refers to a time setting per number of hours when an application-consistent snapshot should be created. Think of consistency-dependent applications like SQL databases, Exchange Server database, or similar.

- *Initial Replication Time:* The default setting is Immediately. This means immediately from when this wizard is completed. If you are working in a production scenario, it might be a good idea to move this initial replication to an off-hour time.

17. Select Create and Associate a Replication Policy from the configuration blade, as shown in Figures 7-23 and 7-24.

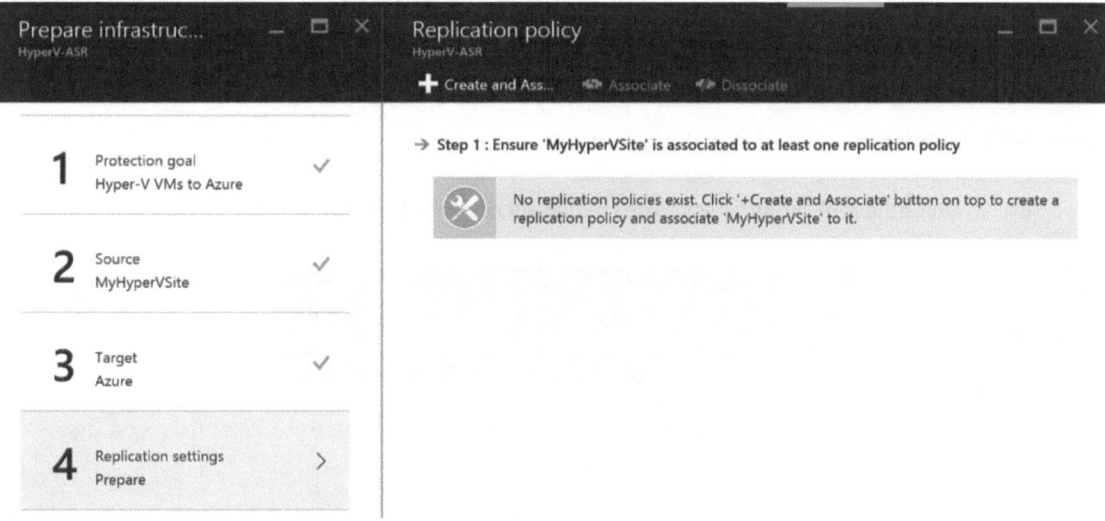

Figure 7-23. *Creating and associating a replication policy*

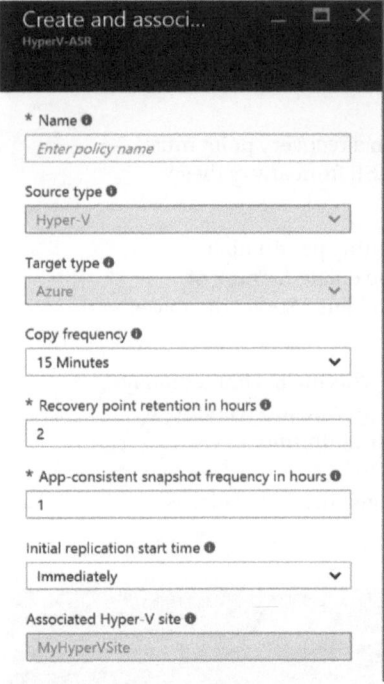

Figure 7-24. *Defining the replication policy parameters*

18. Wait for the replication policy to be created successfully (see Figure 7-25).

Figure 7-25. *Replication policy created successfully*

19. Figure 7-26 shows the final step in this section. It's a more informational
    step, pointing you to the ASR Capacity Planning Tool and asking if you have
    completed that step. (To me personally, this feels more like some sidebar to avoid
    complaints about slower replication, and to cover their bases.)

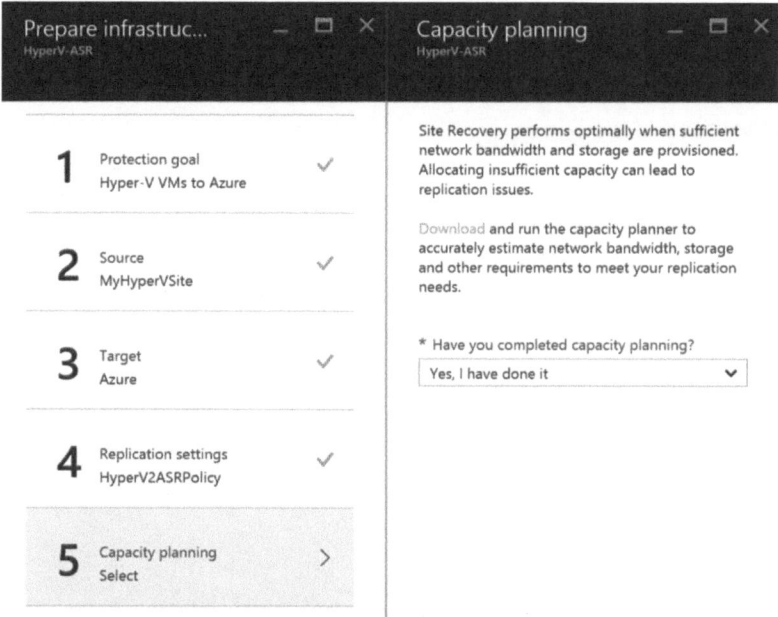

Figure 7-26. *Confirm the capacity planning question*

This completes Step 1↓Prepare Infrastructure—so you can now continue with Step 2—Replicate Application.

Step 2: Replicate Application

This is where you define the source and target environments, as well as select the individual virtual machines that you want to see protected by ASR.

1. In Step 1↓as shown in Figure 7-27, specify the source environment, which is the Hyper-V site that was configured earlier.

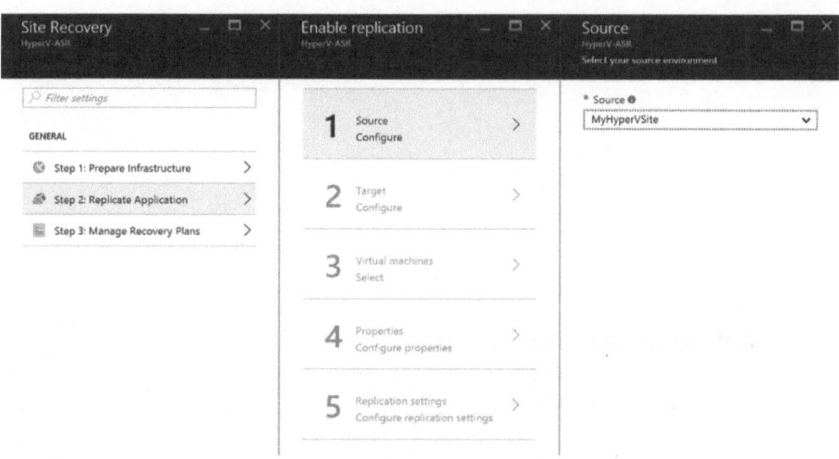

Figure 7-27. *Specify the source environment for replication*

153

2. In Step 2, which looks like Figure 7-28, define the target environment (Azure) by selecting the Azure storage account and virtual network you configured for this before.

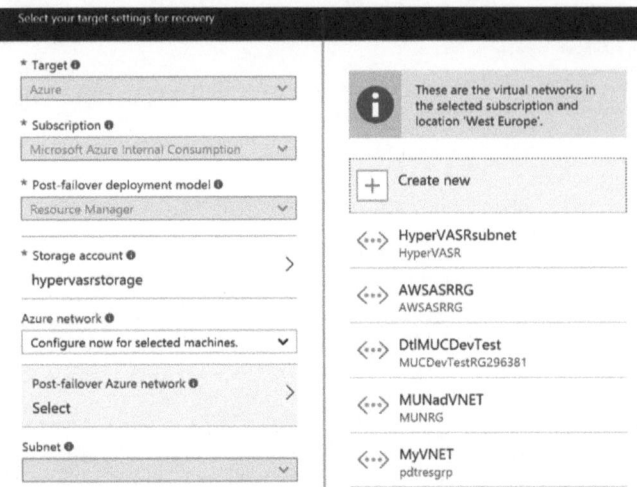

Figure 7-28. *Specify the target environment for replication*

3. This brings you to Step 3, which is displayed in Figure 7-29, where you can select one or several virtual machines that are running in the on-premises Hyper-V environment.

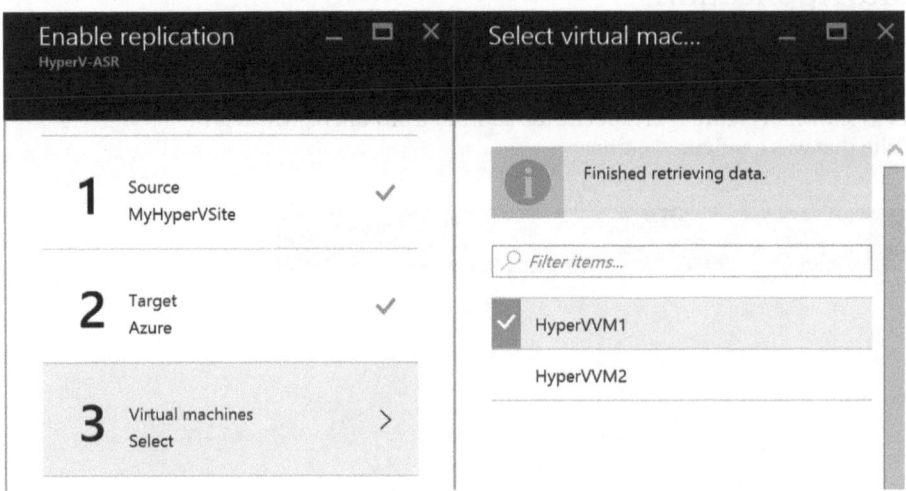

Figure 7-29. *Selecting the virtual machines you want to protect by ASR*

4. For each virtual machine you select, specify the OS Type and OS Disk. My lab configuration is shown in Figure 7-30.

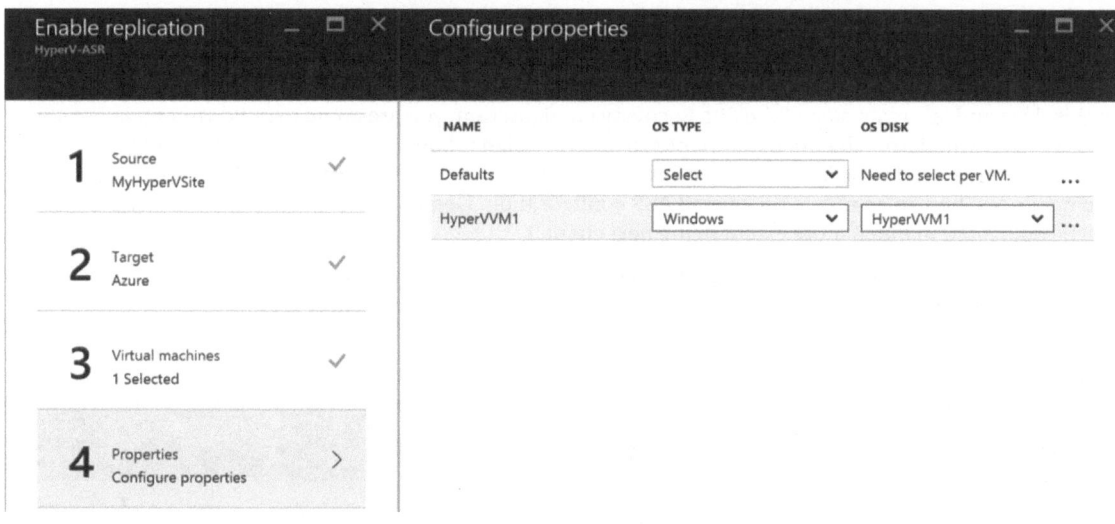

Figure 7-30. *Configure the virtual machine OS type and OS disk properties*

5. In Step 5, the screen should look like Figure 7-31, Select the replication policy you created before and confirm all selections by clicking OK.

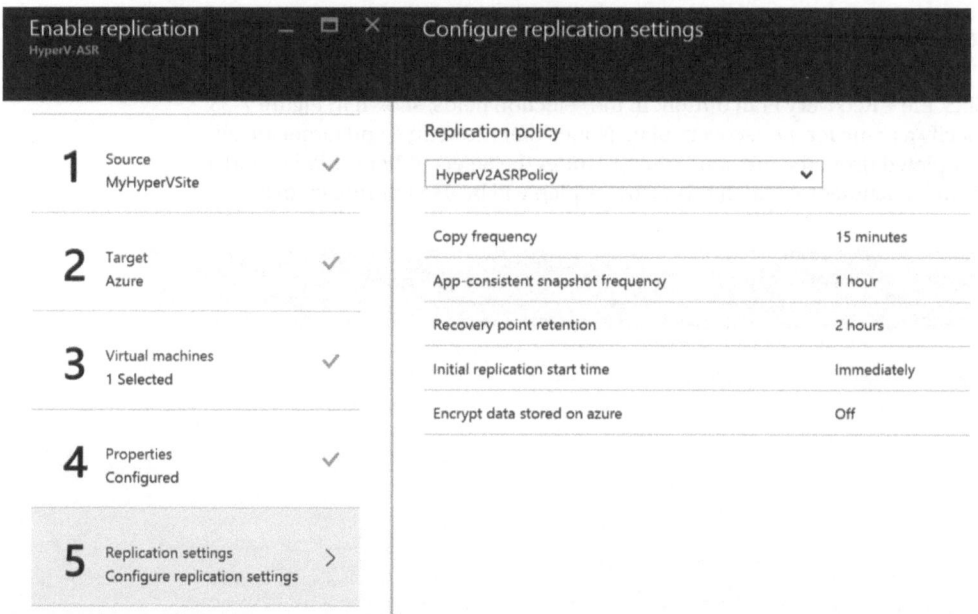

Figure 7-31. *Configure replication settings*

This completes Step 2↓Replicate Application—in which you configured the source and target environment parameters, made a selection of on-premises virtual machines you want to protect, and determined which replication policy settings should be applied.

Step 3: Manage Recovery Plans

In this third and last main step of the Site Recovery configuration, you are going to build your recovery plan.

As you learned from the previous chapter, a recovery plan is basically the configuration of the step-by-step actions that need to occur in case of a failover. Without going into too much detail on recovery plans, you create one here to complete the overall ASR configuration. Details and specifics about the recovery plan will be addressed in much more extent in the next chapter.

1. By selecting Step 3—Manage Recovery Plans—you are asked to create a new recovery plan (this can be changed later once your recovery plans exist). See Figure 7-32.

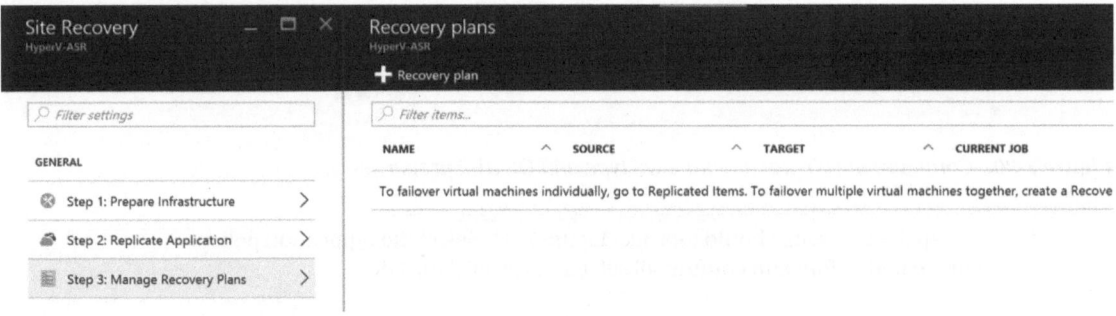

Figure 7-32. *Step 3: Manage Recovery Plans*

2. Click the + Recovery Plan button. In the selection fields, shown in Figure 7-33, specify a name for the recovery plan. Notice that the source and target are already completed (from the previous Step 2). Under the Selected Items blade, mark the virtual machines for which this recovery plan will be used during failover.

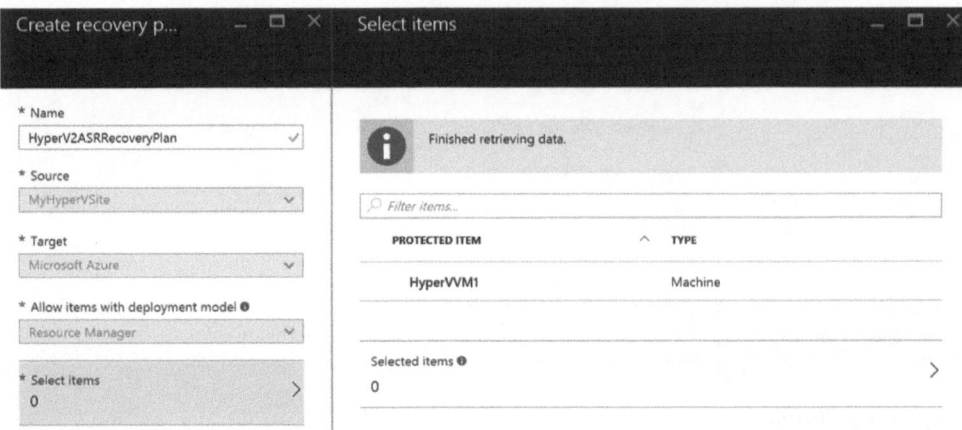

Figure 7-33. *Create the recovery plan and select items*

3. Once the recovery plan is selected, you will see that the virtual machine(s) will start replicating (depending on the replication settings you defined earlier in the replication policy). See Figure 7-34.

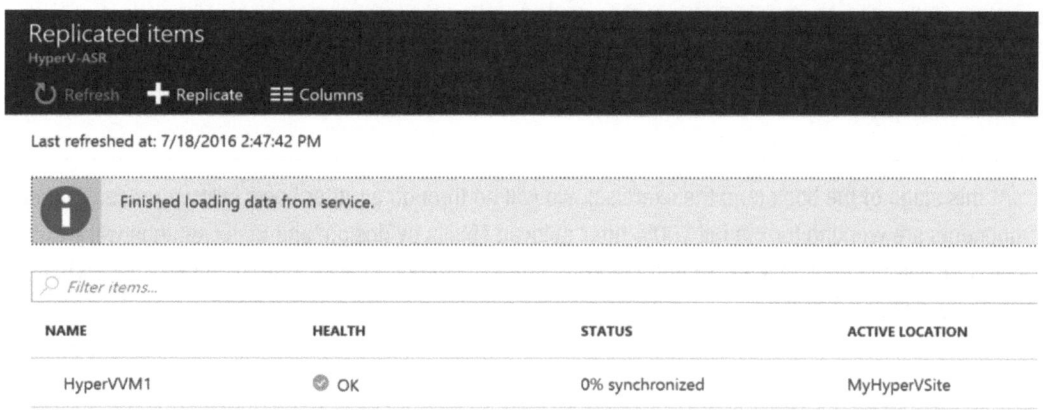

Figure 7-34. *Replicated items are being synchronized to Azure*

4. Wait for the synchronization of the virtual machine(s) to finish. Once it's finished, the virtual machine will have a status Protected (see Figure 7-35), which means it is now fully operational as an ASR item, for which you can execute a failover.

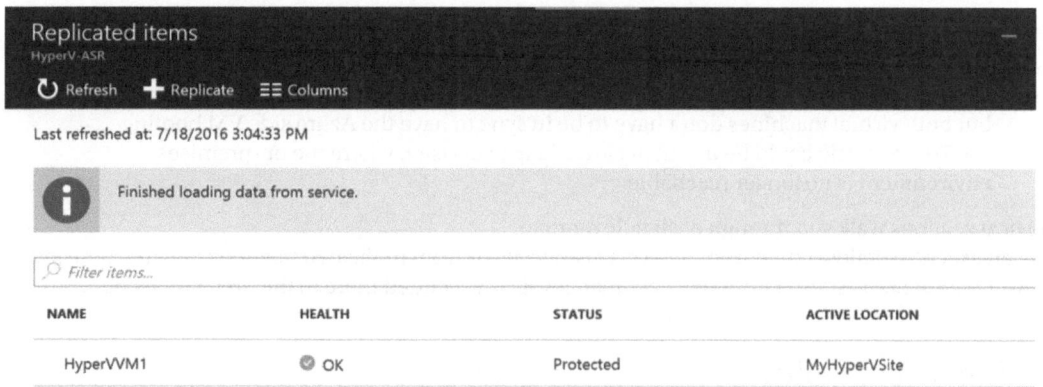

Figure 7-35. *Replicated items↓synchronization is complete and item is protected*

This completes the initial three-step configuration of the ASR; the next part of this exercise will go through a failover simulation.

Performing a Failover

Now that you have set up an ASR configuration by going through the different steps of the wizard, and your virtual machine(s) are in a protected state, you can move to the next step↓and basically the ultimate goal of ASR↓executing a failover.

In short, a failover means that (simulating as a test or as part of a a true production situation disaster scenario) you will complete final replication from the on-premises infrastructure to Azure, starting the virtual machine(s) and testing your applications for running successfully on the Azure side.

■ **Note**   At this stage of the book (and the exercise), we will go through a rather basic failover process, where not all components are working for the full 100% after failover. This is by design, and these settings will be fine-tuned in more detail in the next chapter. So don't worry if not all is working yet in your lab environment when you finish this exercise at the end of this chapter.

When initiating a failover in ASR, there are three possible scenarios:

- *Test Failover:* Running through a full test failover plan, where the communication between the source and target is validated, and a dummy virtual machine is configured to validate the Azure storage account and Azure Virtual network configuration. This test has no impact on your own production environment.

- *Planned Failover*: In case of a planned failover, a proper sequence of actions is followed, by which final machine synchronization will be initiated. Once both virtual machines are in sync, the on-premises VM is shut down and the Azure side VM is started up and ready for use. This failover is ideal when downtime can be foreseen, for example, during a planned electricity outage in the business park.

- *Unplanned Failover*: The understanding here is the same as with a planned failover, but both virtual machines don't have to be in sync to have the Azure side VM booting up. This scenario could be useful in case of a true disaster, where the on-premises environment is no longer reachable.

The next sections walk you through each failover plan.

You can execute a failover plan from recovery plan level, or from replicated items/virtual machine level. The following sequence is started from recovery plan level, as we ended there in the previous section.

Executing a Test Failover

Follow these steps to execute a test failover:

1. After selecting your recovery plan, the Recovery Plan Settings blade will appear. It shows the different failover options available on the top (Test Failover and Planned Failover are visible; Unplanned Failover is hidden behind the ... button).

    Choose Test Failover, which will open the Test Failover blade, as shown in Figure 7-36. The only selection to be made here is the Azure Virtual Network. Select the ASR VNet you configured before.

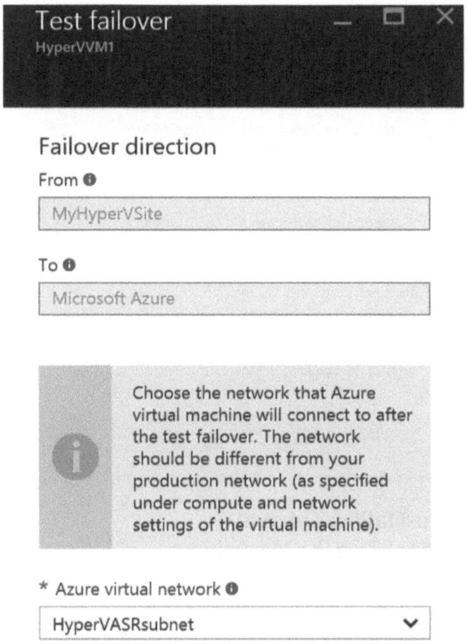

Test failover
HyperVVM1

Failover direction

From ❶

MyHyperVSite

To ❶

Microsoft Azure

> ℹ️ Choose the network that Azure virtual machine will connect to after the test failover. The network should be different from your production network (as specified under compute and network settings of the virtual machine).

* Azure virtual network ❶

HyperVASRsubnet ⌄

Figure 7-36. *Configuring a test failover*

2. This will immediately trigger a Test Failover job. Click on the notification button (the bell) to see what happens more in detail. (See Figure 7-37.)

- Prerequisite checks
- Creating the test environment
- Creating the test virtual machine/starting the virtual machine
- Completing the testing
- Cleaning up the environment

■ **Note** Notice that there is an interruption between starting up the virtual machine and completing the testing. This is by design, and actually foreseen to give the administrator an opportunity to do some more detailed validation and testing of the virtual machine to make sure it is working correctly.

Job

NAME	STATUS	START TIME	DURATION	
Prerequisites check for test failover	✓ Successful	7/18/2016 3:05:55 PM	00:00:01	...
Create test environment	✓ Successful	7/18/2016 3:05:56 PM	00:00:00	...
Create test virtual machine	✓ Successful	7/18/2016 3:05:57 PM	00:00:22	...
Preparing the virtual machine	✓ Successful	7/18/2016 3:06:19 PM	00:00:00	...
Start the virtual machine	✓ Successful	7/18/2016 3:06:20 PM	00:01:08	...
Complete testing	⚠ User Input Requir...	7/18/2016 3:07:28 PM		...

Figure 7-37. *Running through a test failover plan*

3. Confirm the complete testing step. This will trigger the test failover plan to continue testing and cleaning up the environment and finalizing the test failover. The result from my lab setup is shown in Figure 7-38.

🖥 HyperVVM1-test	Creating	HyperVVM1-test	West Europe	
Complete testing	✓ Successful	7/18/2016 3:07:28 PM	00:01:47	...
Clean up the test virtual machine	✓ Successful	7/18/2016 3:09:19 PM	00:03:40	...
Clean up the test environment	✓ Successful	7/18/2016 3:12:59 PM		...
Finalizing test failover	✓ Successful	7/18/2016 3:13:00 PM		...

Figure 7-38. *Completing a test failover plan*

Executing a Planned Failover

In an identical way, you can execute a planned failover, by following these steps:

1. From the recovery plan level or from the recovery items/individual virtual machine level, click the Planned Failover button.

    This will open the Planned Failover blade, as shown in Figure 7-39. Confirm the execution by clicking the OK button, as there is nothing more to be configured here.

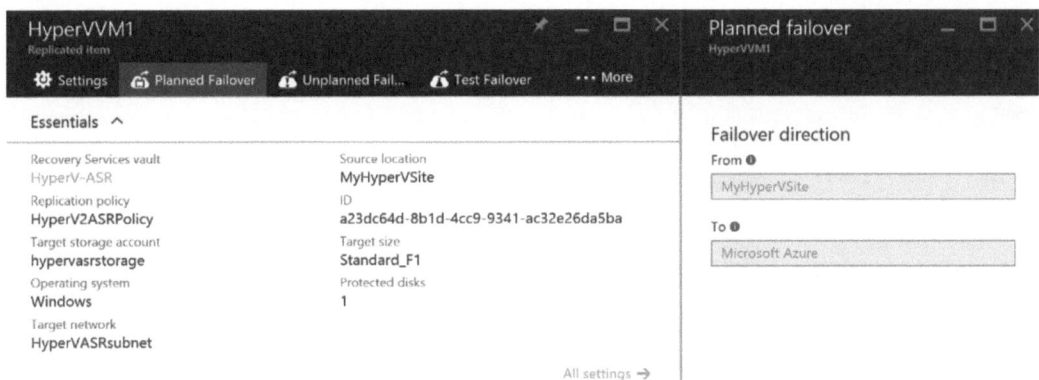

Figure 7-39. *Executing a planned failover*

2. This will again trigger a planned failover, which can be monitored by clicking the notification (bell) button, as shown in Figure 7-40. As you can see, this process is identical to the test failover.

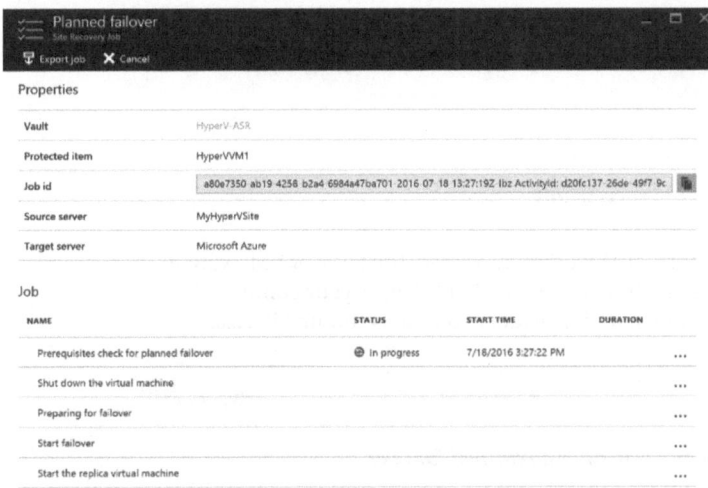

Figure 7-40. *Executing a planned failover*

3. During the failover process, the second step is to shut down the virtual machine. When checking back on your on-premises Hyper-V host, like Figure 7-41 in my setup, you will notice the respective VM (HyperVVM1 in my case) is indeed being shut down properly by ASR.

Virtual Machines

Name ▲	State	CPU Usage	Assigned Memory	Upt
HyperVVM1	Off			
HyperVVM2	Running	0 %	4096 MB	01:
HyperVVM3	Running	6 %	4048 MB	00:

Figure 7-41. *ASR shutting down an on-premises VM as part of the failover*

4. Wait for the failover process to be finished (successfully). The result should look like Figure 7-42.

Job

NAME	STATUS	START TIME	DURATION	
Prerequisites check for planned failover	✓ Successful	7/18/2016 3:27:22 PM	00:01:39	...
Shut down the virtual machine	✓ Successful	7/18/2016 3:29:02 PM	00:00:34	...
Preparing for failover	✓ Successful	7/18/2016 3:29:37 PM		...
Start failover	✓ Successful	7/18/2016 3:29:49 PM	00:02:56	...
Start the replica virtual machine	✓ Successful			...

Figure 7-42. *ASR planned failover completed successfully*

5. From the Azure portal, go to Virtual Machines and select the failover VM. Notice it now has a status of Running, as shown in Figure 7-43. This is your confirmation that the failover process went fine and the virtual machine is running in Azure.

HyperVVM1	Running	HyperVVM1

Figure 7-43. *Virtual machine is running in Azure after a planned failover*

6. As a logical approach, you not only want to verify that the virtual machine is starting up fine, but maybe you also want to verify the services are running, applications are starting up, and so on. There is a natural tendency to connect to this failed over virtual machine from a remote desktop (RDP) session.

   It might be a surprise to you that this is not (yet) possible though, since the Connect button is grayed out, as you can see from Figure 7-44.

Figure 7-44. *Virtual machine running in Azure after a planned failover*

Be confident, however, that this does not mean something is wrong with your virtual machine. Remember the note from the beginning of this chapter, where I mentioned we would focus on getting ASR configured and perform an initial failover, but not all things would work yet? This is one of the examples. Again, this is by design.

The good news is that there is not only a logical explanation for this, but I also have a solution. Learn all about how to solve this issue and successfully connect to your server (as well as some other interesting aspects of ASR plans) in the next chapter.

Summary

This chapter was a technical one, wasn't it? You learned how to configure a Azure Site Recovery Vault, deployed the ASR provider onto a Windows Hyper-V host, configured ASR protection for virtual machines, and ran through a test failover and a planned failover scenario.

In the next chapter, we take it to an even more advanced level by zooming in on protection plans and learning how to automate certain tasks as part of the failover plan, as well as explaining the reason and fixing the issue as to why an RDP session is not available by default after performing a failover of a virtual machine.

CHAPTER 8

■ ■ ■

Configuring ASR for Non-Hyper-V Infrastructures

If you just read Chapter 7, "Configuring ASR for an On-Premises Hyper-V Infrastructure," I have to tell you there is about 80% overlap between configuring ASR for Hyper-V or for non-Hyper-V infrastructures. So I hope you want to learn about the 20% that is different and that this is not a disappointment. In the end, we are talking about Azure Site Recovery, and the beauty is that it is pretty similar in configuration across different platforms. That is how most organizations operate their IT environment anyway, using different platforms.

If you skipped the previous chapter because you are not running a Hyper-V (or SCVMM) infrastructure and are want to get Azure Site Recovery (ASR) configured and integrated in your Vmware-based infrastructure, you are reading the right chapter.

But what about the other platforms? Let me briefly list again which non-Hyper-V infrastructures are supported:

- VMware vSphere virtual machine replication to Azure Virtual Machines

- Amazon AWS virtual machine replication to Azure Virtual Machines

- Azure Virtual Machine replication to Azure Virtual Machines (in a different region)

- Physical server 2012 R2 to Azure Virtual Machines

And for all of them, if the operating system is supported in Azure, they are supported in ASR replication and migration.

This chapter basically contains a full end-to-end exercise on how to configure ASR, this time by using Amazon AWS as a source environment. If you are wondering why I decided to use Amazon AWS, here are a few reasons:

- It is another Cloud service like Azure and it's always good to understand the competition.

- You can go through the full exercise by using the free trial subscription (if you are not doing too crazy on virtual machine specs).

- It is easier to work with in a learning scenario, since not everyone has a VMware infrastructure available for testing.

- The way the configuration of ASR works for Amazon AWS is nearly identical for VMware vSphere environments, physical servers, and Azure-to-Azure setups.

Obviously, depending on your specific situation and testing environment, I leave it up to you to go through this exercise using any of the supported infrastructures mentioned here.

By going through the detailed steps in this chapter, you will learn how to:

- Configure the Azure Site Recovery Vault in Azure

- Install the Azure Site Recovery Unified Agent

- Configure Azure Site Recovery protection for a non-Hyper-V based source infrastructure

- Perform a test failover and an unplanned failover

The chapter walks you through the steps that are required to complete the end-to-end configuration, along with screenshots and some additional explanation as needed to help you understand what you are doing.

Prerequisite Check

To make sure you can start configuring ASR services in Azure right away, here are some of the prerequisites needed to go through the exercises:

- An active Azure subscription (a free trial will do fine)

- An active Amazon AWS subscription (a free trial will do fine)

- Or an active VMware vSphere infrastructure

- Or a few physical servers running Windows Server 2012 R2

- A good understanding of Azure Virtual Machines, storage, and networking

- A good understanding of Amazon AWS, or VMware, or Windows Server 2012 R2

- A few virtual machines running in each environment (three is recommended) or three physical machines running Windows Server 2012 R2

- An Internet connection (direct or proxied) from the source infrastructure hosts to Azure (https/443)

Create an Azure Site Recovery Vault

Although this might sound obvious, you need an active Azure subscription, as well as administrative access rights to this subscription, before you can create the Azure Site Recovery Vault.

1. Log on to the Azure Resource Manager portal (new portal) from https://portal.azure.com. From there, select New and type recovery in the search box. This will present you with a list of all possible Azure resources that you can deploy, related to recovery. (See Figure 8-1.)

Figure 8-1. *Search for Azure Recovery resources*

2. From the results list, select Backup and Site Recovery (OMS). This is the one that allows you to deploy ASR from the new portal, also known as the Azure Resource Manager. The portal is shown in Figure 8-2.

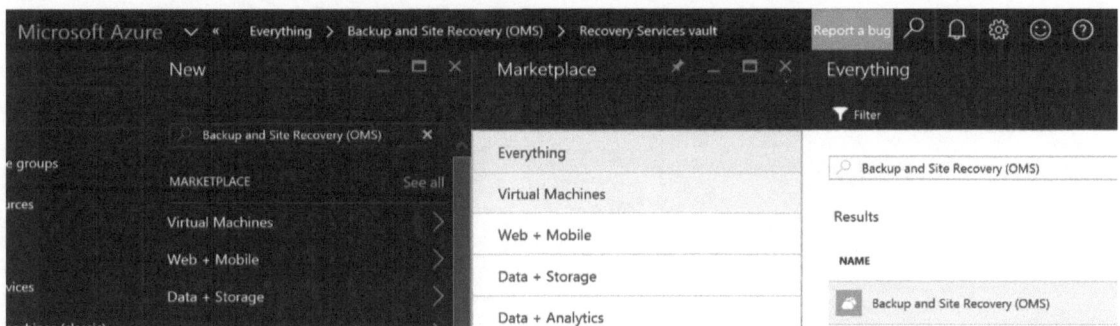

Figure 8-2. *Backup and Site Recovery (OMS) selected*

3. Select Backup and Site Recovery (OMS). This will start the configuration wizard blade (see Figure 8-3) to create the recovery services vault.

- Provide a descriptive name, such as AWS-ASR.

- Select your Azure subscription.

- Preferably, create a new resource group by giving it a name (e.g., AWSASRRG).

- Select the Azure region closest to your location.

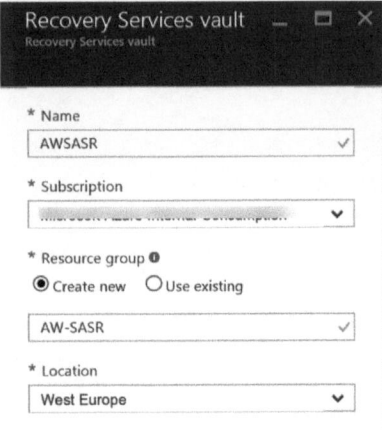

Figure 8-3. *Create a recovery services vault by entering the required parameters*

4. Wait for the recovery services vault to be created. Once it's finished, it will show up in the portal under the new resource group that was created. Select this resource group (see Figure 8-4).

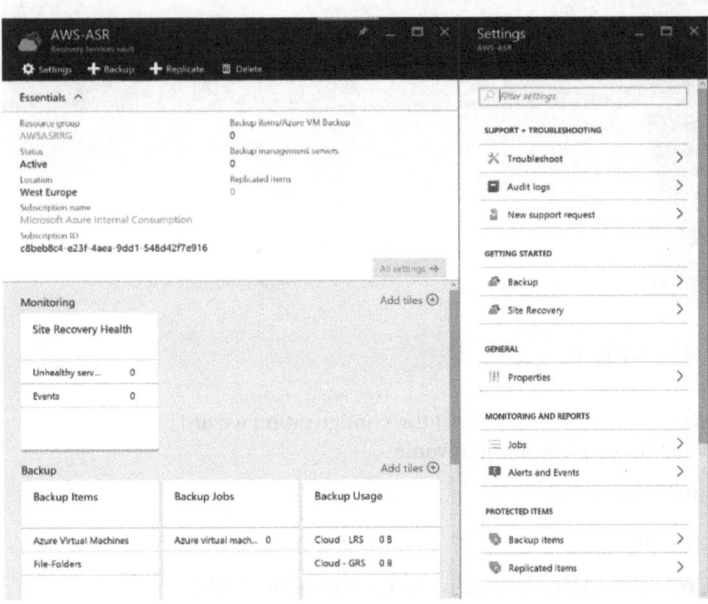

Figure 8-4. *Azure Resource Group HyperVASR with recovery service HyperV-ASR*

This completes the base deployment of a new Azure Site Recovery Vault. We will now continue with the configuration itself.

Configuring the Azure Site Recovery Vault

Use the steps in the following sections to configure the ASR Vault.

Step 1: Prepare Infrastructure

Now that the ASR Vault is created, we can continue configuring it. This is overall a three-step process, where each is split into different substeps.

1. Select the Recovery Services Vault that was created. Browse to the Getting Started option and select Site Recovery. This will launch the Site Recovery configuration blade, which displays the three-step scenario (see Figure 8-5).

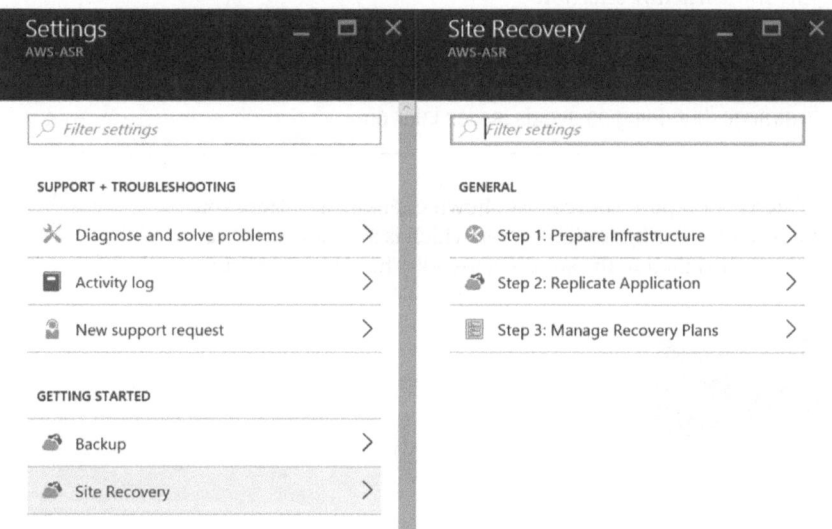

Figure 8-5. *Site Recovery configuration blade*

2. In Step 1—Prepare Infrastructure—you define the replication source and target parameters (see Figure 8-6).

- Specify To Azure as the target.
- Specify whether you are using virtual machines.

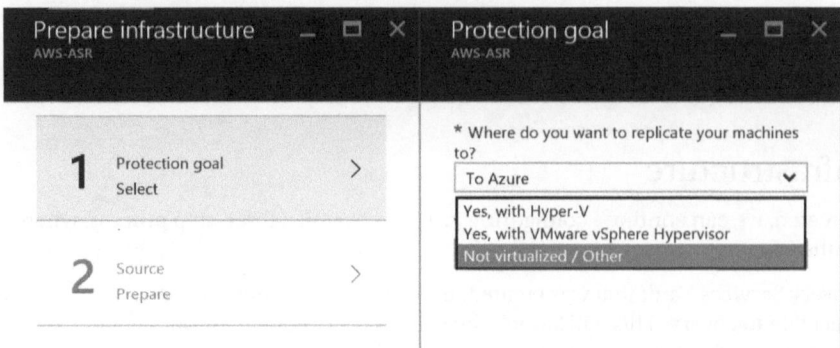

***Figure 8-6.** Step 1 of the Prepare Infrastructure selection*

■ **Note** If your source environment is Amazon AWS or Azure, you also have to indicate that you are *not* using virtual machines. I know this is strange, but doing so avoids issues later on.

---

3.   This brings you to Step 2—Prepare Source—as shown in Figure 8-7. Here you start by adding the so-called configuration server, which is a Windows Server 2012 R2 machine that is installed in the source network. This can be a virtual machine or a physical one.

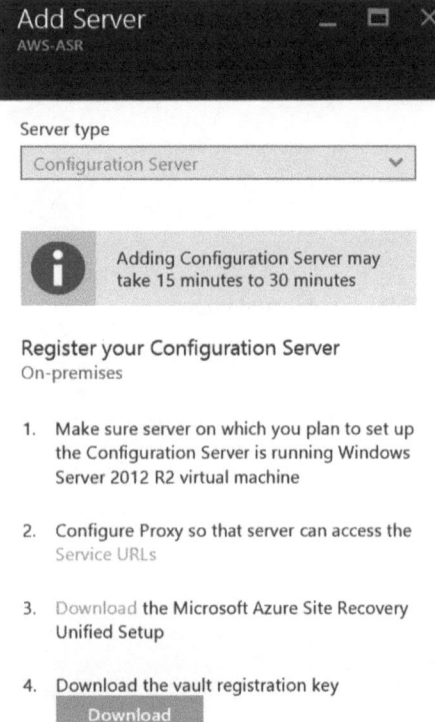

***Figure 8-7.** Prepare source—add a configuration server*

4. In the next step, which is shown in Figure 8-8, you download the Azure Site Recovery Unified Setup, as well as the Azure Site Recovery registration key. You can download these directly to the "configuration server to be" or to your local workstation. Then copy the install files or connect to them remotely from the configuration server.

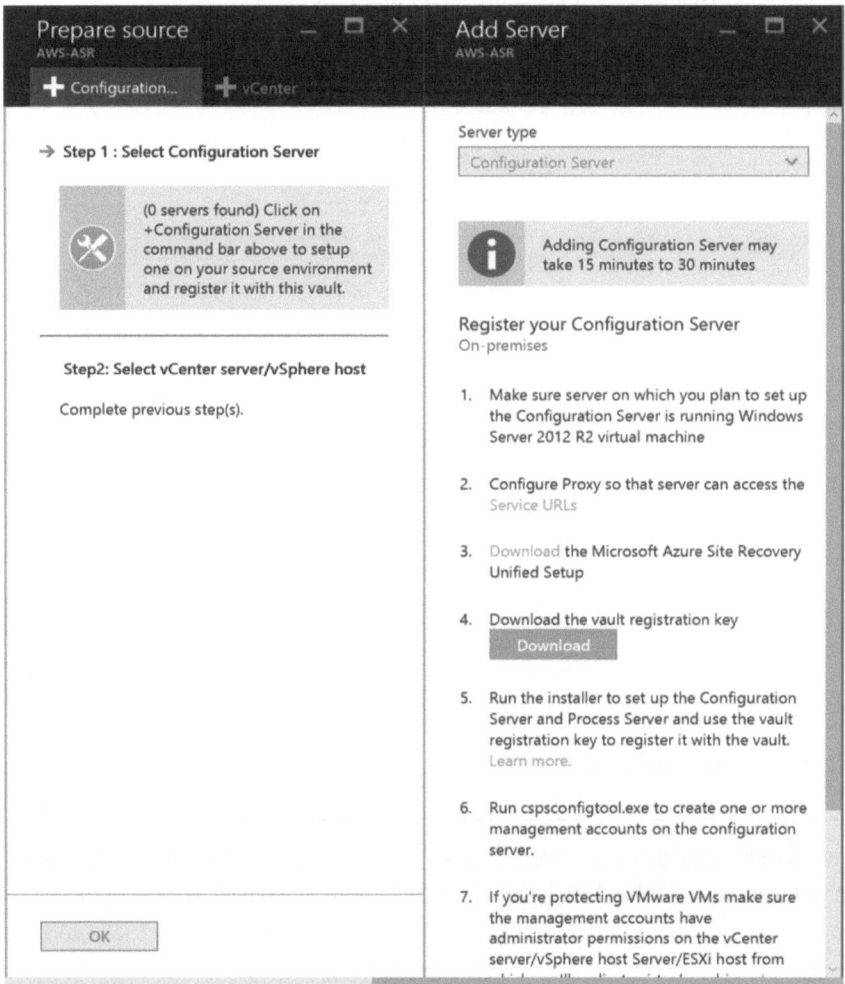

Figure 8-8. *Prepare source—download configuration server setup files*

5. Log on to the configuration server machine with administrative credentials and start the AzureSiteRecoveryUnifiedSetup.msi installation file. This will launch the Azure Site Recovery Unified Setup, which configures this machine as the ASR configuration server/process server/management server.

■ **Note** In the Azure classic ASR setup, this needed to be separate machines in both environments, source and target. Thank you Microsoft product team for optimizing this component to the maximum!

6. In the first section, select Install the Configuration Server and Process Server (see Figure 8-9). Click Next to continue.

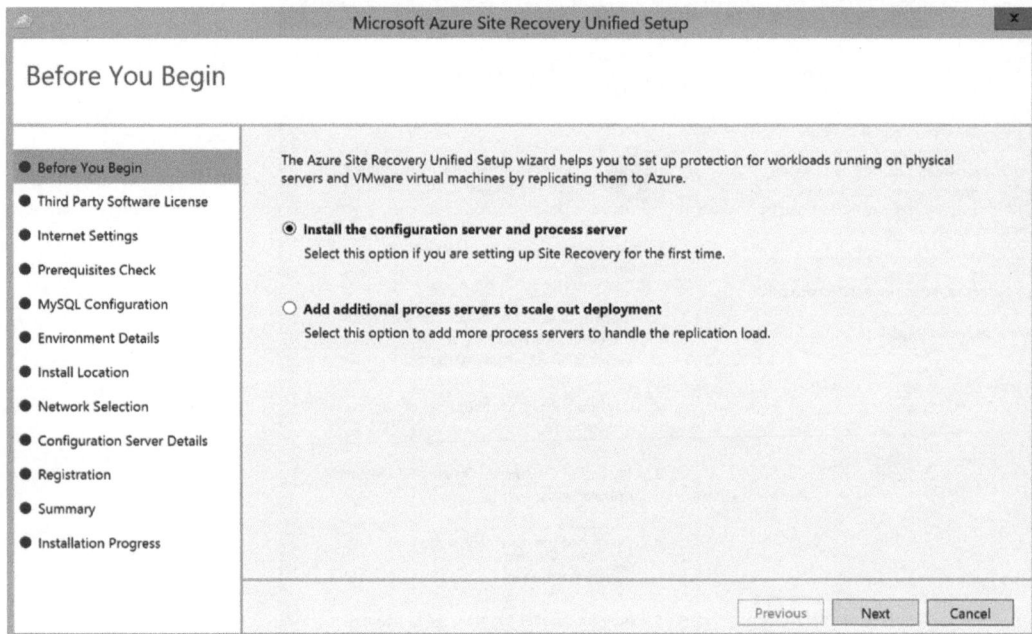

Figure 8-9. *Install the configuration server and process server*

■ **Note** Notice the option to add additional process servers to scale out deployment; this is very useful when you have a large install base you want to protect in ASR. It can also help in providing a high available process server setup.

7. Next, you have to accept the third-party license agreement for the installation of the MySQL Community Server; see Figure 8-10. Click Next to continue.

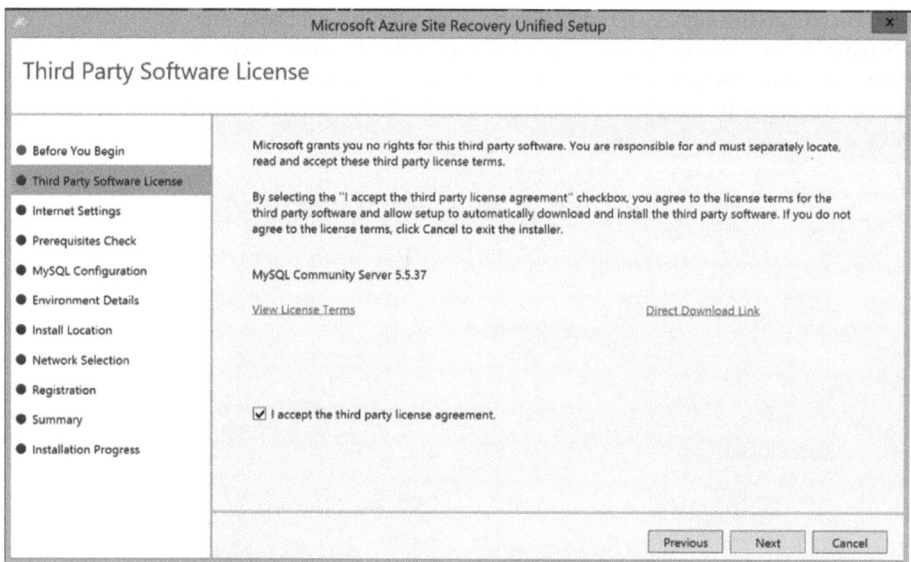

Figure 8-10. *MySQL license agreement*

8. In the step that follows, shown in Figure 8-11, you are asked how the configuration server and process server connect to the Internet (and thus the ASR backend in Azure). If your source network requires an in-between proxy with authentication, you can enter the credentials here too. Click Next to continue.

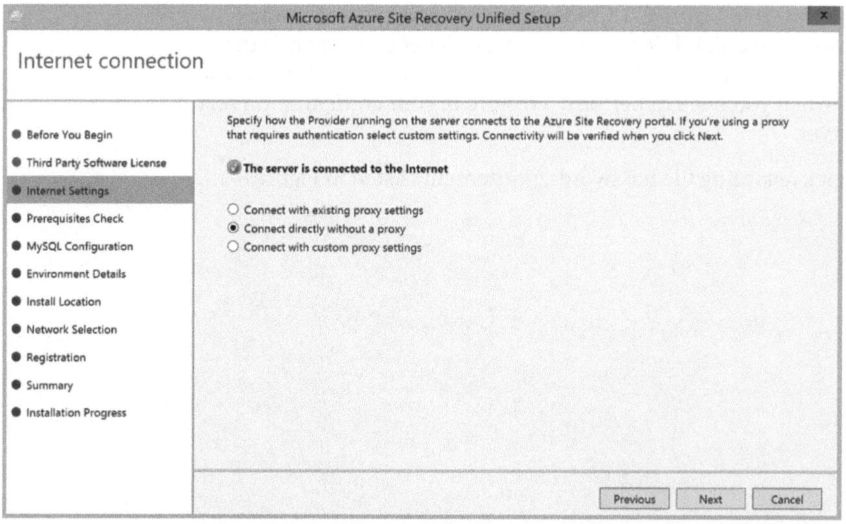

Figure 8-11. *Specify the Internet settings*

9.   The installation will go through a prerequisite check to validate that the source machine is ready to be set up as the configuration server and process server. Fix any errors here and restart the setup. You can ignore the warning about free space requirements from my demo setup (see Figure 8-12). Click Next to continue.

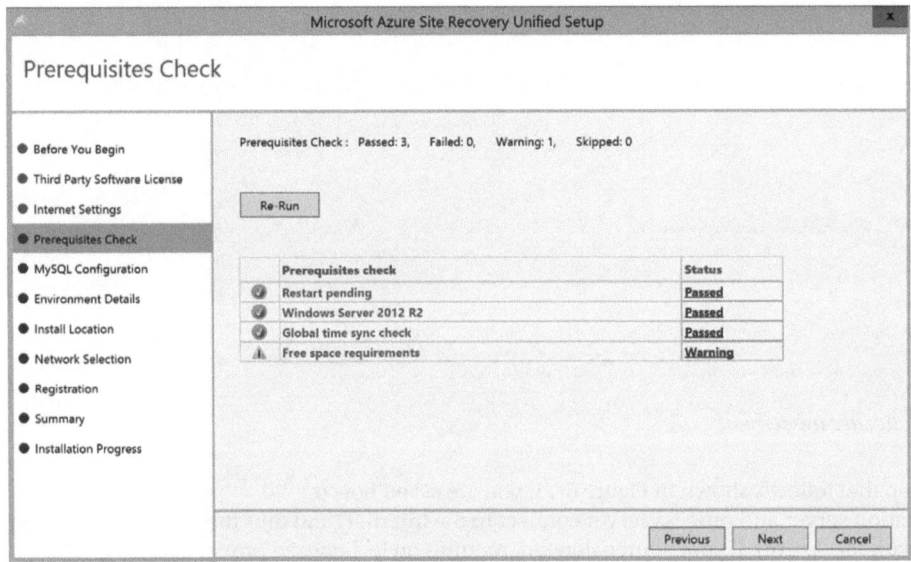

Figure 8-12. *Prerequisites check*

10.   In the next step, shown in Figure 8-13, enter a MySQL root password and a MySQL database password. While you normally don't need to log on to the MySQL software, it's best to store these credentials in a safe place. This might become handy when you need to perform a restore of your configuration server and process server.

Note the feedback regarding the password requirements listed in Figure 8-13.

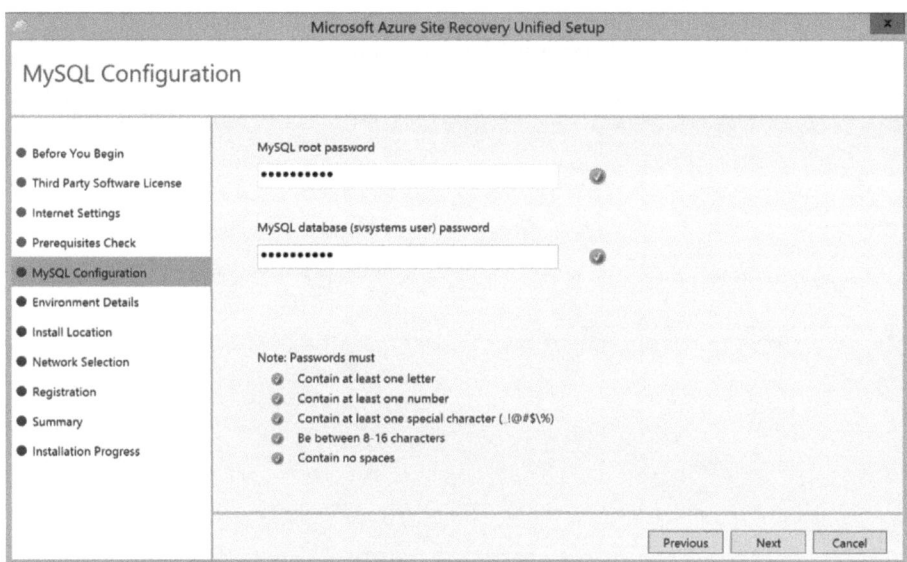

Figure 8-13. *Enter the MySQL root password and database password you want to use*

11. The next step is to inform the Unified Setup if you are protecting VMware virtual machines. This helps in knowing if any VMware-to-VHD process needs to be set up in the background (see Figure 8-14). Again, click Next to continue.

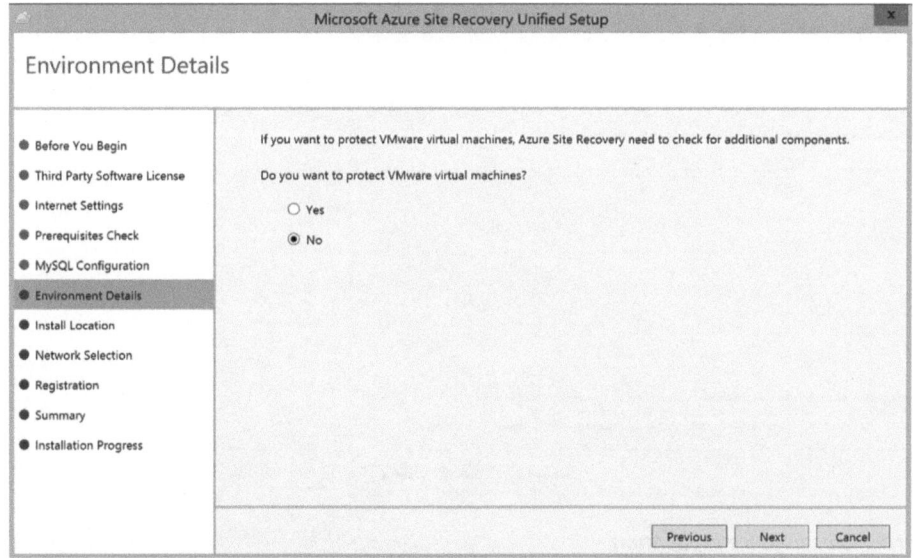

Figure 8-14. *Do you want to protect VMware virtual machines?*

12. Now you can define your install location, as displayed in Figure 8-15. Feel free to keep the default or change it when needed. Click Next to continue.

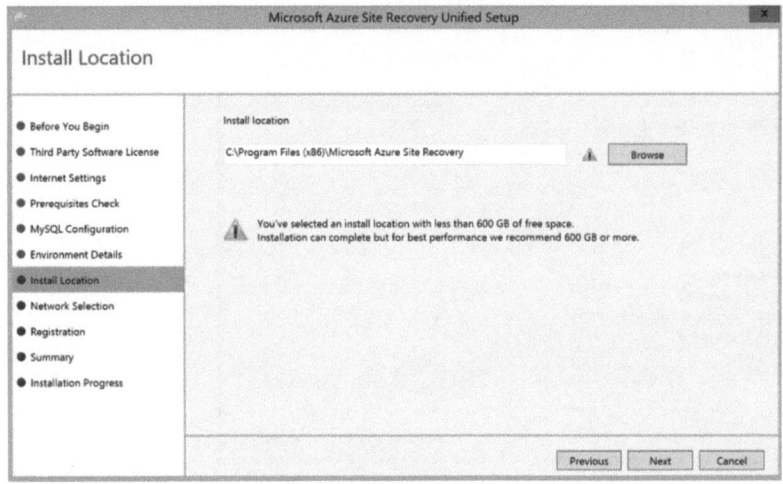

Figure 8-15. *Install location definition*

13. Specify the NIC of the machine (see Figure 8-16), which will be used to receive replication traffic. Notice the default port 9443 that is being used. If your network and firewall have other requirements, make sure you change them on all ends.

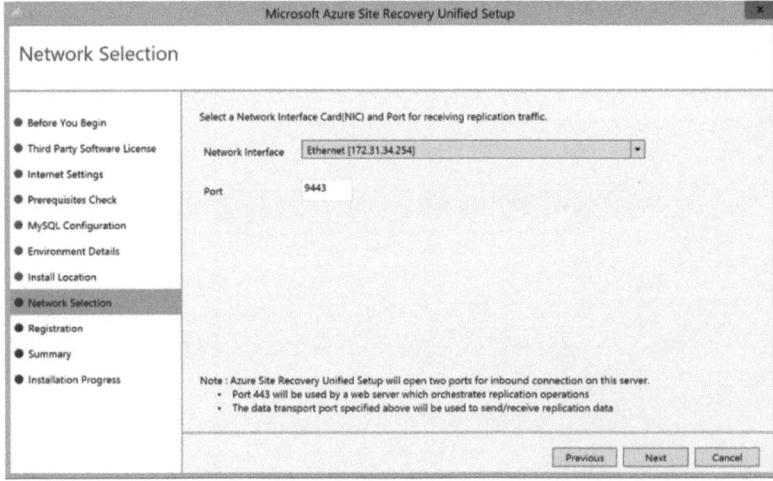

Figure 8-16. *Specify NIC to be used for replication*

14. In the next step, you are asked for the registration file. This has normally been downloaded together with the ASR Unified Setup install files. Browse to the file and validate the information. Figure 8-17 shows how the file is named.

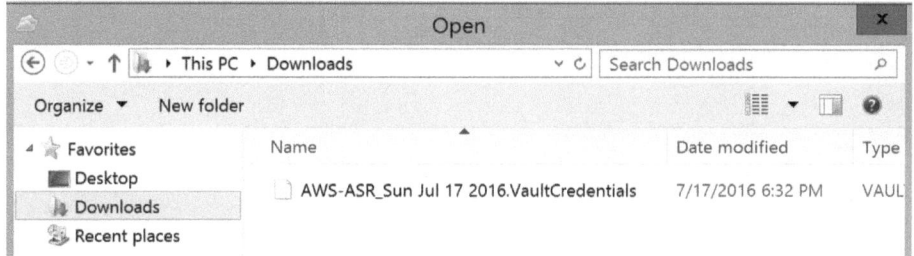

Figure 8-17. *The downloaded ASR registration key*

15. The last screen (see Figure 8-18) shows a summary of all selections you've made. If all is okay, click the Install button to install the software on your machine.

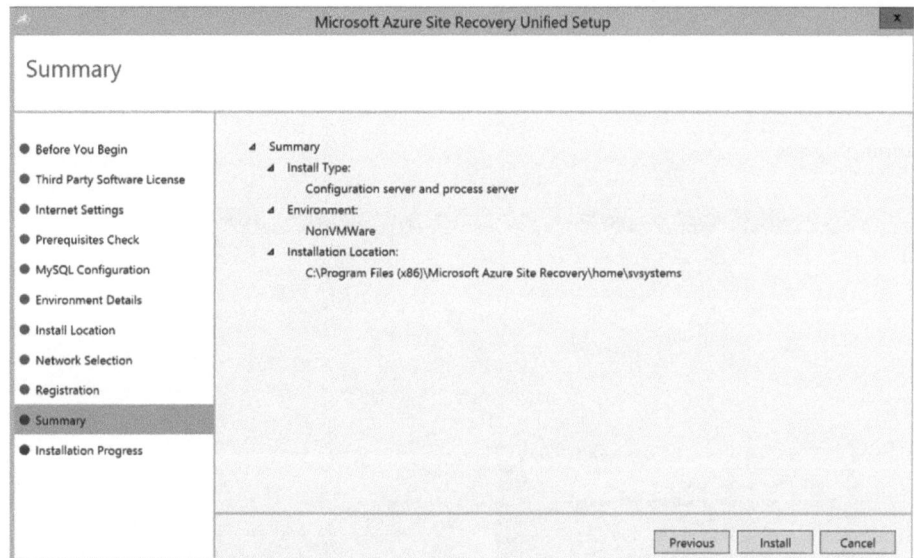

Figure 8-18. *Summary of your choices*

16. The installation will start, and it goes through a few different steps. Wait for the steps to be done. Click the Finish button to close the installation wizard. (See Figures 8-19 and 8-20 to get an idea of the installation progress.)

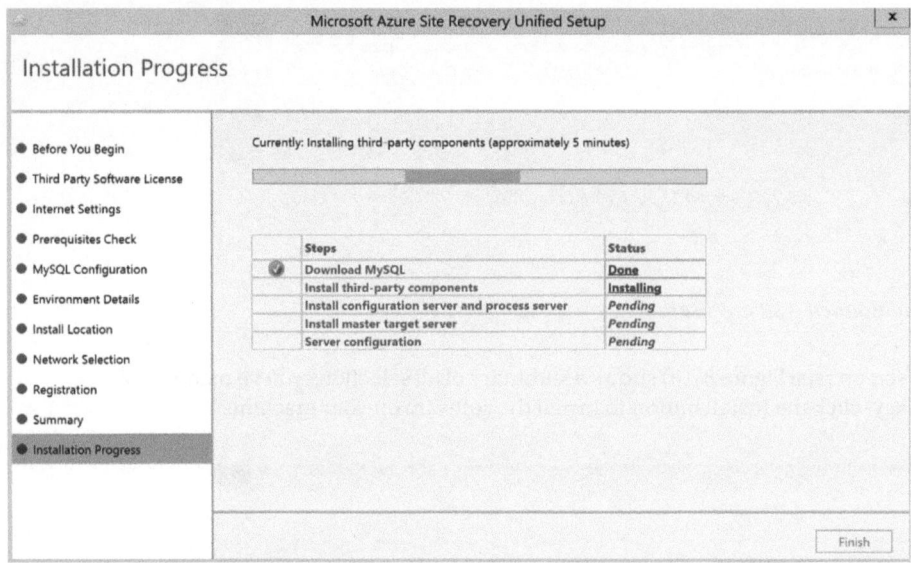

Figure 8-19. *Installation progress*

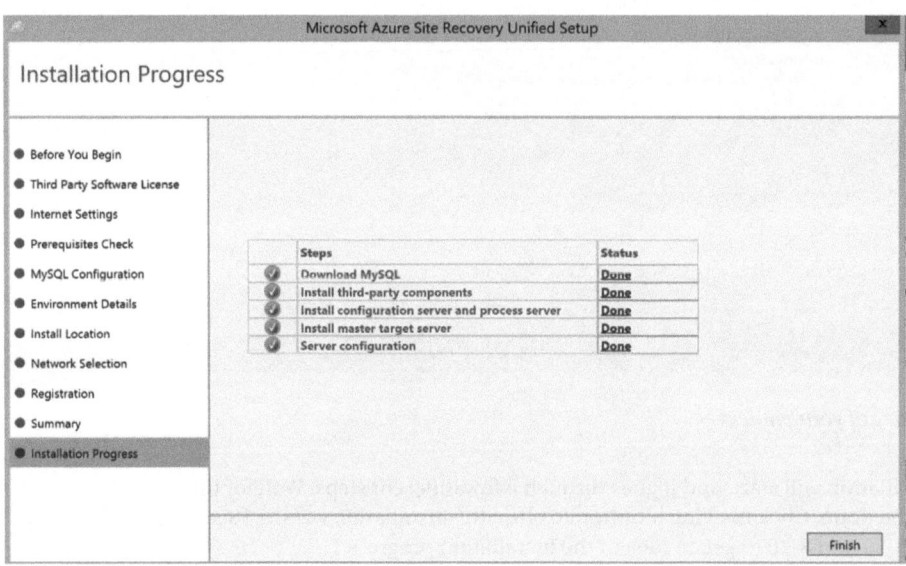

Figure 8-20. *Installation finished successfully*

17. After closing the installation wizard, you are asked to restart the server. Although nobody likes reboots, as they feel like they are a waste of time, I recommend you do this. It will save you from troubleshooting later on. (To emphasize the importance of rebooting, I included the message in Figure 8-21.)

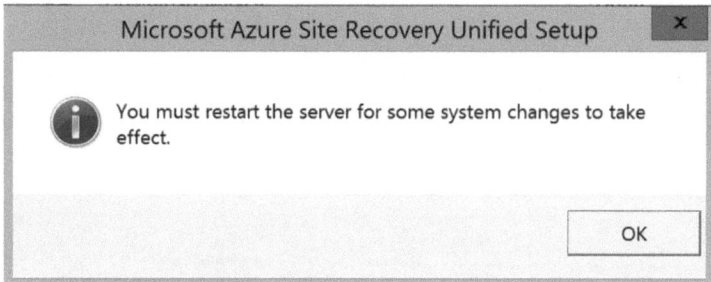

Figure 8-21. *Prompt for restart*

18. After the server has restarted, the setup of the configuration server and process server should continue automatically (if not, there should also be a shortcut on the desktop for this). As part of the setup, a random configuration server connection passphrase will be created, which should be copied to the clipboard (see Figure 8-22). (I also recommend saving this file in a separate Notepad file in a secure location. This phrase is required when registering the server in the Azure Site Recovery vault.)

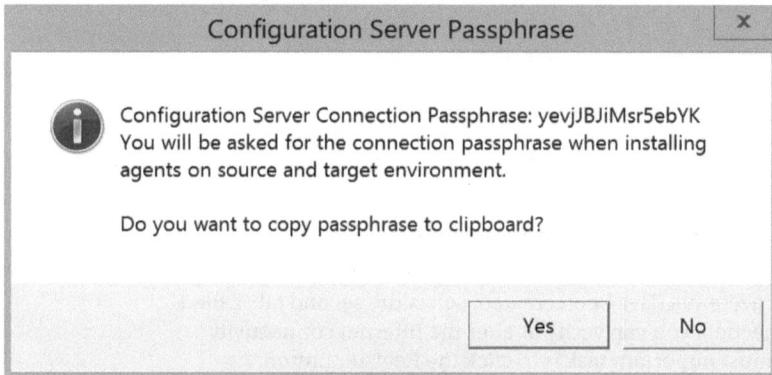

Figure 8-22. *Copy the passphrase to the clipboard*

19. In the actual ASR configuration server configuration, shown in Figure 8-23, there are only a few minor steps left before the server will be registered in ASR. From the Manage Accounts tab, click the Add Account button. Here you need to specify all account credentials of all source machines you want to protect/migrate to ASR. This can be local administrative account credentials, domain administrative user account credentials, Linux root user account credentials, and so on, as shown in Figure 8-24.

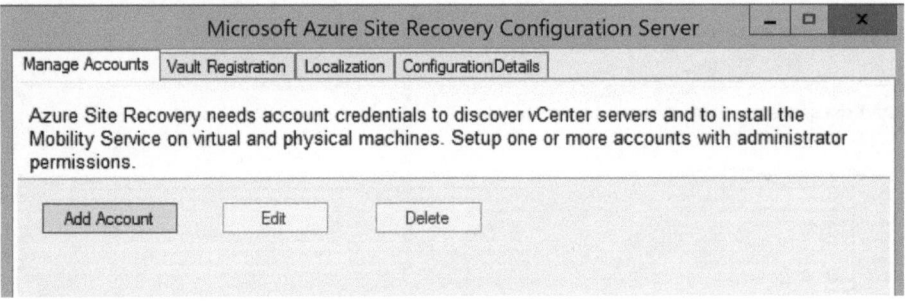

Figure 8-23. *Manage accounts—add account*

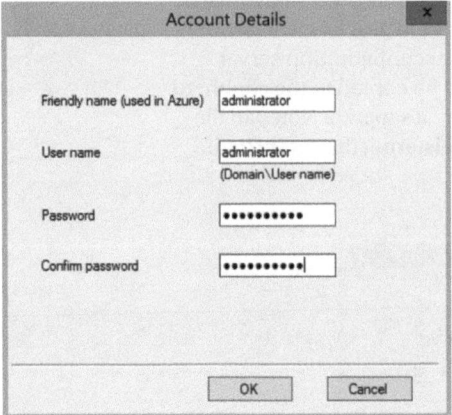

Figure 8-24. *Manage accounts—add account and specify credentials*

20. When all the required accounts have been created, select the second tab, called Vault Registration. If needed, you can verify or alter the Internet connectivity settings here, but the most important task is to click the Register button.

This will set up a connection (https/port 9433 by default) from the source configuration server and process server to the Azure Site Recovery Vault and register this server. The flow is visible in Figure 8-25.

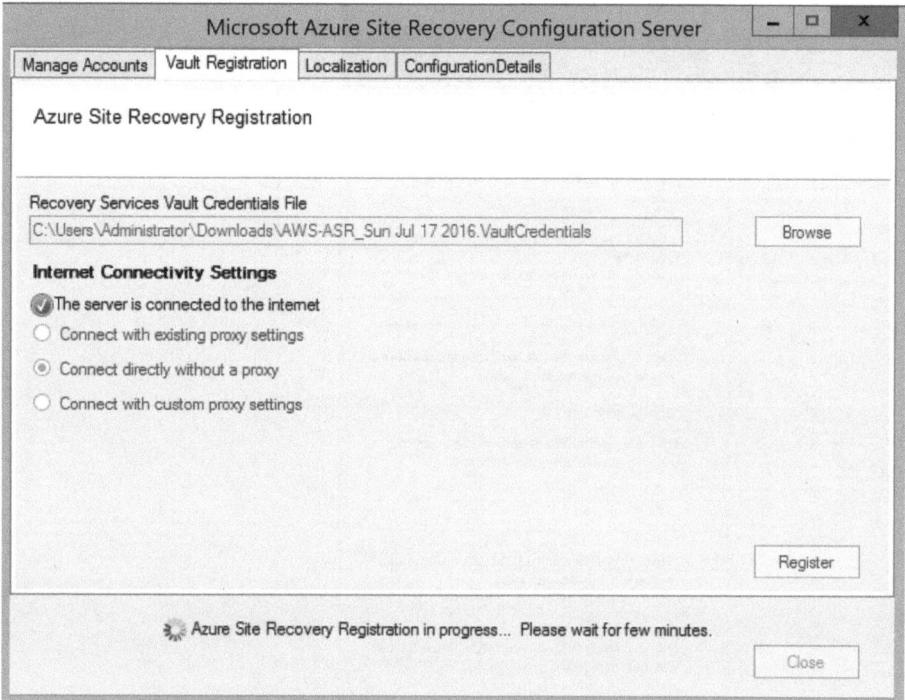

Figure 8-25. *Register button to get the server registered in ASR Vault*

This completes the installation and configuration of the ASR configuration server and process server in our source network. You can log off this server now and get back to the Azure portal to continue the setup steps from there.

If you didn't close the Azure portal in between, you should now see that the source ASR configuration server and process server are registered successfully in ASR. (This process might still take up to 15 minutes before the server is actually listed there.) If you did close the portal, log back on to http://portal.azure. com, select the resource group you created, and from there select the Azure Recovery Vault you configured. Go back to Step 1—Prepare Infrastructure in Section 1—Protection Goal.

21. You are now at Step 3 of the Prepare Infrastructure configuration, as shown in Figure 8-26. The goal is here to configure/select an Azure storage account as well as an Azure Virtual Network. Both will be used for the virtual machines that are being failed over to Azure during a disaster scenario. If you have already configured these, feel free to reuse them. However, in most production environments I have deployed at customers, a dedicated one will be created for each, thereby isolating the site recovery virtual machines. Both options work though.

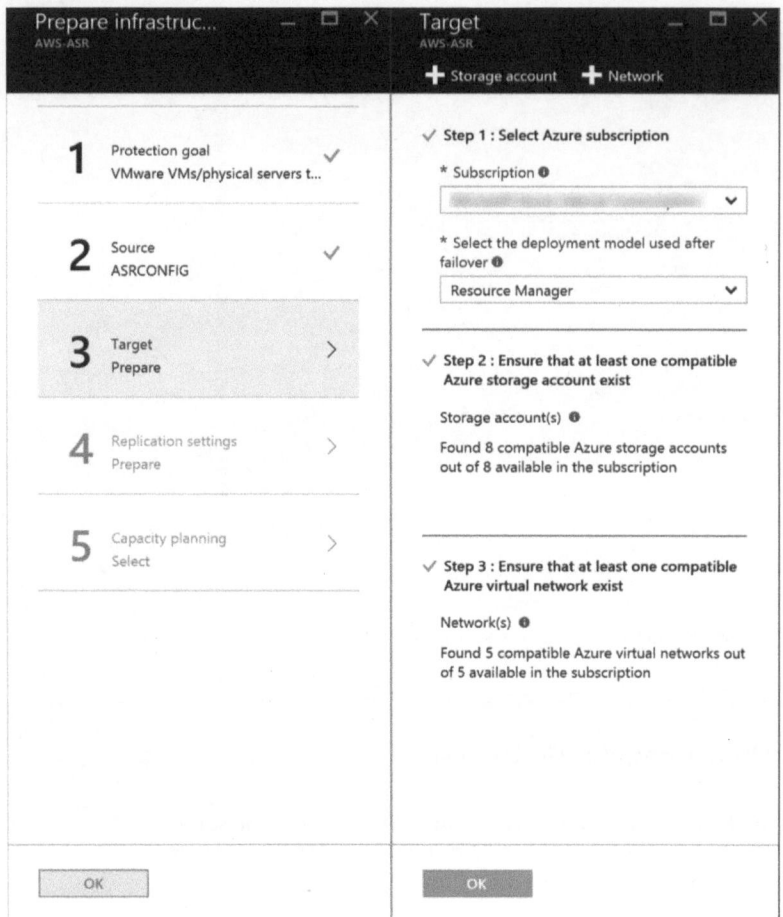

Figure 8-26. *Step 3—prepare the target*

- Select your Azure subscription.
- Select Resource Manager as the deployment model; this means the virtual machines and related resources will be created in the new Azure portal, not in classic mode.

22. If you don't have a storage account, now is a good time to create one.

- Provide a unique name (unique among all Azure subscriptions…).
- Select Standard as the storage performance type.
- Select LRS as the replication type.

(You can use Figure 8-27 as a reference on how to configure these settings.)

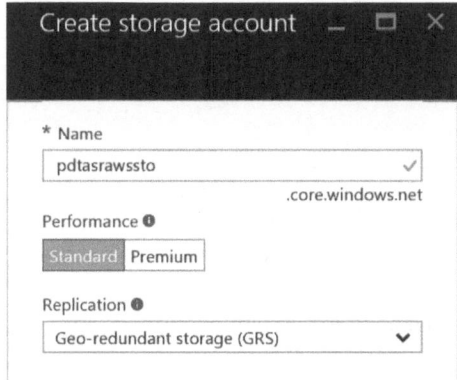

Figure 8-27. *Creating a storage account for ASR*

23. Next, fill in the options for the Azure Virtual Network, where I suggest you create a dedicated one for the ASR resources.

- Specify a unique name for the VNet as well as the subnet.

- Provide the address space (IP range) of addresses that can be used and the related subnet.

   (Use Figure 8-28 as a reference.)

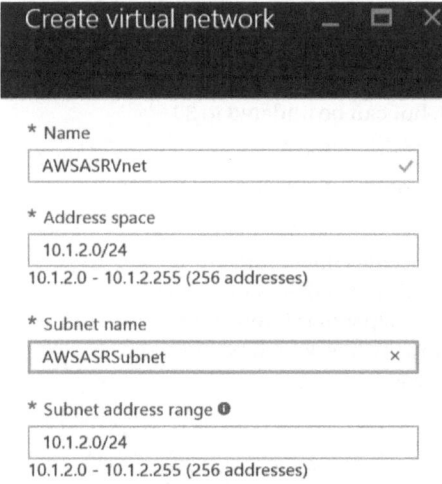

Figure 8-28. *Creating a virtual network for ASR*

This brings you to the next section in this step, creating a replication policy.

A replication policy is a configuration that defines how the replication should be treated, the time interval for the VM changes synchronization, and the initial replication start time.

In the real world, these settings depend on specific customer scenarios, application and operating system characteristics, and the like. In this lab environment, most of the default settings are acceptable for what you want to achieve:

- *Copy Frequency:* The default is 15 minutes, which can be lowered to 30 seconds. This points to the time interval of when changes are being synchronized from on-premises to Azure. This has no impact on the source virtual machine, as it stays active during the synchronization.

- *Recovery Point Retention:* This is the retention time for when a recovery point must be created. This allows you to restore a virtual machine in ASR from any of these recovery points, if needed.

- *App-Consistent Snapshot:* This parameter refers to a time setting per number of hours when an application consistent snapshot should be created. Think of consistency dependent applications like SQL databases, Exchange Server database, or similar.

- *Initial Replication Time:* The default setting here is Immediately. This means immediately from when this wizard is completed. If you are working in a production scenario, it might be a good idea to move this initial replication to an off-hour time.

24. Select Create and Associate a Replication Policy (as shown in Figure 8-29) from the configuration blade and complete the parameters. You can use my example settings as a good start.

- Provide a unique and descriptive name for the policy, such as `ASRAWS Policy`.

- The source and target are completed automatically.

- RPO Threshold in Minutes: 15 minutes by default, but can be updated to 30 seconds.

- Recovery Point Retention: Specifies the number of hours a recovery point should be kept.

- App-Consistent Snapshot Frequency in Minutes: Specifies the number of minutes an application-consistent snapshot should also be taken, next to the recovery point retention. An application-consistent snapshot is interesting for a SQL Server, Exchange Server, SharePoint Server, and the like, which benefit from having a consistent snapshot in case a restore is needed.

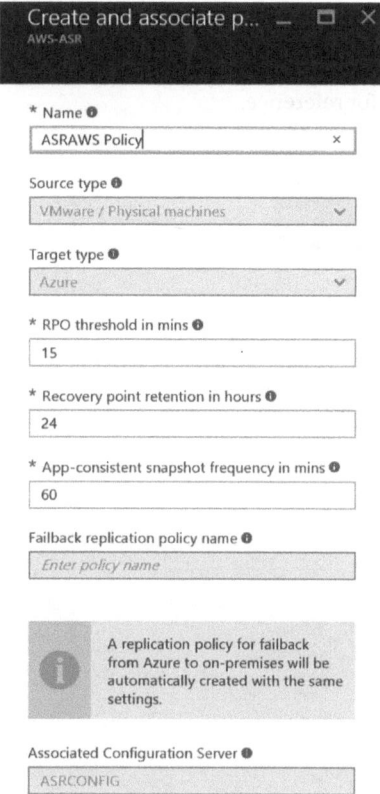

Figure 8-29. *Creating and associating a replication policy*

25. Wait for the replication policy to be created successfully, as shown in Figure 8-30.

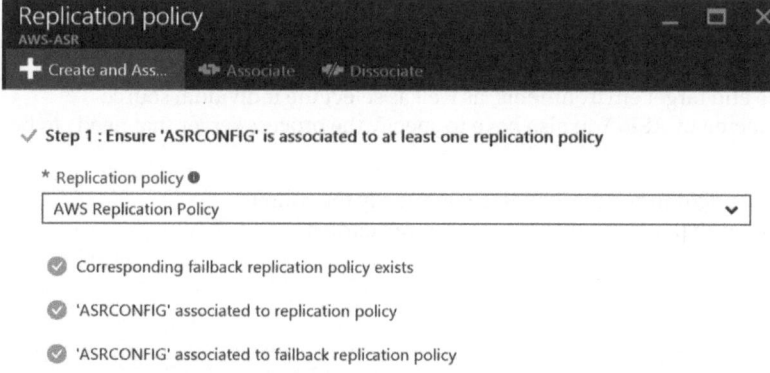

Figure 8-30. *Replication policy has been created successfully*

26. The final step in this section is more informational. It points you to the ASR Capacity Planning tool and asks if you have completed that step. (To me personally, this feels more like a sidebar to avoid complaints about slower replication and to cover their bases.) I included Figure 8-31 for reference.

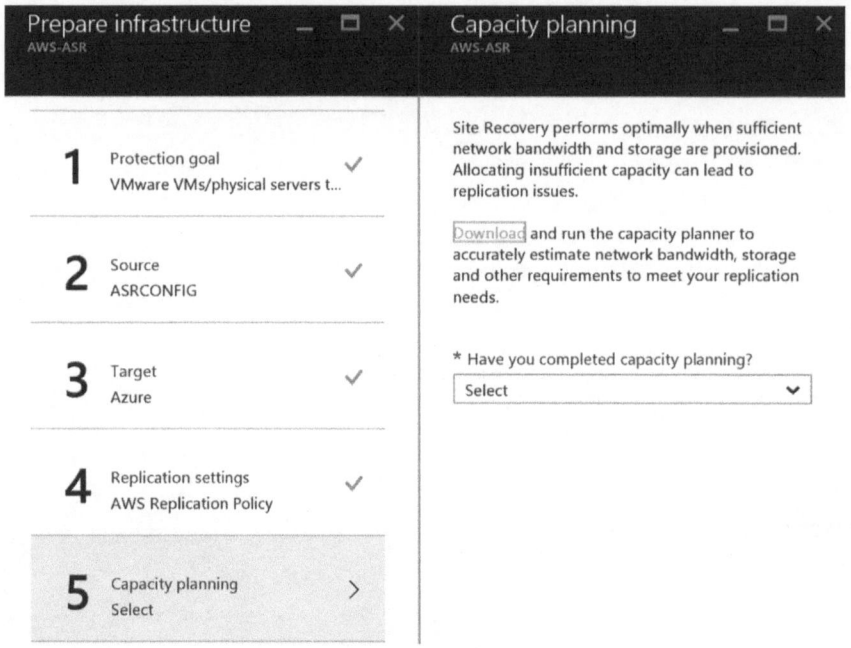

Figure 8-31. *Confirming the capacity planning question*

This completes Step 1—Prepare Infrastructure—so you can now continue with Step 2: Replicate Application.

Step 2: Replicate Application

This is where you define the source and target environments, as well as select the individual source machines that you want to see protected by ASR. You also have to specify the process server that needs to be used for this replication.

1. Figure 8-32 shows the configuration Step 1, where you specify the source environment, which is the Hyper-V site that was configured earlier.

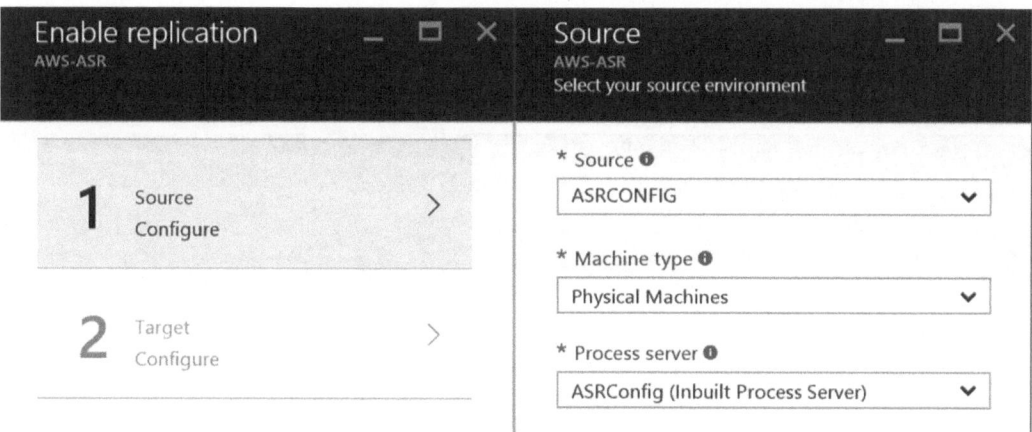

Figure 8-32. *Specify the source environment for replication*

2. In Step 2, displayed in Figure 8-33, define the target environment (Azure) by selecting the Azure storage account and virtual network you configured for this.

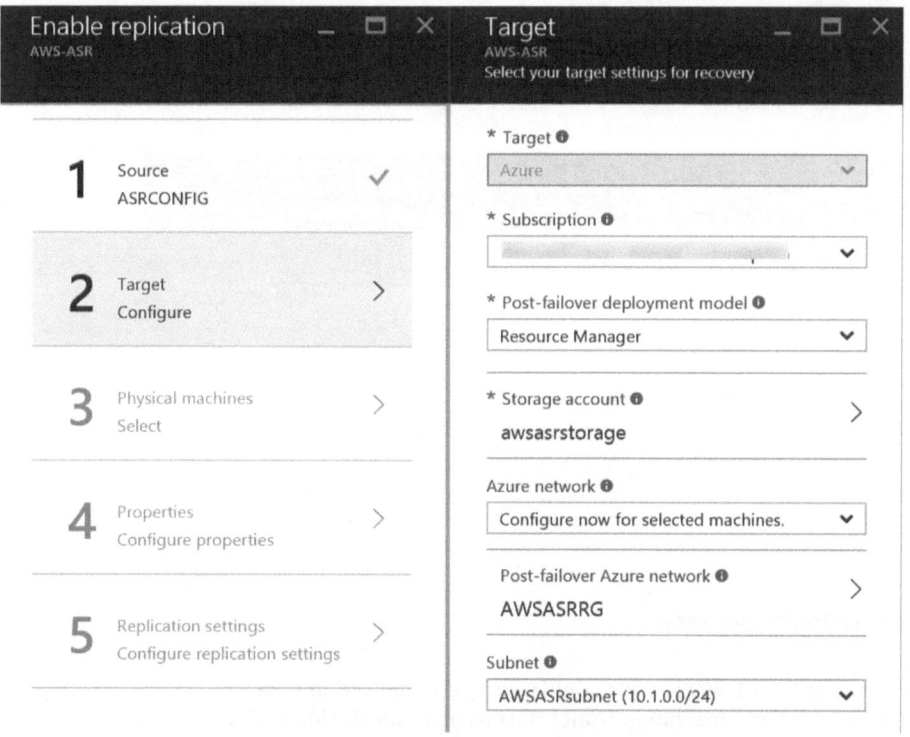

Figure 8-33. *Specify the target environment for replication*

3. This brings you to Step 3, where you can select one or several source machines. Specify their hostname, IP address, and OS type. (see Figure 8-34 for an example from my lab setup.)

Figure 8-34. *Specifying the source machines you want to protect using ASR*

4. In Step 4, configure the additional properties for each selected machine. (Specify the local admin account to be used and optionally exclude disks you don't want to be replicated.) See Figure 8-35.

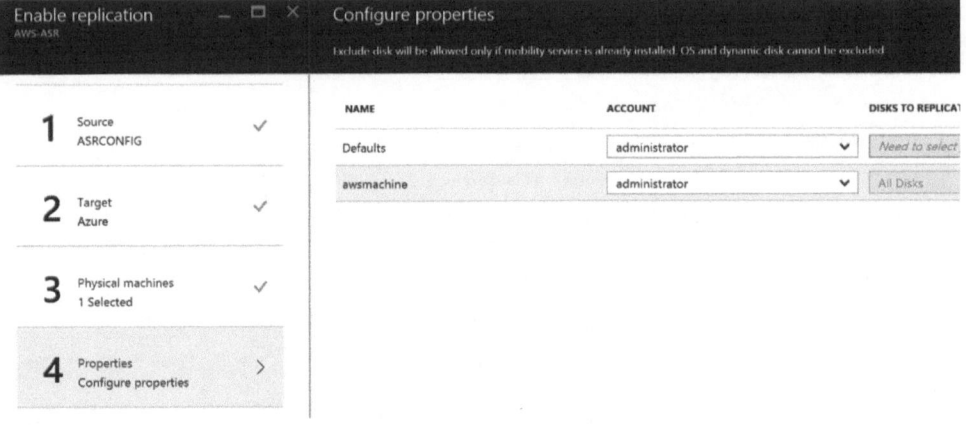

Figure 8-35. *Configure replication properties*

5. This brings you to Step 5, where you should specify the replication policy you want to use for these machines. Notice the option to specify Multi-VM replication, as shown in Figure 8-36.

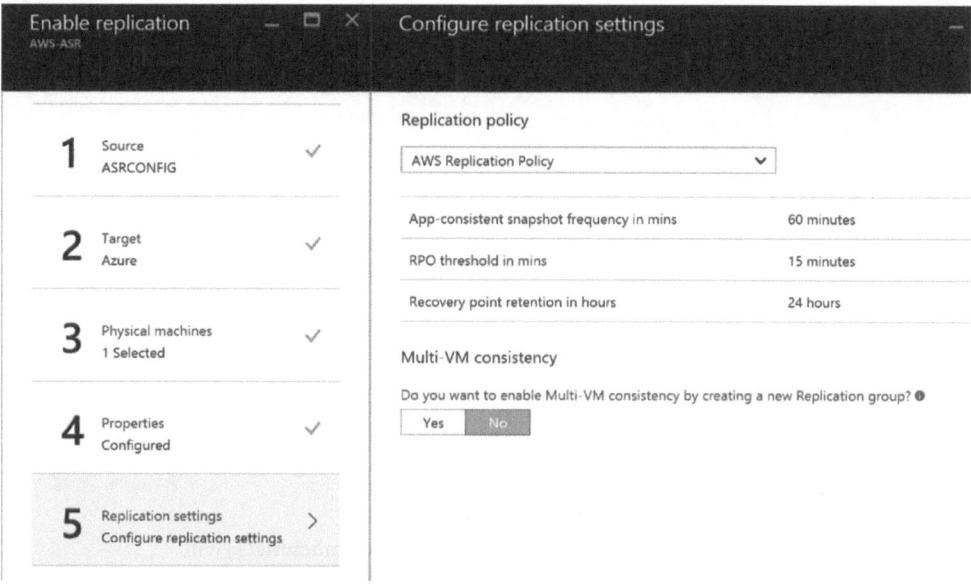

Figure 8-36. *Configure replication settings*

This completes Step 2—Replicate Application—in which you configured the source and target environment parameters, chose which source machines you want to protect, and determined what replication policy settings should be applied.

Step 3: Manage Recovery Plans

In this third and last main step of the site recovery configuration, you are going to build your recovery plan.

As you learned in Chapter 4, a recovery plan is basically the configuration of the step-by-step actions that need to occur in case of a failover. You'll create a recovery plan to complete the overall ASR configuration.

1. Select Step 3—Manage Recovery Plans. You are asked to create a new recovery plan (this can be changed later).

2. Click the + Recovery Plan button. In the selection fields, specify a name for the recovery plan. Notice that the source and target are already completed (from Step 2). Under the selected items, mark the machines for which this recovery plan will be used during failover. See Figure 8-37 for details.

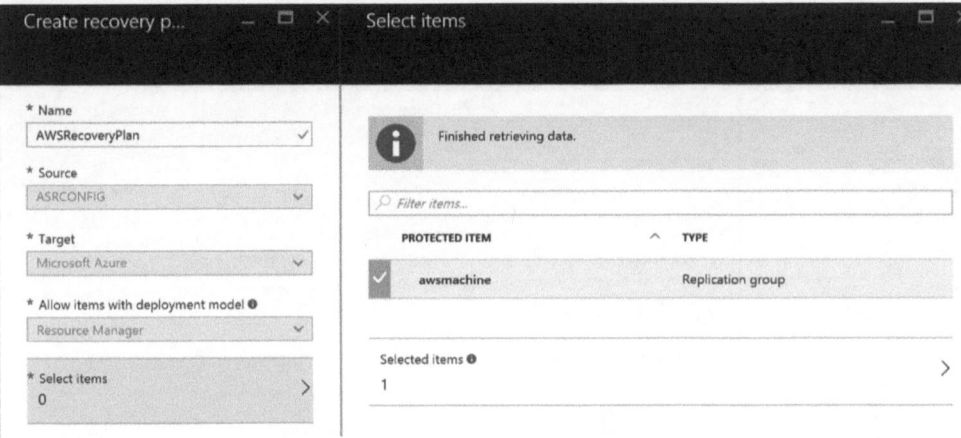

Figure 8-37. *Create the recovery plan and the select items*

3. Once the recovery plan is selected, you will see that the source machine(s) will start replicating (depending on the replication settings you defined earlier in the replication policy). You can go to the job details to see more. This should look similar to Figure 8-38.

Properties

Vault	AWS-ASR
Protected item	awsmachine
Job id	b5b2e499-1479-4655-8df8-f8909f572483-2016-07-17 19:10:19Z-lbz ActivityId: d9bf4a44-af8b-41b0-ae
Source server	ASRCONFIG
Target server	ASRCONFIG

Job

NAME	STATUS	START TIME	DURATION	
Prerequisites check for enabling protection	✔ Successful	7/17/2016 7:10:21 PM	00:00:05	...
Installing Mobility Service and preparing target	◷ In progress	7/17/2016 7:10:26 PM		...
Enable replication				...
Starting initial replication				...
Updating the Provider states				...

Figure 8-38. *Replicated items are being synchronized to Azure*

4. Wait for the synchronization of the virtual machine(s) to finish. Once finished, the virtual machine will have a status Protected, which means it is now fully operational as an ASR item, for which you can execute a failover. (See Figure 8-39.)

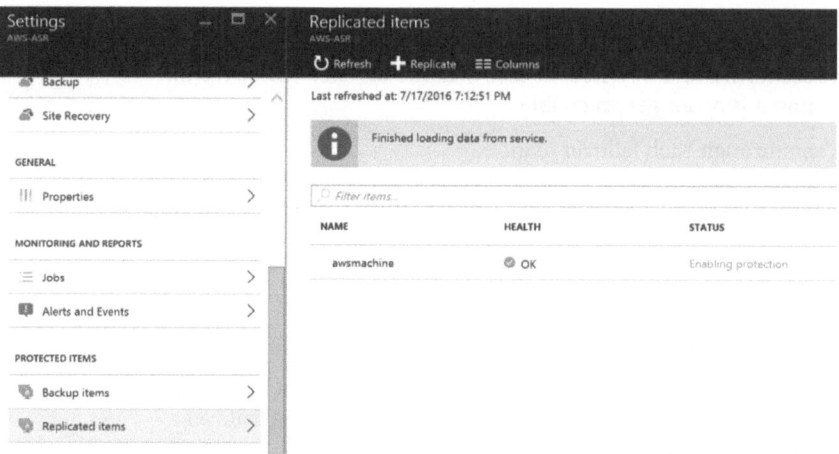

Figure 8-39. *Replicated items—synchronization is complete and the item is protected*

This completes the initial three-step configuration of ASR; the next part of this exercise goes through a failover simulation.

Performing a Failover

Now that you have set up an ASR configuration and your source machine(s) are in a protected state, you can move to the next step—basically the ultimate goal of the ASR—executing a failover.

In short, a failover means that (simulating as a test or as part of a true production situation disaster scenario) you will complete final replication from the on-premises infrastructure to Azure, starting up the virtual machine(s) and testing your applications for running successfully on the Azure side.

■ **Note**   At this stage of the book (and the exercise), we go through a rather basic failover process, where not all components are working 100% after failover. This is by design, and will be fine-tuned in more detail in the next chapter. So don't worry if not all is working yet in your lab environment when you finish this exercise.

When initiating a failover in ASR, there are three possible scenarios:

- *Test Failover:* Running through a full test failover plan, where the communication between the source and target is validated. A dummy virtual machine is configured to validate the Azure storage account and Azure Virtual Network configuration. This test has no impact on your own production environment.

- *Planned Failover*: In case of a planned failover, a proper sequence of actions is followed, by which a final machine synchronization will be initiated. Once both virtual machines are in sync, the on-premises VM is shut down, and the Azure-side VM is started up and ready for use. This failover is ideal when downtime is foreseen, such as during a planned electricity outage in a business park.

- ***Unplanned Failover:*** The understanding here is the same as with a Planned Failover, but the virtual machines don't have to be in sync to have the Azure-side VM booting up. This scenario could be useful in case of a true disaster, where the on-premises environment is no longer reachable.

The next sections walk you through each failover plan.

You can execute a failover plan from the recovery plan level or from replicated items/virtual machine level. The following sequence is from the recovery plan level, as we ended there in the previous section.

Executing a Test Failover

Follow these steps to execute a test failover:

1. After selecting your recovery plan, the Recovery Plan Settings blade will appear, listing the different failover options on top (Test Failover and Planned Failover are visible; Unplanned Failover is hidden behind the ... button).

   Choose Test Failover, which will open the Test Failover blade. The only selection to be made here is the Azure Virtual Network. Select the ASR VNet you configured.

2. This will immediately trigger a Test Failover job. Click on the notification button (the bell) to see what happens more in detail.

   - Prerequisite checks

   - Creating the test environment

   - Creating the test virtual machine/starting the virtual machine

   - Completing the testing

   - Cleaning up the environment

     You can see the outcome of this in Figure 8-40.

■ **Note**   Notice that there is an interruption between starting up the virtual machine and completing the testing. This is by design, and actually foreseen to give the administrator the opportunity to do some more detailed validation and testing of the virtual machine to make sure it is working correctly.

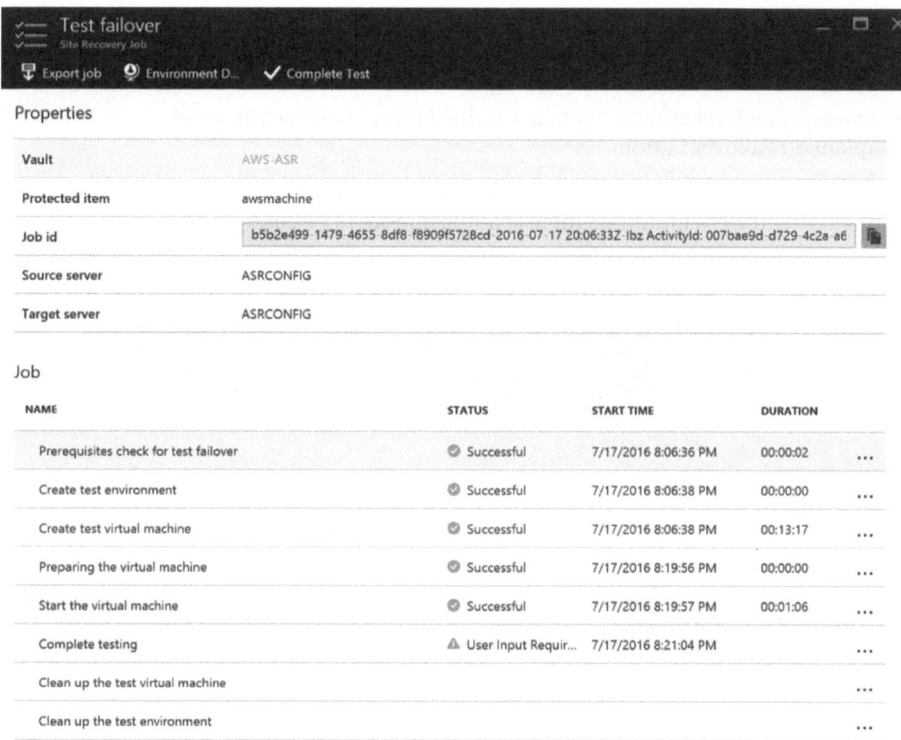

Figure 8-40. *Running through a test failover plan*

3. Confirm the Complete Testing step. This will trigger the test failover plan to continue testing and cleaning up the environment and finalizing the test failover, as shown in Figure 8-41.

Job

NAME	STATUS	START TIME	DURATION	
Prerequisites check for enabling protection	✅ Successful	7/17/2016 7:10:21 PM	00:00:05	...
Installing Mobility Service and preparing target	✅ Successful	7/17/2016 7:10:26 PM	00:14:27	...
Enable replication	✅ Successful	7/17/2016 7:24:54 PM	00:00:40	...
Starting initial replication	✅ Successful	7/17/2016 7:25:34 PM		...
Updating the Provider states	✅ Successful	7/17/2016 7:25:38 PM		...

Figure 8-41. *Completing a test failover plan*

This completes the test failover. Let's try the same for another machine and go through an unplanned failover process.

Executing an Unplanned Failover

In an identical way, you can execute an unplanned failover, which is comprised of the following steps:

1. From the recovery plan level or recovery items/individual source machine level, click the Unplanned Failover button.

   This will open the Unplanned Failover blade (see Figure 8-42). Confirm the execution by clicking the OK button, as there is nothing more to be configured here.

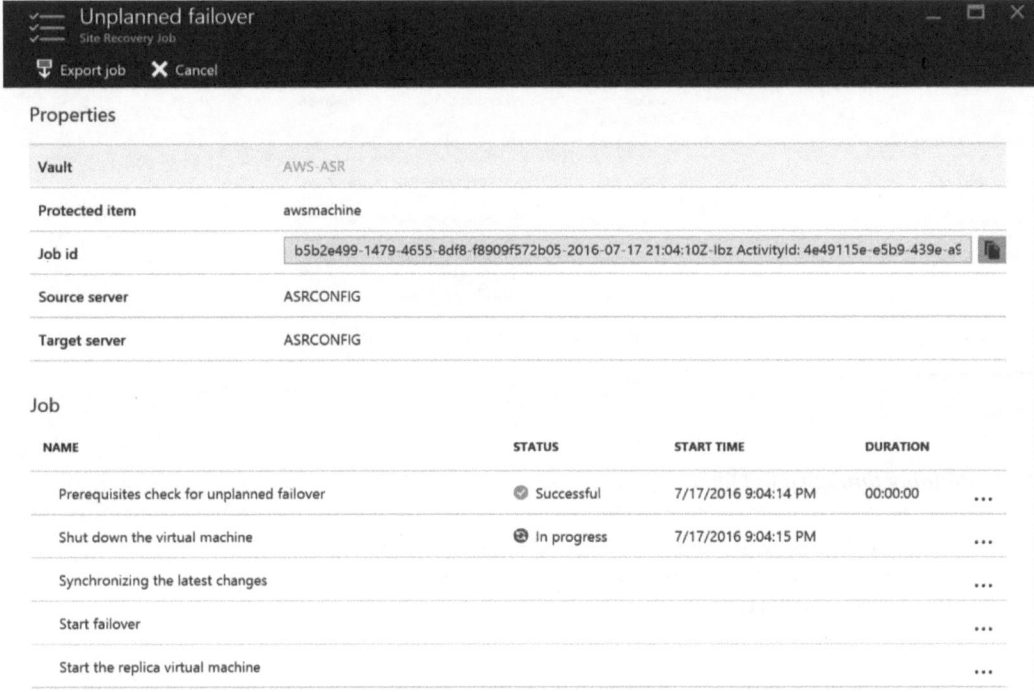

Figure 8-42. *Executing an unplanned failover*

2. This will trigger the unplanned failover, which can be monitored by clicking the notification (bell) button, as shown in Figure 8-43. As you can see, this process is identical to the test failover process.

■ **Note** For a (yet) unknown reason, ASR can't force an Amazon AWS machine to shut down properly. Although this logged as "failed," it is not blocking the failover mechanism itself. This is a good sign in case of a true disaster recovery failover needs to occur, where the source environment would not be reachable.

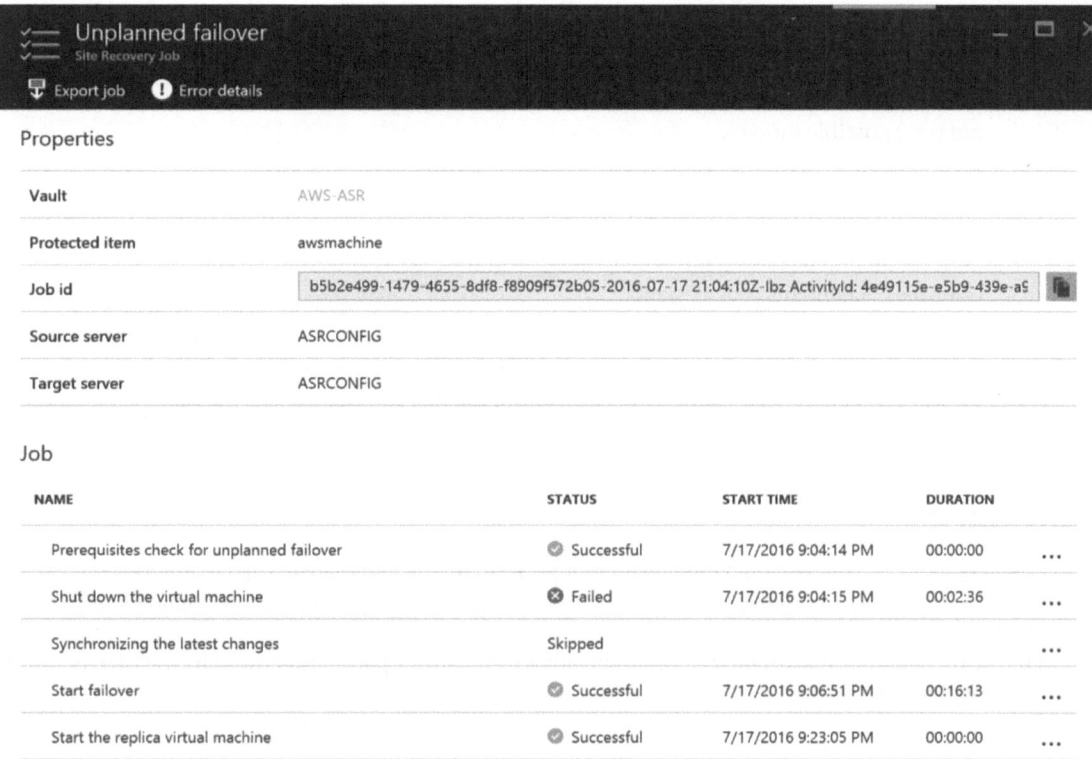

Figure 8-43. Executing a planned failover

3. Wait for the failover process to finish (successfully).

4. From the Azure portal, go to Virtual Machines and select the failover VM. Notice it now has a status of Running. This is your confirmation that the failover process went fine, and the virtual machine is running in Azure. (Figure 8-44 shows what it should look like.)

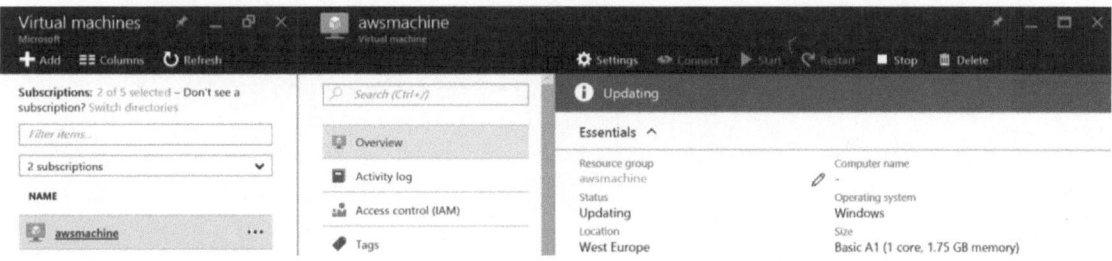

Figure 8-44. Virtual machine running in Azure after a planned failover

5.   As a logical approach, you not only want to verify that the virtual machine is starting up fine, but you might also want to verify that the services are running and the applications are starting up fine too. The natural tendency is to connect to this failed-over virtual machine from a Remote Desktop (RDP) session. This is not (yet) possible though.

Be confident, however, that this does not mean something is wrong with your virtual machine. Remember the note from the beginning of this chapter, where I mentioned we would focus on getting Azure Site Recovery configured and perform an initial failover, but not all things would work? This is one of the examples. Again, this is by design.

The good news is, there is not only a logical explanation for this, but I also have a solution. You will learn all about how to solve this issue and successfully connect to your server (as well as some other interesting aspects of ASR plans) in the next chapter.

Summary

In this chapter, I guided you through configuring ASR for non-Hyper-V infrastructures, using Amazon AWS as a source environment. After going through the full configuration, you performed a test failover and unplanned failover.

In the next chapter, you learn how to configure advanced failover plans and how to fix the RDP issue so you can connect to your VMs.

CHAPTER 9

■ ■ ■

Azure Site Recovery: Recovery Plans and Advanced Configurations

After going through the exercises in Chapters 7 and 8 (nice one if you did both!), you know the basics of Azure Site Recovery plans. But you just touched the surface.

In this chapter, you will learn how to make your recovery plans more intelligent, how to structure your failover VMs in groups and why, and how to integrate automation scripts into your failover plan. So for the first time in this book, you will meet your future best friend—PowerShell.

As part of what I call "advanced configurations," you will also learn how to set up a site-to-site VPN connection between an on-premises Hyper-V host and an Azure Virtual Network. Not that it is needed for ASR replication or failover to work, but you will find out that it helps in building your overall disaster recovery strategy and solution plan, when part of the applications are still running on-premises, where some other applications are failed over to Azure.

Another component that will be discussed is how to modify the VM machine specs after failover, allowing you to run your failed over Azure VM having other machine characteristics (think of CPU, memory, and disk type) than the on-premises running source machine. This can be of interest when you don't need the full machine power during a failover scenario, or when you're migrating to a more powerful machine in Azure.

The next topic I go through is the "mystery" from Chapters 7 and 8, where you could not connect with an RDP session to your Azure VMs in ASR failover state.

At the end of this chapter, I walk you through a failback scenario, from ASR VMs to the on-premises Hyper-V host, and discuss how it works for Amazon AWS.

After going through each of these topics, you should have enough knowledge and experience to start implementing ASR in just about any scenario possible, not only in a test/demo scenario shown in the exercises in this book, but also in a full production environment.

Enjoy!

Introduction to Recovery Plans

In my personal opinion, recovery plans are the most critical part of the overall Azure Site Recovery failover process. It is like the center of intelligence, a recipe in a cookbook if you will, in which you define step-by-step what tasks and activities need to happen during failover. By design, a recovery plan is split into different groups, allowing you to combine those virtual machines that belong together. (Think of the example of a two-tier application, running on a web server and a separate database server. If any of these fail over to Azure, you want to guarantee the other machine follows in the failover process.)

© Peter De Tender 2016
P. De Tender, *Implementing Operations Management Suite*, DOI 10.1007/978-1-4842-1979-9_9

The default structure of a recovery plan looks like this:

All groups shut down	Performs a shutdown of all members of this group
All groups fail over	Performs a failover of all members of this group
Group 1: Start	Starts the VMs that are members of this group

You can extend this structure by adding up to six groups, as shown in Figure 9-1.

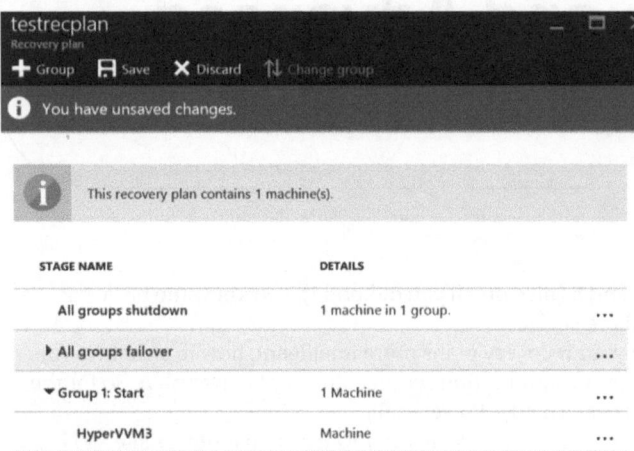

Figure 9-1. *Recovery plans group structure*

Each virtual machine that is protected as part of ASR must be linked to a recovery plan and belong to any of the "Group *x*: Start" classifications. A protected virtual machine can belong to multiple recovery plans, allowing you to establish different failover scenarios for different situations, like a planned or unplanned failover.

For each group, protected items (VMs) can be added and removed, and you can add pre-actions and post-actions.

For each pre- or post-action, the activity that can be defined is a manual action or a script.

Customizing Recovery Plans

As a starter, let's go back to the recovery plan you created as part of the exercise in the previous chapter(s), add an additional group, and then add a protected item to this group.

1. From within the Azure portal, browse to the ASR resource group you created.

2. From within the ASR resource group, select the Azure Site Recovery Vault.

3. Click the Settings button.

4. From within the Settings blade, scroll down to Manage/Recovery Plans. See Figure 9-2.

Figure 9-2. Recovery Plans—settings

5. This will show all your existing recovery plans for this ASR Vault. My demo lab setup looks like Figure 9-3.

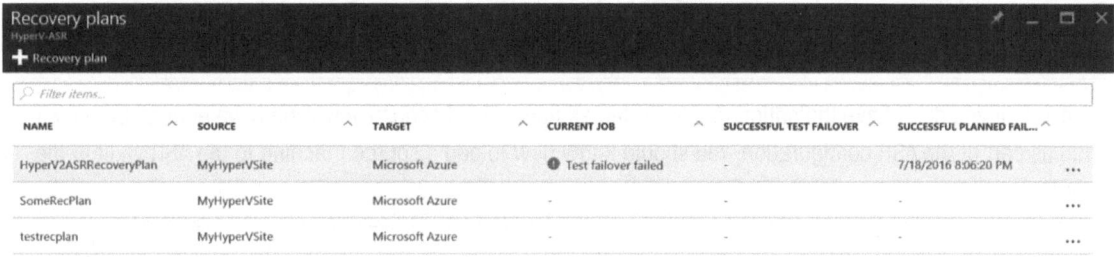

Figure 9-3. Recovery plans

6. Select the recovery plan you created before (see Figure 9-4 for an example) and click Customize. This will open the blade with the recovery plan group structure.

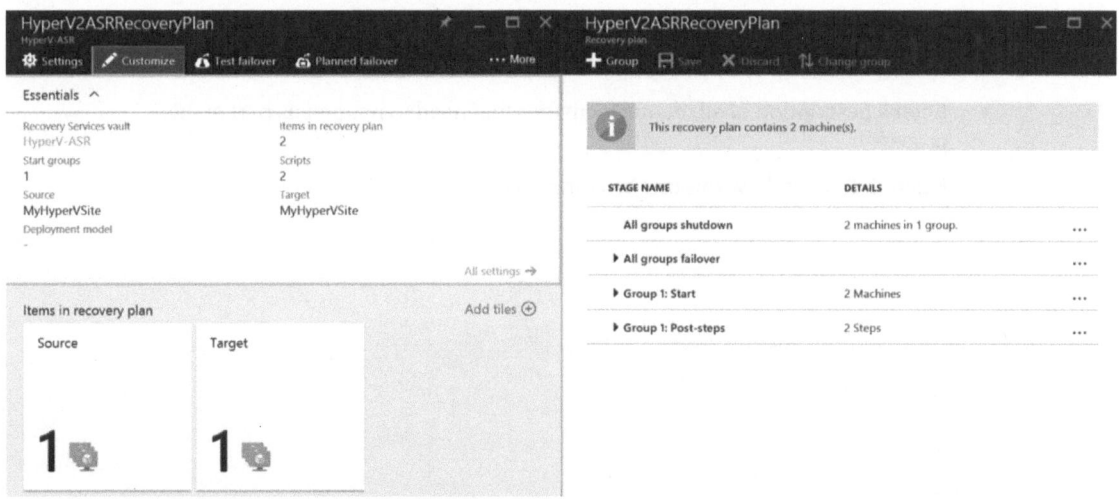

Figure 9-4. Customize a recovery plan

7. From the top menu, click the +Group button to add a second group, as shown in Figure 9-5.

8. Before saving the changes, click the ... next to the Group 2 and choose Add Protected Items, as shown in Figure 9-5.

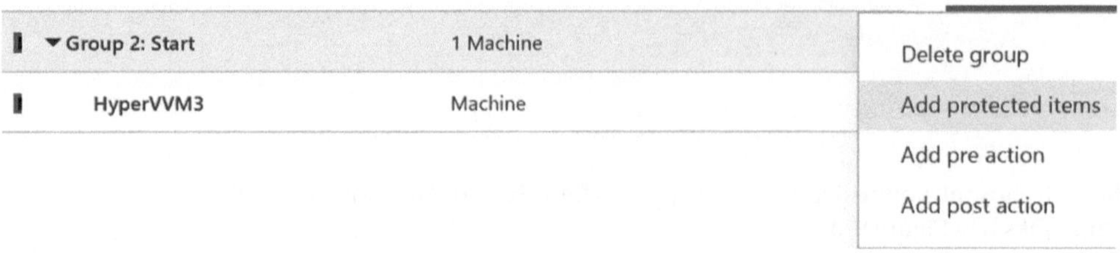

▼ Group 2: Start	1 Machine		Delete group
HyperVVM3	Machine		Add protected items
			Add pre action
			Add post action

Figure 9-5. *Adding protected items to a recovery plan group*

■ **Note**   If you don't have the option to add protected items, it is because you don't have enough protected items as part of the ASR configuration. You should know how to add a source machine to the ASR vault in the meantime.

Adding Manual Actions to a Recovery Plan

Follow these steps to add manual actions to your recovery plan:

1. Select Group 2: Start again, click the ..., and choose Add Pre Action. This opens up the Insert Action blade.

   • Switch the action to Manual

   • Give a descriptive name for the action

   • Enter a description of all manual activities that need to happen as part of this process

   Figure 9-6 shows how this can be completed.

Figure 9-6. *Insert manual actions for the recovery plan*

2. Mark it to execute the action during a test failover. Click OK to close this blade.

   Notice, as shown in Figure 9-7, how Group 2 is extended with pre-steps, showing the manual actions you defined.

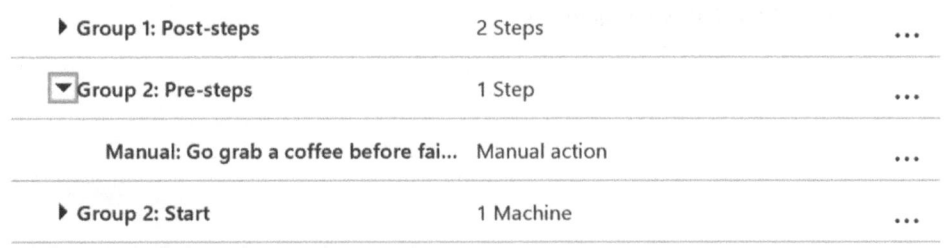

Figure 9-7. *The pre-steps are now listed*

3. Save the configuration.

4. Save the changes made to the recovery plan. Close this blade.

   If you run a failover, you will now notice it will go through and will wait for manual action (confirmation by IT admin). It will show the comments you entered in the Group 2: Pre-Steps phase, before failing over the machine that is a member of Group 2.

Adding Automated Actions to a Recovery Plan

Where you can see the potential and use case for manual actions, I assume you are more interested in learning about how to automate certain actions. This is possible by using the "script action," which allows you to inject any PowerShell script you can think of, having it execute that action. Think of validating network settings, copying certain files over, verifying all machines are available in Azure before moving over to the next group, and so on. The sky is the limit here.

The automation part is driven out of OMS automation, which was briefly mentioned in Chapter 1. As the name says, it is the automation engine across Azure. First of all, you create an Azure automation account, which will be used to fire off the automation scripts. These scripts are PowerShell-based. All scripts are stored in the Azure automation repository and can be reused from there.

As you can imagine, the harder part of the configuration is building the script itself. To help you here, there is an integration with the Automation Gallery, a community-based repository of pre-built scripts that are at your disposal to reuse as-is or as a baseline for building your own customized scripts.

To learn how easy it is to inject these scripts, go through the following steps:

1. Create an OMS automation account.

2. Select your script from the Gallery or build a custom one.

3. Link this script to the ASR recovery plan group pre- or post-action.

Creating an OMS Automation Account

1. From the Azure portal, select New and type `automation` in the search field.

2. From the result list, select Automation from Publisher Microsoft and click the Create button in the next blade (see Figure 9-8).

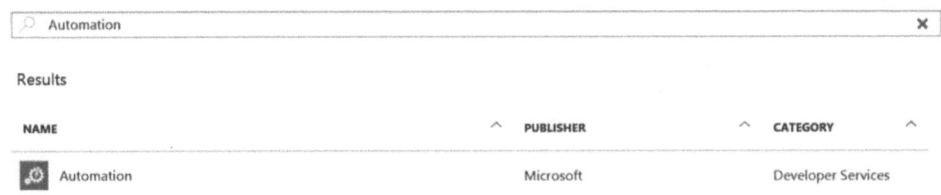

Figure 9-8. *OMS automation*

3. This will open up the Add Automation Account configuration blade. (See Figure 9-9 for an example of how it is done in my lab setup.)

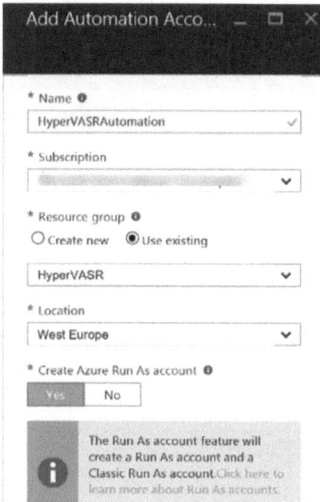

Figure 9-9. *Add Automation Account blade*

4. Provide a unique name for the automation account. I prefer using separate automation accounts for different purposes, that's why I use HyperVASR... as a reference. This is not required though. Link it to the ASR resource group and create the account created as a Run As Account.

The Azure Run As Account allows this service account contributor rights to your Azure subscription, giving it access rights to execute runbooks on behalf of that service account. The authentication behind the scenes is relying on the certificate-based service principle.

Therefore, if you say "No" to the question to create the Azure Run As Account, the account itself will be created, but it won't have access to Azure resources within your subscription. This will result in failing runbooks, as they can't see the resources.

During the creation of the Azure automation account, the following items will also be created in the background:

- ***AzureAutomationTutorial Runbook***, which is a sample PowerShell runbook

- ***AzureAutomationTutorialScript Runbook***, which is another sample PowerShell runbook

- ***AzureRunAsCertificate***, a one-year valid SSL certificate used as authentication validator for the Azure Automation account

5. Go back to your resource group and select the Azure automation account you just created (see Figure 9-10). This will publish its details.

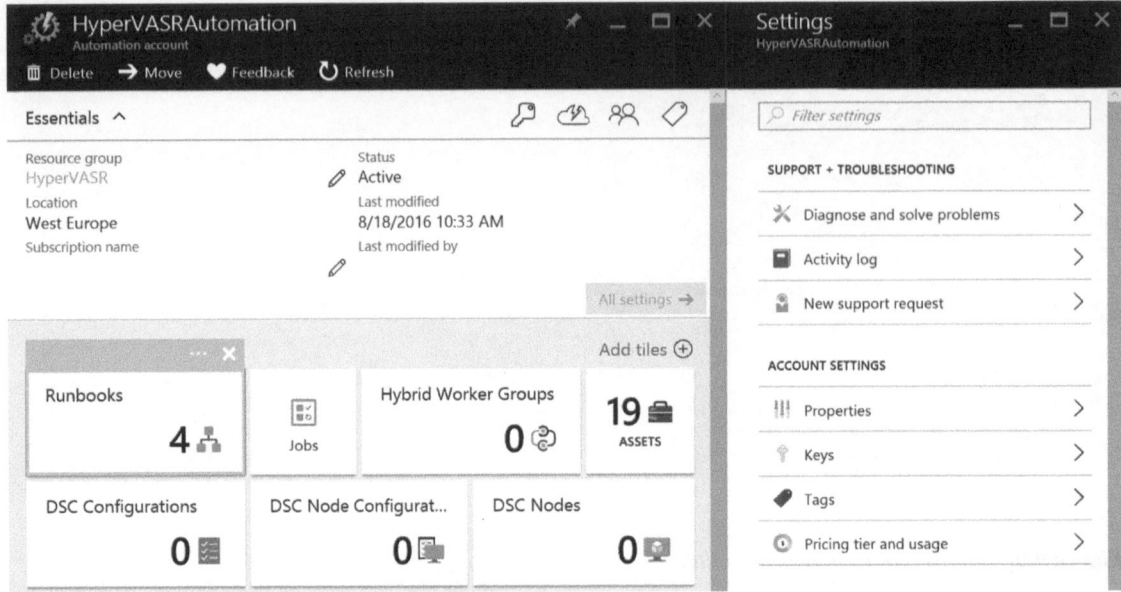

Figure 9-10. *Azure automation account settings*

Creating a Runbook

1. Click the Runbooks box; Notice the preconfigured runbooks, as mentioned. See Figure 9-11.

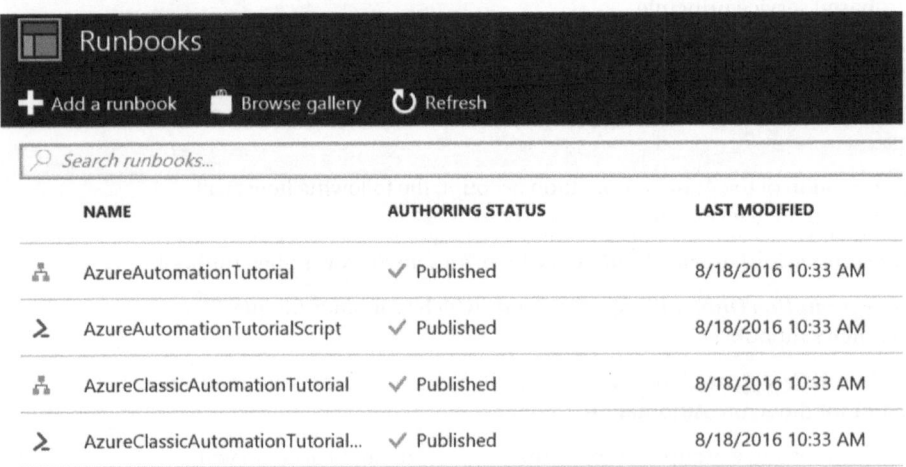

Figure 9-11. *Azure automation runbooks*

2. Click the Browse Gallery button.

3. In the search field, type Recovery. This will show an extensive list of prebuilt (PowerShell) scripts specifically related to Azure Site Recovery operations, as can be seen in Figure 9-12.

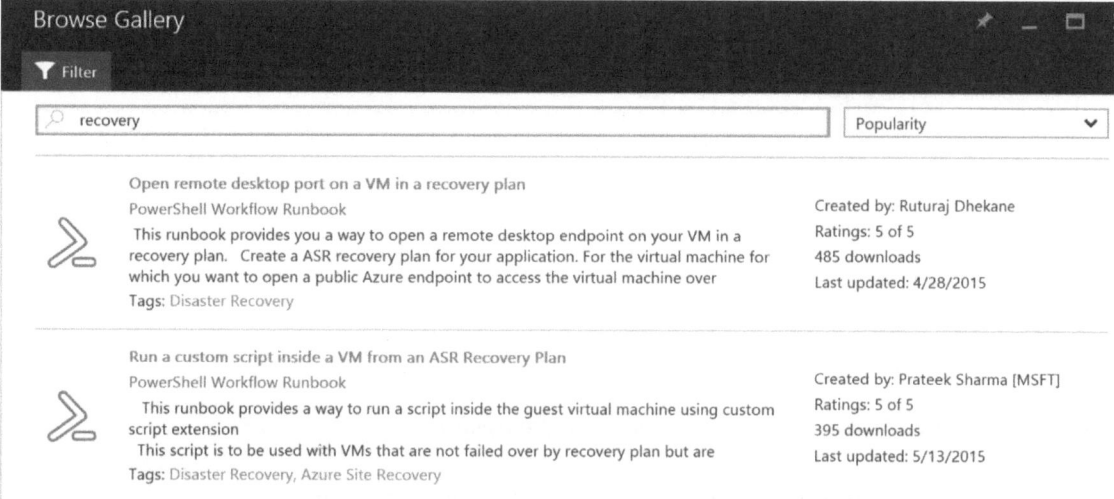

Figure 9-12. *Azure Automation Gallery—recovery scripts*

4. Browse through the list of scripts in the gallery to get an idea of what is available. Find the script called "Open Remote Desktop Port on a VM in a Recovery Plan," created by Ruturaj Dhekane. (See Figure 9-13.)

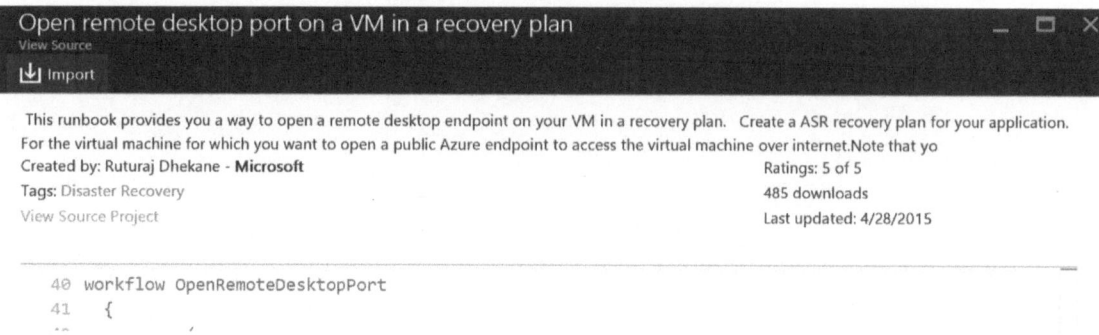

Figure 9-13. *Azure Automation Gallery—import script from gallery*

5. Click the Import button. This opens the Import blade, which looks like Figure 9-14.

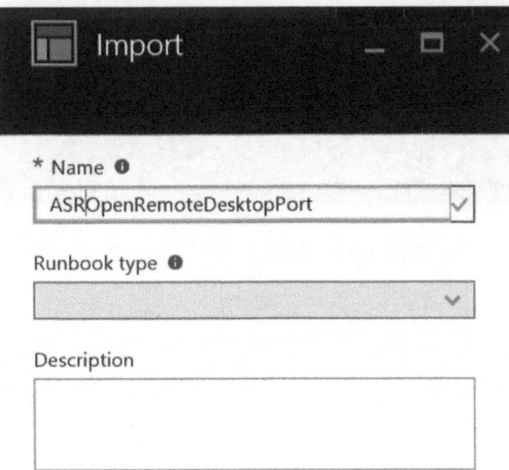

Figure 9-14. *Azure Automation Gallery—import script from gallery*

6. Give the script a descriptive name and click OK. Wait for the script to be imported, which will result in showing the details pane for the script, as you can see in Figure 9-15.

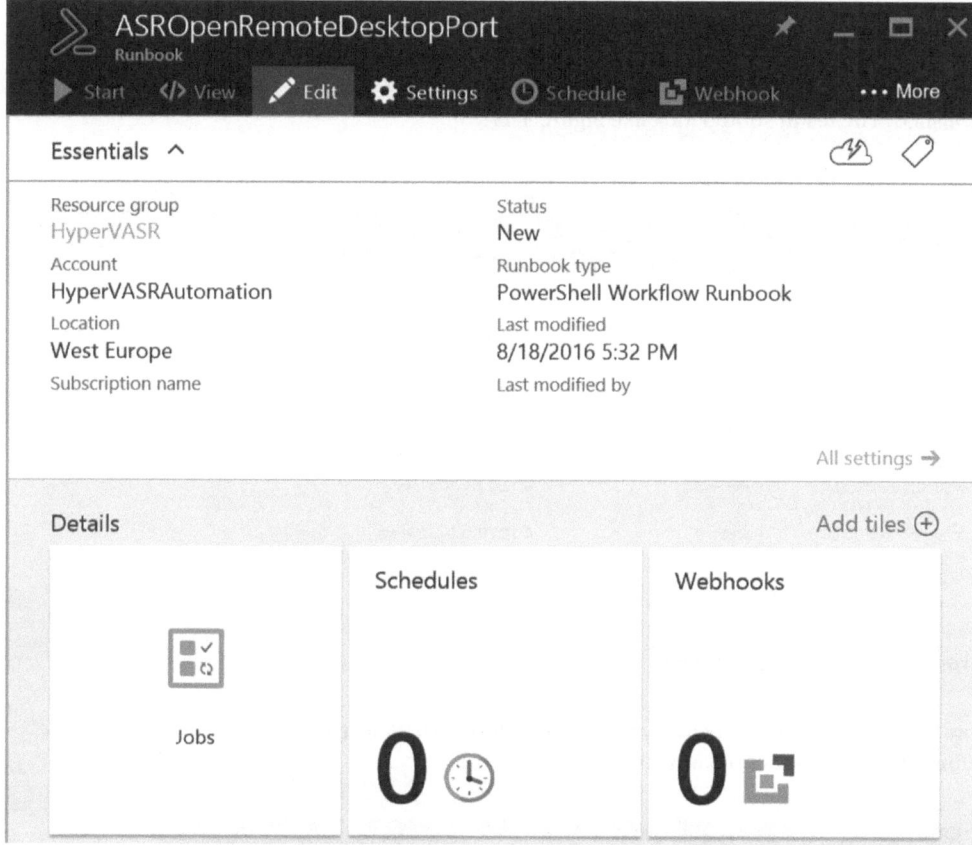

Figure 9-15. *Azure Automation Gallery—edit script from gallery*

7. From the details pane, click the Edit button. This brings up the PowerShell code, where you would normally make modifications. For now, just accept the script as it is. Although the script is imported, it is not yet available as a workbook. Therefore, click the Publish button from the top menu. (Use Figure 9-16 to find your way around in the portal.)

Figure 9-16. *Publish the workflow runbook*

8. Confirm the popup question to publish the script with Yes.

Adding the Automation Script to the Recovery Plan

1. Close the Edit blade and the Gallery blade, which should bring you back to the overall Runbooks blade. Notice that the script has been added and marked as published. The result should look like Figure 9-17.

	NAME	AUTHORING STATUS	LAST MODIFIED	TAGS
	ASROpenRemoteDesktopPort	✓ Published	8/18/2016 5:50 PM	
	AzureAutomationTutorial	✓ Published	8/18/2016 10:33 AM	
	AzureAutomationTutorialScript	✓ Published	8/18/2016 10:33 AM	
	AzureClassicAutomationTutorial	✓ Published	8/18/2016 10:33 AM	
	AzureClassicAutomationTutorial...	✓ Published	8/18/2016 10:33 AM	

Figure 9-17.   Workflow runbook is published

2. Now browse back to your recovery plan and customize it. Select a group and define a pre- or post-action, as shown in Figure 9-18.

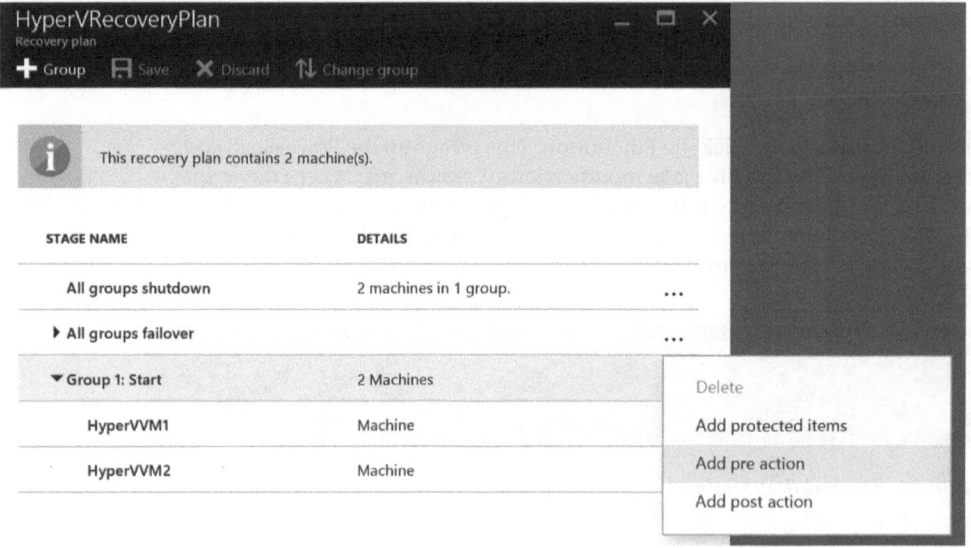

Figure 9-18.   Add a pre-action to a recovery plan group

3. This opens the Insert Action blade again. Enter the following parameters:

    - Insert: Script

    - Name: Descriptive name for the script

    - Automation Account Name: Shows your Azure Automation account you created earlier

    - Runbook Name: Shows the list of published runbooks; select the RDP script you created earlier

    Use Figure 9-19 as a reference for how to complete the parameters.

Figure 9-19. *Add a pre-action automated script to a recovery plan group*

4. Click OK to confirm the insert action; save the changed recovery plan.

This completes the configuration of a recovery plan for a manual action or an automation script action.

Of course, the true power comes when you are able to integrate your own custom PowerShell scripts, thereby building true intelligence into your failover plan.

Providing Network Connectivity to ASR Failed Over Virtual Machines

In this section, I'm taking a step away from ASR as such, because for replicating the machines from source to target, or even migrating, there is no need for anything else but SSL port 443 by design, as you have learned and experienced throughout the previous chapters.

So why am I dedicating a lot of this chapter to network connectivity?

Because in my opinion, ASR is only half of the story when thinking about how and what kind of disaster recovery solution organizations need. Yes, ASR is the medium that replicates machines from about any source environment to Azure Virtual Machines as the target. And thanks to recovery plans, you can automate this process to a serious extent, starting up your virtual machines and running your applications. So far, so good. But how are your users going to connect to these applications? Well, that's where network connectivity comes in.

To allow private/internal connectivity from your on-premises network to the Azure Virtual Network (VNET) and the virtual machines and applications that are running there, you should configure a site-to-site VPN connection between both. Another solution is ExpressRoute, but I'm not covering this here, as it is set up and configured by telecom providers in a lot of cases. For more information on ExpressRoute though, head over to the following web site:

https://azure.microsoft.com/en-us/services/expressroute/

To allow public/external connectivity from the Internet to the Azure Virtual Network (VNET) and the virtual machines and applications running there, you can rely on the built-in firewall functionality of Azure, called Network Security Groups (NSG). Similar to a typical firewall, NSG is a collection of inbound and outbound traffic rules, defining what communication is allowed toward which VNets and virtual machines in Azure. Besides network security, Azure can also provide load-balancing functionality out of the Azure Load Balancer, Azure Traffic Manager, or several third-party load balancers that are available through the Azure marketplace. Or maybe the organization is already using a geo-load balancing solution themselves on-premises today, allowing them to redirect traffic from one datacenter to the other, even between geographical dispersed regions. In that case, this solution might be reused pointing toward public IP endpoints in Azure.

For the core of this section, I focus on Azure site-to-site VPN. You will learn how to build the VPN connectivity between an on-premises Hyper-V network and an Azure VNet, allowing for full traffic communication between both networks and all VMs running at each end of the tunnel. I'm using Hyper-V as an example, since I've been using it for working on the chapters in this book, but nothing holds you back from using other solutions. If you have a firewall appliance available that supports Azure Site-to-Site VPN, feel free to challenge yourself and get it working.

■ **Tip**   For an overview of validated VPN devices for Azure Site-to-Site VPN, head over to the following web page:

https://azure.microsoft.com/en-us/documentation/articles/vpn-gateway-about-vpn-
devices/#devicetable

Network Topology Drawing

To give you a clear view on what we are trying to achieve, take a look at the basic network schema in Figure 9-20.

On-Premises (Hyper-V) -to- Azure

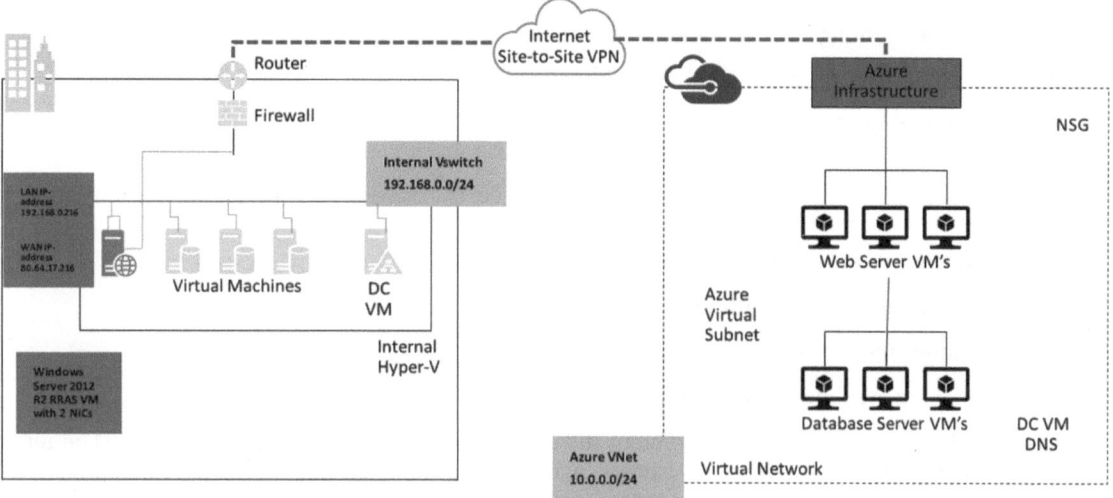

Figure 9-20. *Network schema of the site-to-site topology we are building*

Our exercise/demo environment has the following characteristics.
For the on-premises network:

- Internet-facing router/firewall with public IP address 80.64.19.1

- Local on-premises subnet/HyperV switch 192.168.0.0/24

- Physical Hyper-V machine, host IP 192.168.0.10

- A couple of virtual machines (192.168.0.50/51/52/53)

- We will build an additional Windows Server 2012R2 VM as Routing and Remote
  Access Server (RRAS), having two virtual NICs, one for internal LAN communication
  (192.168.0.216) and the other with direct public IP address (NAT is supported)
  (80.64.19.216)

For the Azure network:

- Virtual Network 10.0.0.0/24

- A couple of virtual machines, ASR protected or directly deployed in Azure
  (10.0.0.20/21/22)

- We will configure the Azure VPN gateway and local subnet and integrate them with
  the on-premises RRAS server VPN endpoint

Preparing the Azure Network for Azure Site-to-Site VPN

Deploying a site-to-site VPN from the Azure side involves the following steps:

1. Creating/editing a virtual network

2. Verifying or adding virtual subnets to the virtual network

3. Configuring a DNS server

4. Creating the gateway subnet

5. Creating the virtual network gateway

6. Creating a local network gateway

7. Integrating with your VPN device

8. Creating the site-to-site VPN tunnel

9. Verifying the connections in both directions

Although this might feel like a lot of different and complex steps, it shouldn't take more than 20 minutes, of which 15 minutes is waiting for the VPN gateway to be deployed and the connections to be set up. So I hope I didn't scare you away yet, but rather got you enthusiastic about making this work.

1. From the Azure portal, browse to your ASR resource group and select the virtual network that you created.

2. From the settings of the virtual network, browse to Subnets. There should already be a subnet available, which was created at the same time you created the virtual network (see Figure 9-21 as an example).

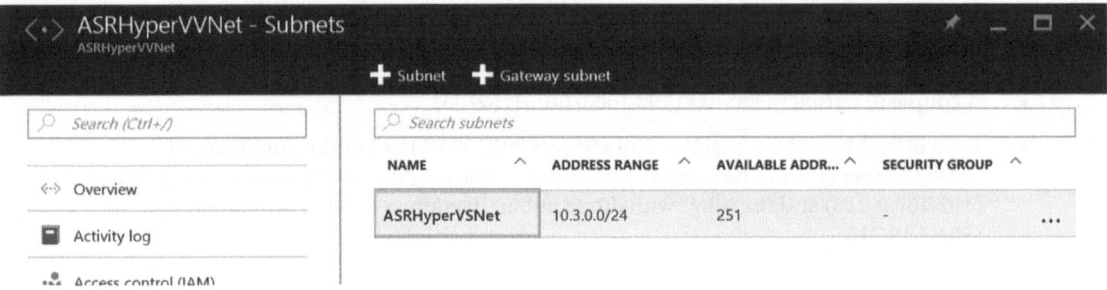

Figure 9-21. *Virtual network and virtual subnet*

3. Click the +Gateway Subnet button to add a gateway subnet, which opens the Add Subnet blade, as shown in Figure 9-22.

   • Notice that the name will be created automatically, having "gateway" as part of the name. This is for Azure to recognize this is a gateway subnet in background.

   • The address range/CIDR block will also be prepopulated; you can change this if you need to, but that is not required in this example.

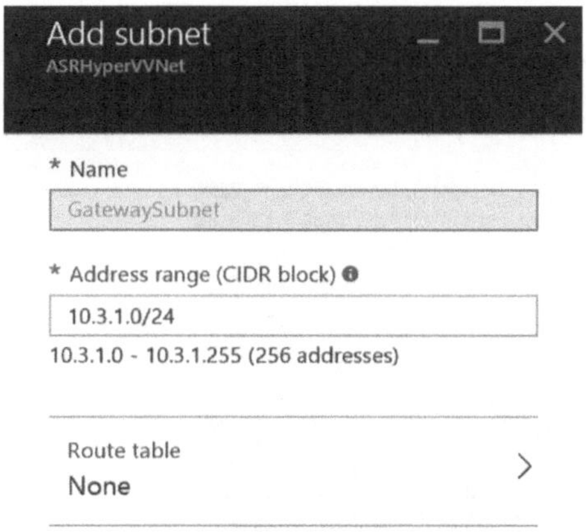

Add subnet — ▢ ✕
ASRHyperVVNet

* Name

GatewaySubnet

* Address range (CIDR block) ❶

10.3.1.0/24

10.3.1.0 - 10.3.1.255 (256 addresses)

Route table
None   〉

Figure 9-22. *Add gateway subnet*

4. Besides the subnet and gateway subnet, we will also add a DNS server setting to our virtual network. Close the Virtual Subnet blade and select DNS Servers from the virtual network settings. The configuration pane looks like Figure 9-23.

5. Here you can choose between Azure DNS and Custom DNS. Since we want to use our own Active Directory integrated DNS servers, select Custom DNS.

    Add the IP addresses for the primary DNS (the Azure VM acting as the ADDS/DNS server) and secondary DNS server (the on-premises VM acting as the ADDS/DNS server).

ASRHyperVVNet - DNS servers   ☆ — ▢ ✕
ASRHyperVVNet

💾 Save   ✕ Discard

🔍 Search (Ctrl+/)

DNS servers ❶

Azure DNS Custom DNS

* Primary DNS server

10.3.0.5   ✓

‹⋅› Overview

Secondary DNS server

192.168.0.50   ✕

■ Activity log

.▪ Access control (IAM)

🏷 Tags

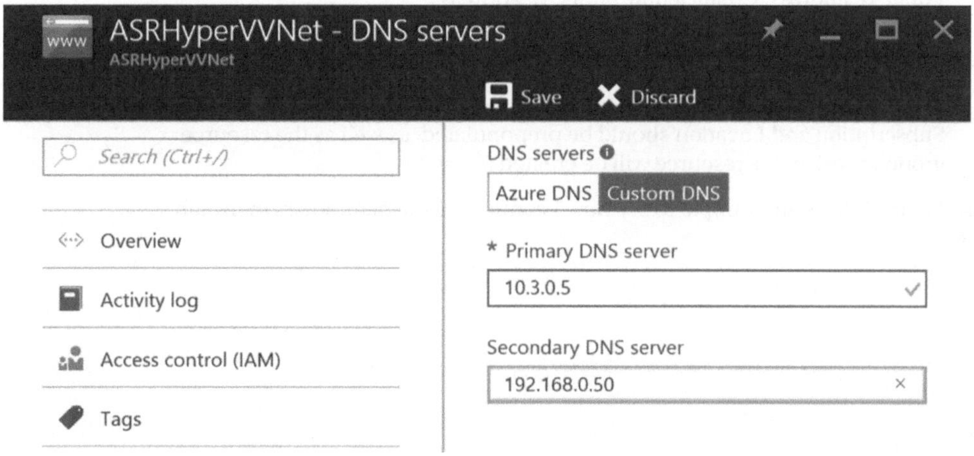

Figure 9-23. *Configure a custom DNS*

6. Now we are going to create our virtual network gateway. From the Azure portal, select New/Networking/Virtual Network Gateway (see Figure 9-24 to get an idea how this looks like from the Azure portal).

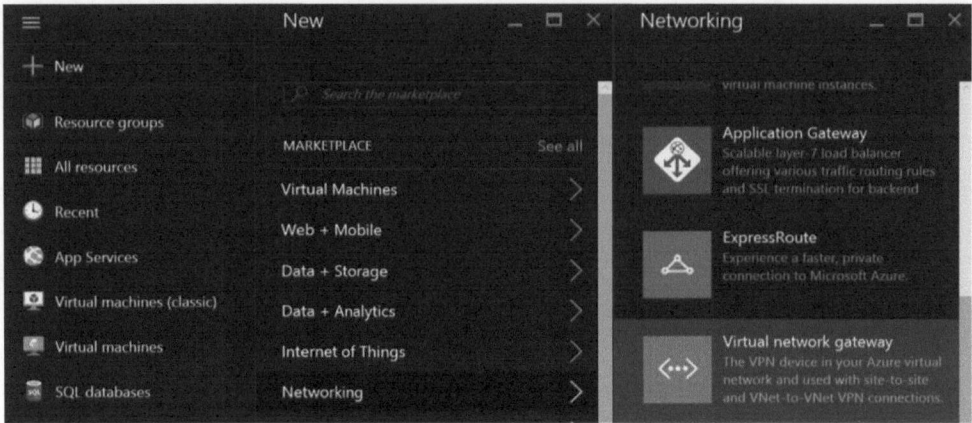

Figure 9-24. *Create a new virtual network gateway*

7. This opens the Create Virtual Network Gateway blade. Here you specify the following parameters:

   - Unique name for the virtual network gateway (e.g., ASRHyperVVNetGW)

   - Virtual Network: Select the virtual network you created earlier

   - Public IP address: Create a new public IP address

   - Gateway Type: VPN

   - VPN Type: Policy Based

   - Subscription and Location should be prepopulated, as well as the resource group in which this resource will be created

   Use Figure 9-25 as an example to see how I configured the parameters in my lab setup.

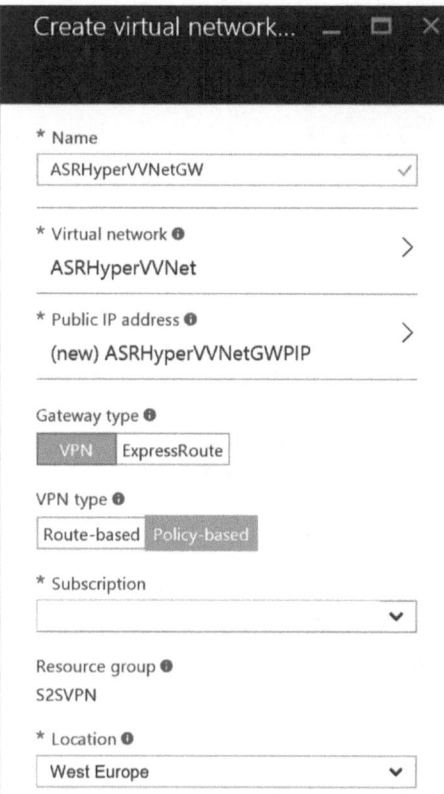

Figure 9-25. *Create a new virtual network gateway*

8. Azure will now create the virtual network gateway in the background. Note this can take anywhere from 15-45 minutes. Until this step is fully completed, we cannot establish the VPN connectivity between both environments. (This might be a good time for a coffee or another drink.)

9. Once the gateway has been created, select it and check the public IP endpoint address out of its settings. Keep note of this address, as you will need it to complete the on-premises RRAS configuration (see Figure 9-26).

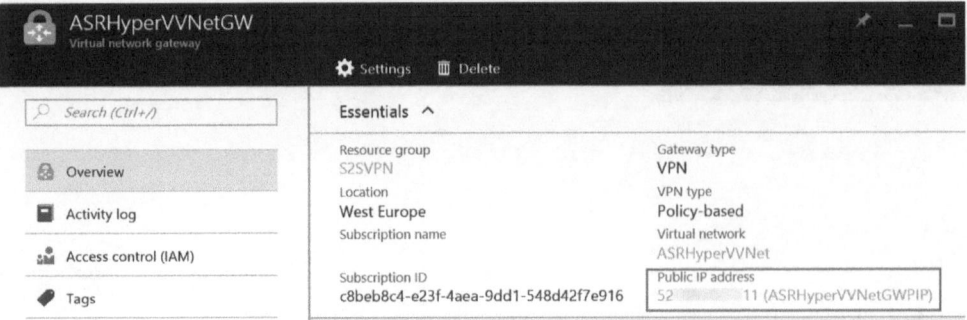

Figure 9-26. *Virtual network is created and the public IP address is defined*

10. Next we have to create a local network gateway. This will represent "the glue" between Azure and your on-premises network. From the Azure portal, select New/Networking/Local Network Gateway.

- Provide a name for this resource

- IP address: This should reflect the public IP address of the on-premises RRAS server connection (the 80.64.19.216 fictional IP address in Figure 9-20)

Figure 9-27 shows what the configuration should look like.

Figure 9-27. *Creating a local network gateway*

11. The last configuration component we need to set up↓as shown in Figure 9-28↓is the VPN connection itself. To do this, browse to your virtual network gateway (the one with the Azure public IP address, which was created in Steps 8-9).

NAME	TYPE	LOCATION	
ASRHyperVLocalNGW	Local network...	West Europe	...
ASRHyperVVNetGWPIP	Public IP addr...	West Europe	...
ASRHyperVVNetGW	Virtual networ...	West Europe	...
ASRHyperVVNet	Virtual network	West Europe	...

Diagnose and solve problems

SETTINGS

Connections

Point-to-site configuration

Properties

Figure 9-28. *The virtual network is created and public IP address is defined*

12. In the Settings, select Connections/Add Connections.

13. This opens the Add Connection blade, where you have to make some selections to get this deployed. Since all required components have been created out of all previous steps we walked through, this should be pretty straightforward:

    - Name: Provide a descriptive name for the VPN connection.

    - Connection Type: Change this to site-to-site (IPSec).

    - Select the virtual network gateway and local network gateway as you created them before.

    - Shared Key: Provide a shared key here; this can be copied from your on-premises VPN device if it provides one, or you can generate one by typing any passphrase you want. In my demo setup, I chose abcdef123456).

    Use Figure 9-29 as a reference for how it will look.

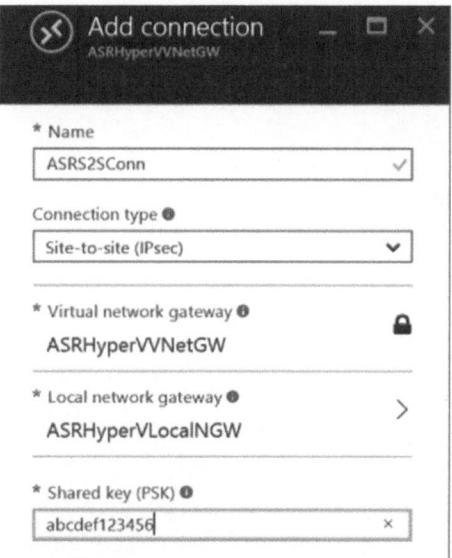

Figure 9-29. *Adding the VPN connection*

14. This completes the configuration of the site-to-site VPN connection on the Azure side for now. The next part of the configuration is to be done on the on-premises VPN RRAS virtual machine.

Preparing the On-Premises Hyper-V Infrastructure for Azure Site-to-Site VPN

The most important things to get arranged in the on-premises network are:

- Direct public IP, bound to the second NIC of the RRAS VM

- Configuring the RRAS VM for Azure site-to-site VPN connectivity

Since I don't have control over your on-premises router/firewall/network topology, I can't write anything meaningful about how to set up the device. In my environment, I directly linked a public IP address (behind my firewall/router for security!!) to the second NIC of the RRAS VM. So nothing more to share on that one, besides I entered the IP address in the TCP/IP IPv4 settings of the NIC as a fixed IP address, pointing to my router/firewall as gateway.

- NIC 1 is an internal LAN 192.168.0.xx: No gateway IP to be specified here

- NIC 2 is a public Internet 80.x.x.216: Gateway IP 80.x.x.1

You can see these settings from my network connections configuration in the control panel in Figures 9-30 and 9-31.

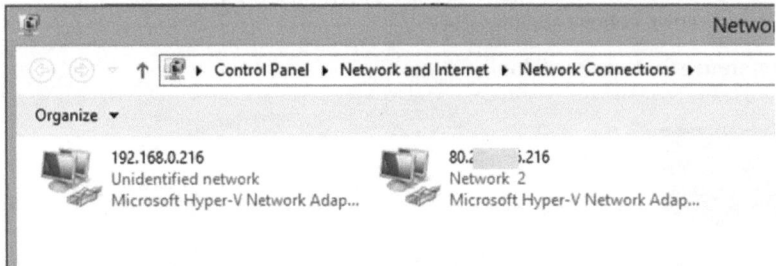

Figure 9-30. *NIC configurations of the VPN RRAS virtual machine*

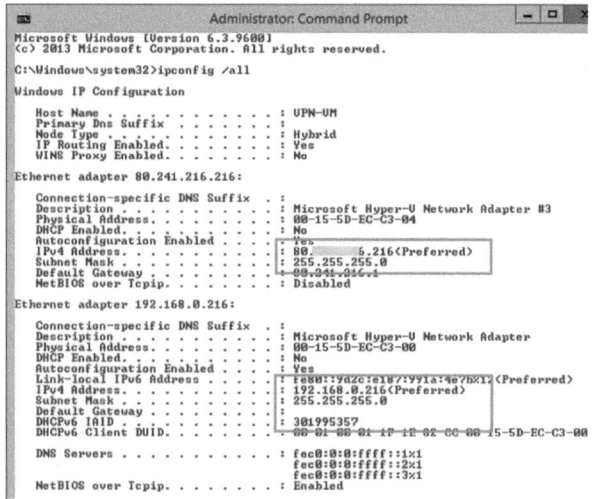

Figure 9-31. *NIC configurations of the VPN RRAS virtual machine*

So let's now guide you through the RRAS VM setup and configuration, as this will emulate the VPN endpoint device for the on-premises network.

1. Have a Windows 2012 R2 VM ready with the two virtual NICs configured with their fixed IP address settings, as mentioned earlier.

2. From within the Server Manager of this virtual machine, add the Remote Access server server role and accept the defaults to install this role (see Figure 9-32).

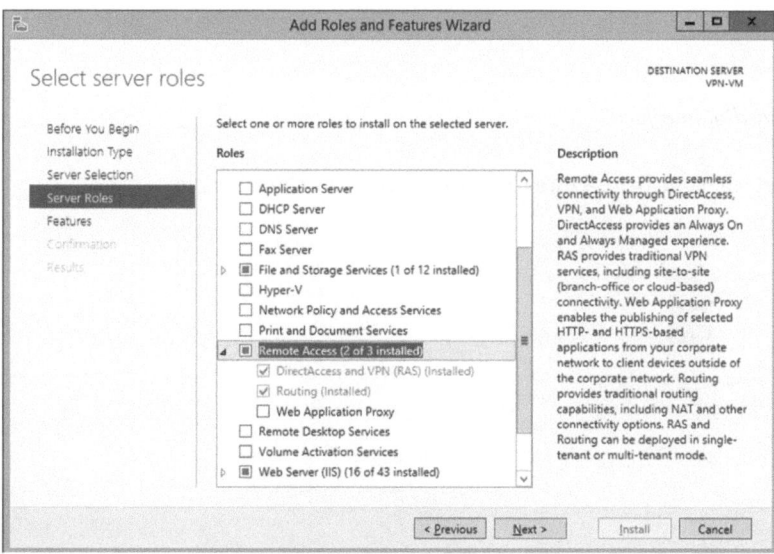

Figure 9-32. *Adding the Remote Access Server role*

3. Once installed, go to the Routing and Remote Access management console. Select your server and then right-click and select Configure and Enable Routing and Remote Access, as shown in Figure 9-33.

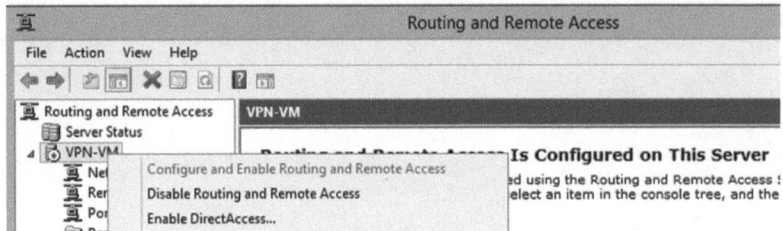

Figure 9-33. *Configure and Enable Routing and Remote Access*

4. Select Network Interface/New Demand-Dial Interface. See Figure 9-34 if it is not clear where to find this option.

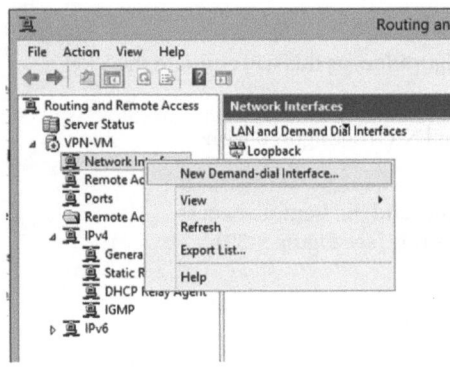

Figure 9-34. *Define a new demand-dial interface*

5. Provide a unique interface name (e.g., Azure S2S). See Figure 9-35. Click Next to continue.

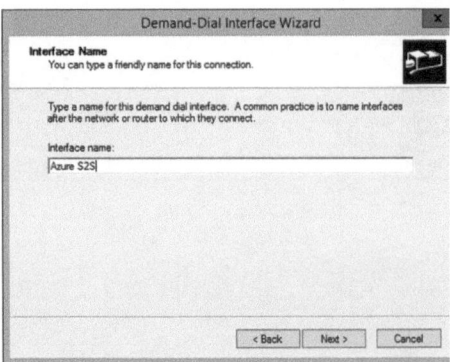

Figure 9-35. *Define a new demand-dial interface↓interface name*

6. Select Connect Using a Virtual Private Network (VPN), as shown in Figure 9-36. Click Next to continue.

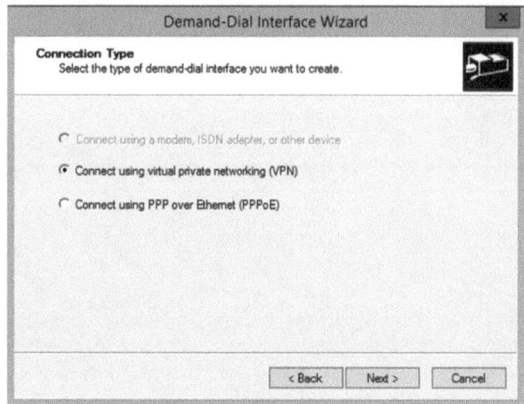

Figure 9-36. *Define a new demand-dial interface↓connect using VPN*

7. In the VPN type step, select IKE v2 as the authentication type (see Figure 9-37). Click Next to continue.

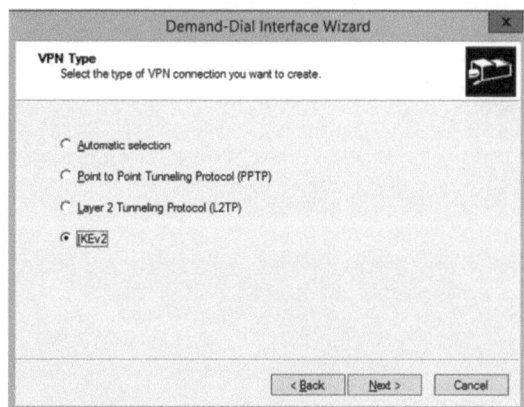

Figure 9-37. *Define a new demand-dial interface↓IKEv2 as VPN type*

8. In the next step, displayed in Figure 9-38, enter the public IP address of the Azure VPN gateway. Click Next to continue.

221

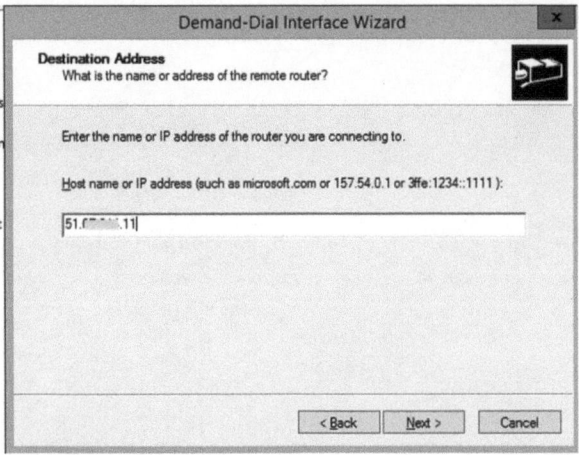

Figure 9-38. *Define a new demand-dial interface↓Azure gateway destination address*

9. In the Protocols and Security step, which is shown in Figure 9-39, uncheck the Route IP Packets option, as we will create our static routes manually later. Also uncheck the Add a User Account option. Click Next to continue.

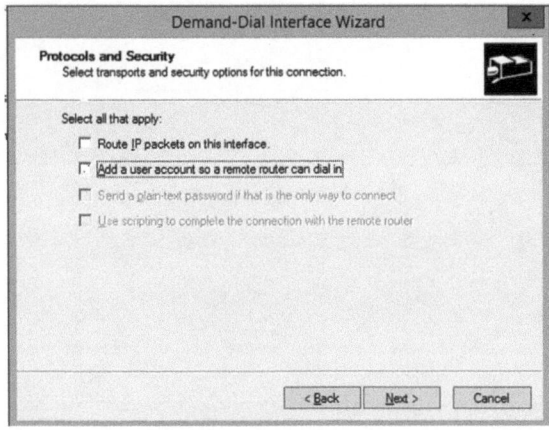

Figure 9-39. *Define a new demand-dial interface↓protocols and security*

10. In the next step, provide a temporary username to continue the configuration. This can be any name, as it will not be used as authentication for the VPN tunnel. Click Next to continue. (See Figure 9-40.)

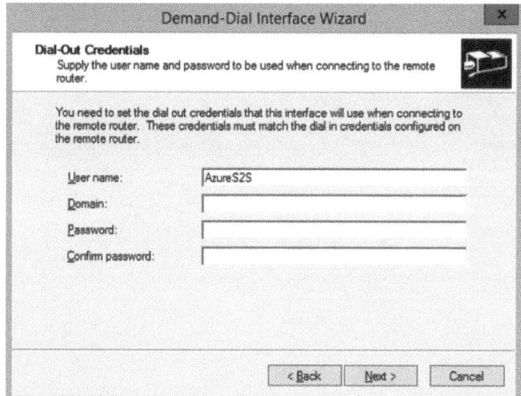

Figure 9-40. Define a new demand-dial interface↓temporary username credentials

11. This completes the demand-dial interface configuration wizard. Click Finish to close it. (See Figure 9-41.)

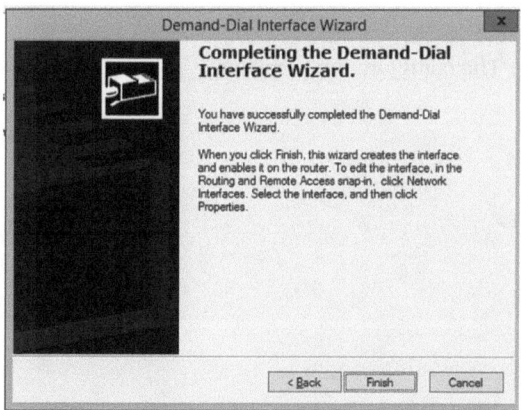

Figure 9-41. Define a new demand-dial interface—finished

12. Once the network interface has been created, go to its properties, as shown in Figure 9-42. In the General tab, verify that the Azure Gateway Public IP address is completed.

Figure 9-42. *VPN Interface↓general settings and Azure gateway public IP address*

13. On the Options tab, no changes are to be made. The configuration in my lab setup looks like Figure 9-43.

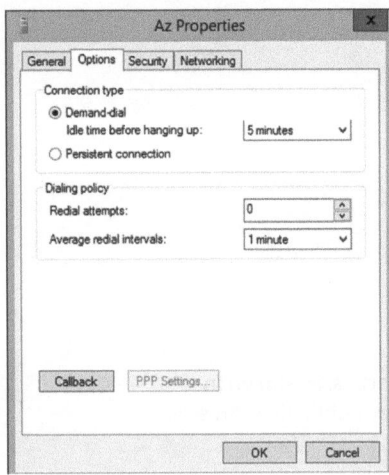

Figure 9-43. *VPN interface↓Options tab*

14. On the Security tab, select Use Preshared Key for Authentication. Here you enter the preshared key as it was defined in the Azure VPN connection configuration (see Figure 9-44).

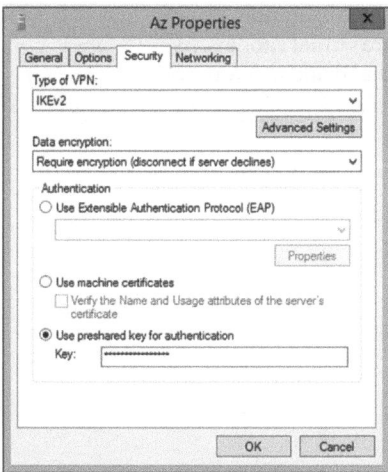

Figure 9-44. *VPN interface ↓Security tab ↓using a preshared key*

15. On the Networking tab, accept and leave the default values as they are. Look at Figure 9-45 for a reference.

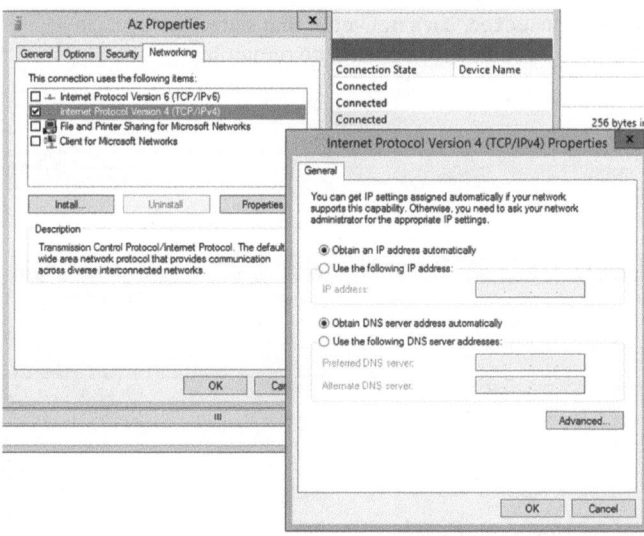

Figure 9-45. *VPN interface ↓Networking tab*

This completes the configuration of the network interface, which provides the Azure site-to-site VPN connection. It could take several minutes before the connection becomes active and shows a status of connected.

16. The last small configuration you must do to wrap up the VPN configuration on the on-premises network is add a static route toward the Azure virtual subnets. As shown in Figure 9-46, to do this, browse to IPv4/Static Routes and add a new route.

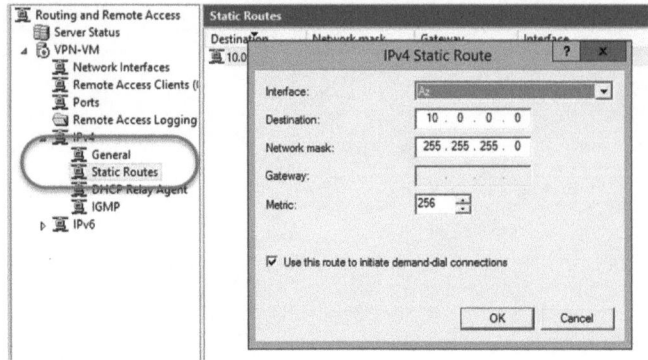

***Figure 9-46.** Static route is being added to the VPN configuration*

This will ensure that virtual machines from the on-premises network (192.168.0.0/24) will find their way to the Azure subnets on the other side of the VPN tunnel (10.0.0.0/24).

17. Wait for the VPN connection to become Connected, if it's not yet in that state. The result should look like Figure 9-47 before you can continue with the remaining steps.

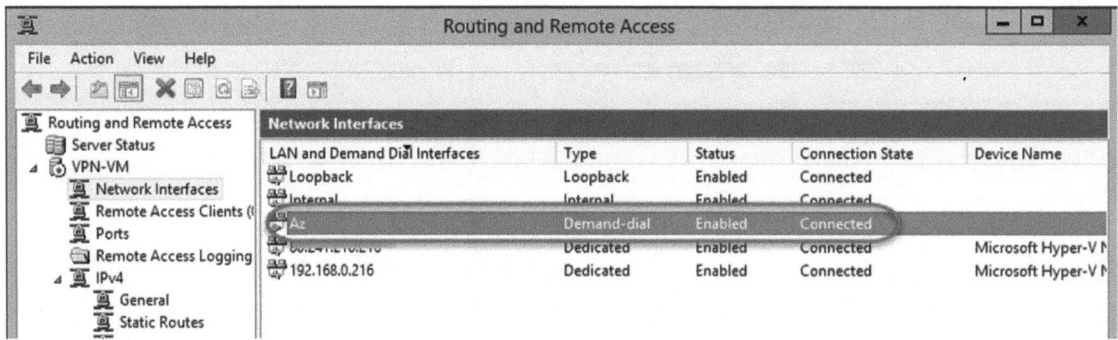

***Figure 9-47.** Azure site-to-site VPN demand-dial interface✓connected*

18. Verify the same from the Azure portal. Browse to the VPN connection that you created earlier, which should also have a status of Connected, as you can see in Figure 9-48.

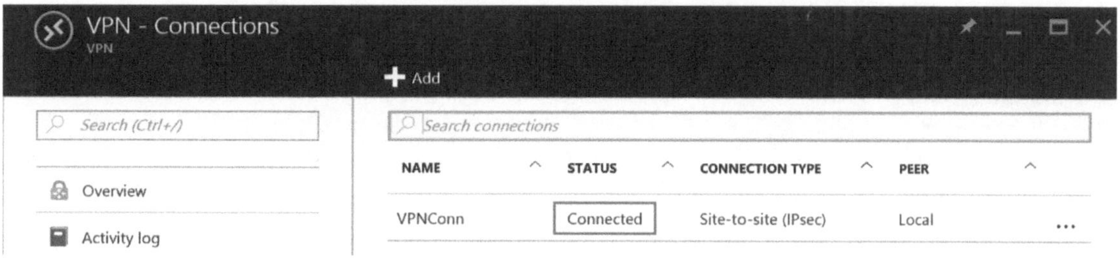

Figure 9-48. Azure site-to-site VPN connection↓connected to on-premises

19. This confirms that the Azure site-to-site VPN tunnel is configured, established, and connected. Let's do a final check to determine if the virtual machines on both ends of the tunnel can communicate with each other, by sending a ping from one VM to the other in both directions (make sure you have the Windows machine firewall disabled or configured as an exclusion to allow ICMP ping traffic). To show you that this is indeed working, I added Figures 9-49 and 9-50. These should be self-explanatory.

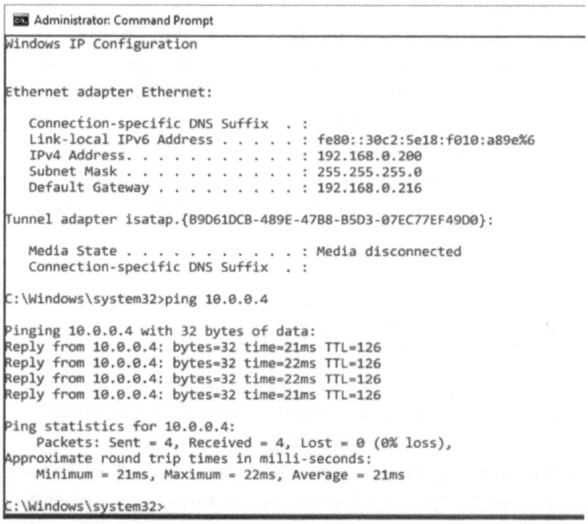

Figure 9-49. Sending/receiving ping reply messages from on-premises VM behind the RRAS VM toward an Azure VM behind the VPN site-to-site subnets

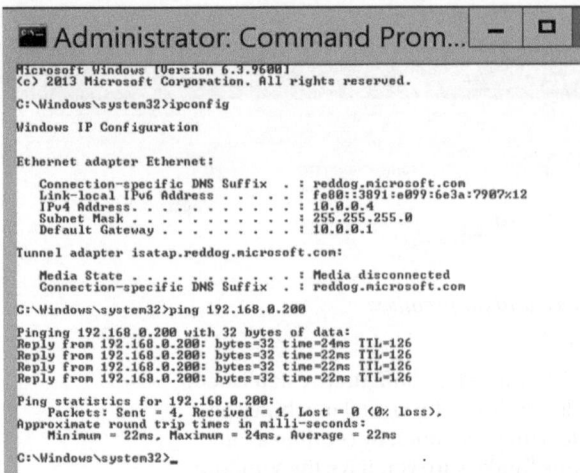

Figure 9-50. *Sending/receiving ping reply messages from an Azure VM behind the VPN site-to-site subnets toward an on-premises VM behind the RRAS VM*

This completes the configuration of the Azure site-to-site VPN.

Congrats, you have now successfully established a site-to-site VPN configuration between an on-premises Hyper-V host and an Azure VPN gateway connection. Bringing it back to the disaster recovery story at the beginning of this chapter… if an application server(s) fails over to an ASR Azure virtual machine, end users who are still active at the on-premises network can now easily connect to the ASR protected machine in Azure. In fact, all communication is allowed by default, including ping, RDP, file share access, and so on.

Remote users connecting to the office or the prime datacenter will also find their way to the ASR protected application servers running in Azure during a disaster scenario, as long as their VPN connection subnet in the office gets routed to the Azure gateway.

Modifying Virtual Machine Sizing as Part of ASR

In this section, I talk about an ASR feature that is so simple but powerful. Once a machine is in a protected state out of ASR, you can modify the detected virtual machine specifications like memory, CPU, and disk.

Let me explain the use case for this in an easy example: You are running a SQL server database application on-premises. The SQL server has 128GB of memory, 16 cores, and 2TB of disk space. The machine gets protected to Azure Site Recovery. The agreement is that in case of disaster happening, not all SQL databases need to become active, and only 30% of the users must be able to connect to the applications. This could mean the machine specs can be changed to 64GB of memory or less and eight or four cores.

The benefit of using this approach is cost management, as a machine with fewer technical specs is a cheaper machine T-shirt size in Azure.

To modify these machine specs, go through the following steps:

1. From within the Azure portal, browse to your ASR resource group and ASR Vault, from which you browse to Protected Items/Replicated Items (see Figure 9-51).

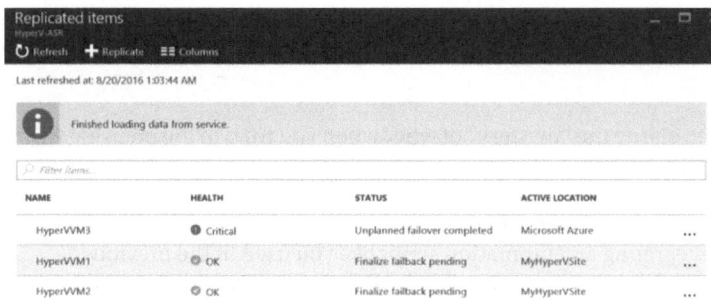

Figure 9-51. *ASR replicated/protected Items*

2. Select any of the protected machines and then choose Settings/Compute and Network. This will show you the current specs of the machine, as shown in Figure 9-52.

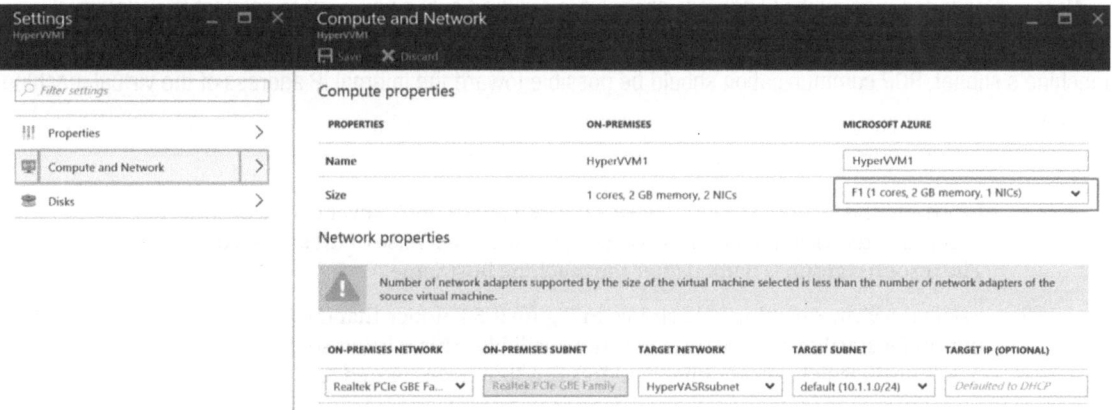

Figure 9-52. *Protected Items ↓compute and network settings*

3. From here, you can change the hostname of the machine, as well as modify the size parameters. Notice that initially, an Azure VM T-shirt size will be mapped with the original source specs of the machine. By making another selection in the listbox, you can change the technical machine specs for this virtual machine once it boots up in Azure.

4. Also notice the ability to modify the target network and target subnet if needed.

This completes the process of modifying the machine sizing parameters of an ASR-protected VM. I told you it was not difficult to configure, but the result is a pretty interesting and powerful one, both technically and financially.

Explaining Why RDP to ASR Virtual Machines Was Not Working After Failover

In this last section of this chapter, I want to clarify the "mystery" of why↓when you tried to log on using RDP to an ASR failed over machine↓it was not working.

First of all, it's no mystery at all; sorry if that disappoints you. There is a purely technical explanation for it, and Microsoft's motivation to use it like that is an interesting one.

The first part of the solution lies in integrating an automation script like you used in the previous section, enabling RDP for an ASR protected machine. Assuming that RDP was already active on the on-premises server before it was replicated with ASR, there must be something else missing from the picture.

The main reasons why RDP is not working from the Internet to ASR protected machines is because there is no public endpoint configured for the virtual machine, as well as no rules defined on the Network Security Group (NSG) level to allow incoming traffic into the virtual network.

So we must fix two things to make RDP work again. I already discussed the first one, so in this section I will guide you through the configuration of the public IP endpoint.

■ **Note**   Configuring the public IP address endpoint is required only if you want to connect to your virtual machine from an external Internet connection. If your site-to-site VPN configuration allows traffic to the virtual machine's subnet, RDP communication should be possible toward the internal IP address of the virtual machine already.

---

1. Browse to the resource group that was created out of the failover of one of your ASR protected virtual machines you ran during the exercise of Chapters 6 or 7. The resource group is named after the machine hostname.

2. Select the virtual machine. As shown in Figure 9-53, notice that the Connect button for starting an RDP session is not available. This is because the virtual machine doesn't have a public IP address endpoint configured to it.

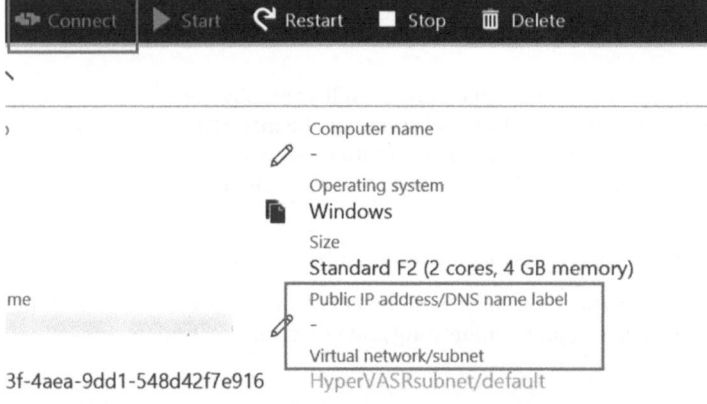

Figure 9-53. *Can't RDP to a failed over VM*

3.   Select the virtual machine's network interface, as shown in Figure 9-54.

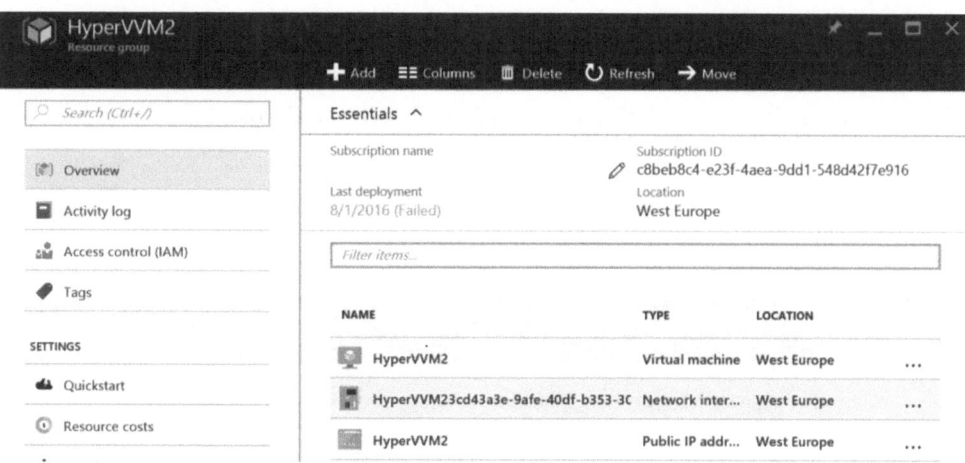

Figure 9-54. *ASR failed over virtual machine resource group↓NIC*

4.   Browse to Settings/IP Configurations. Select the IP configuration that is listed, as shown in Figure 9-55.

Figure 9-55. *Virtual machine's IP configurations*

5. Notice that the public IP address settings are currently set to Disabled. Change this to Enabled.

- Select the IP address field.

- Click Create New in the choose the public IP address blade.

- Specify a name for this public IP address configuration (I typically use the hostname and PIP, e.g., HyperVVM3PIP).

- Define the assignment as Dynamic.

(Figure 9-56 shows how to configure this.)

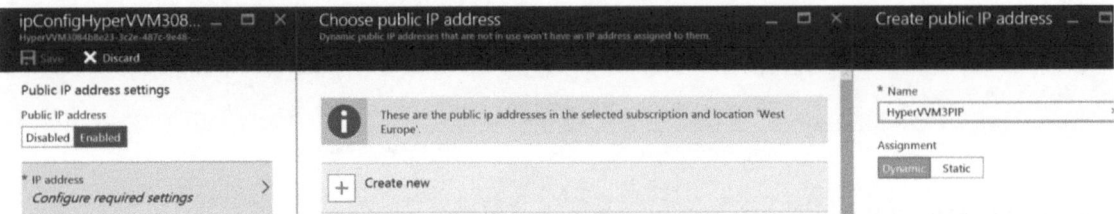

Figure 9-56. *Configuring a public IP address endpoint for the VM*

6. Save the configuration changes.

7. After the configuration is updated, go back to the virtual machine and verify that the Connect button is now active. Also notice that the public IP address was configured. Both items are marked in Figure 9-57.

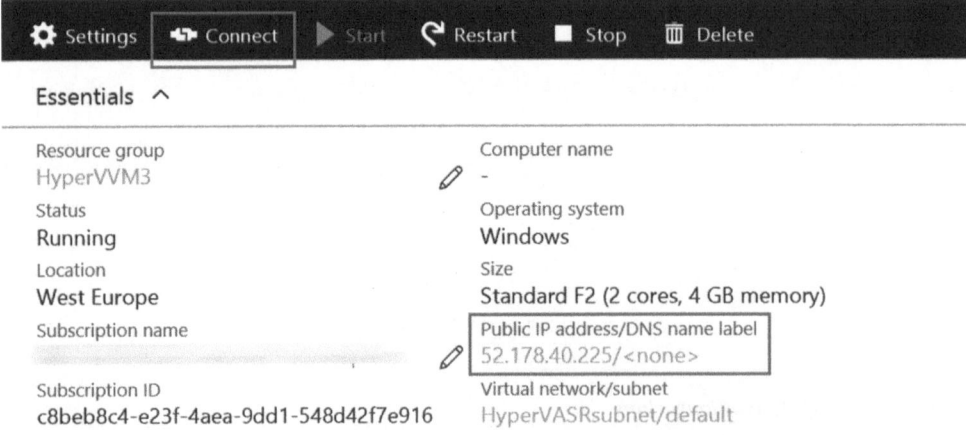

Figure 9-57. *Public IP address endpoint is configured and RDP connect is available*

This completes the procedure on how to configure a public IP address endpoint to allow direct RDP connection to your failed over virtual machine.

Performing a Failback Scenario

In this last section of the chapter, I quickly walk you through performing a failback scenario, which in the end is the whole point of having a disaster recovery solution↓running your systems and applications from another location temporarily and moving everything back to the original datacenter after everything is up and running again. (Unless you decide to leave your virtual machines in Azure and run them as production machines, which would be perfectly fine too!!)

Performing a failback scenario requires the following:

- Initiating a failover from Azure to on-premises

- Committing the change

- Reverse replicating from Azure to on-premises

After doing these steps, the on-premises virtual machine will be the "master" again and will start replicating all changes back to the offline ASR protected virtual machine in Azure. After that, you can again initiate a failover to Azure and start all over again playing with disaster recovery.

Let's run through this failback scenario:

1. From the Azure portal, browse to the ASR Vault/Protected Items and select any of the failed over virtual machines from the previous chapters, as I have done in Figure 9-58.

2. Select Planned Failover. (Notice that there is no failback option here.)

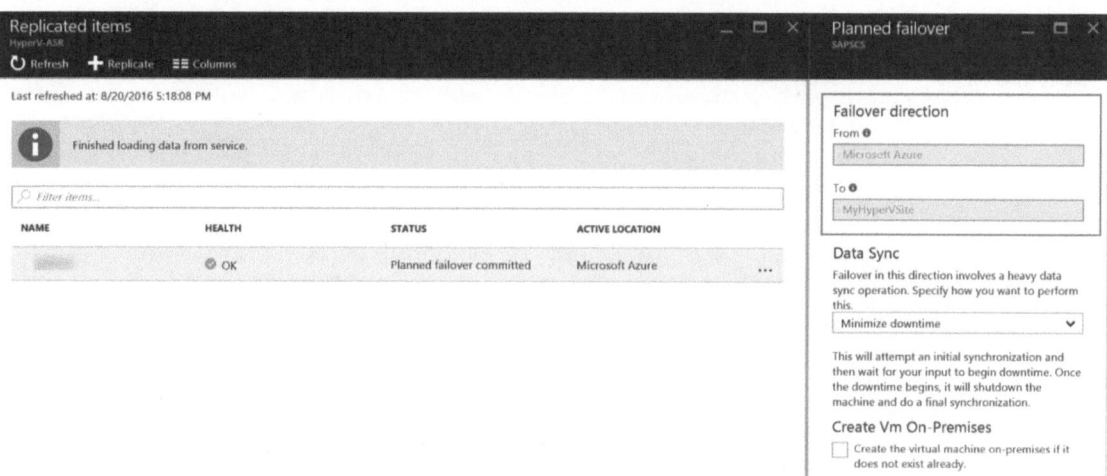

Figure 9-58. *Planned failover, which basically is a failback*

3. Notice the direction will be the opposite, so we are now failing over from Microsoft Azure to the on-premises Hyper-V site.

4. Click OK to start the failover.

5. From the Notification area, click the launched job so you can see the progress.

   A few steps are being executed here:

   - Checking the prerequisites for virtual machine failback
   - Preparing the on-premises virtual machine
   - Initiating data synchronization
   - Monitoring data synchronization
   - Waiting for user input
   - Starting virtual machine failback

After this has been executed successfully, the virtual machine runs back on-premises. Figure 9-59 gives you an idea as to how the job steps should look in your environment.

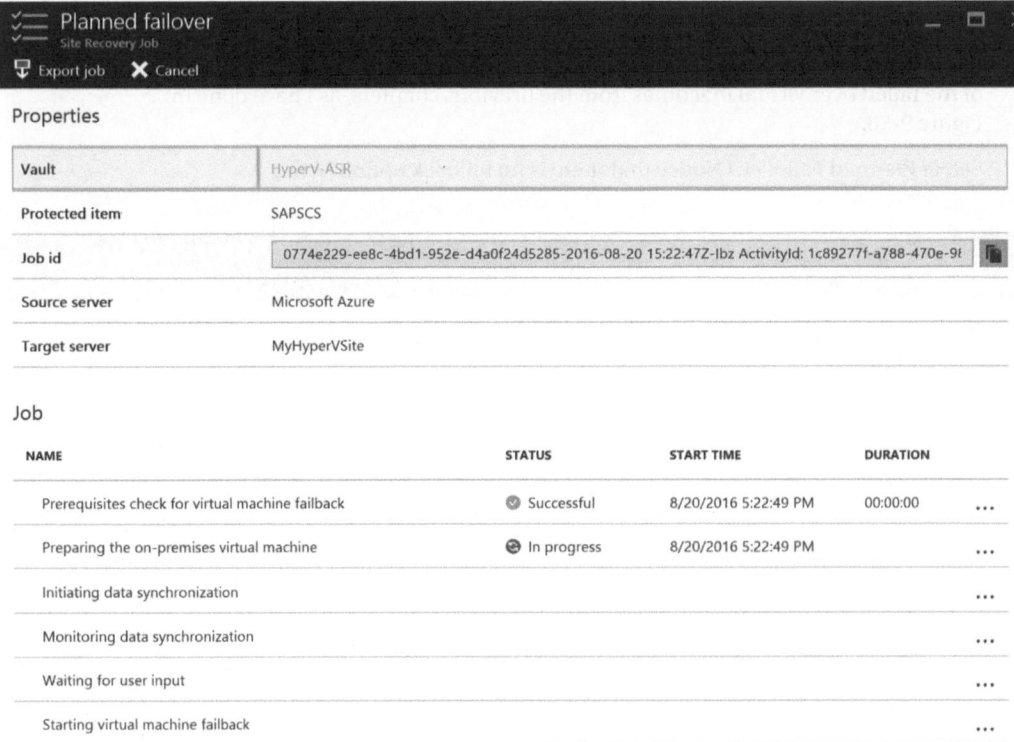

Figure 9-59. *Job progress of a planned failover, which basically is a failback*

6. When you're checking the replication health on the on-premises Hyper-V host, the state should look like Figure 9-60.

Replication Mode:	Replica	**Primary Server:**	
Replication State:	Failback in progress	**Replica Server:**	m1295
Replication Health:	Not Applicable	**Last synchronized at:**	Not Applicable

Figure 9-60. *Failback in progress to the on-premises Hyper-V host*

7. When monitoring the ASR service from the resource monitor on the Hyper-V host (cbengine.exe), it shows the amount of data being pulled down from Azure (site recovery), which refers to the "to-be-synchronized" data changes from Azure to on-premises. Figure 9-61 gives you an idea what this should look like.

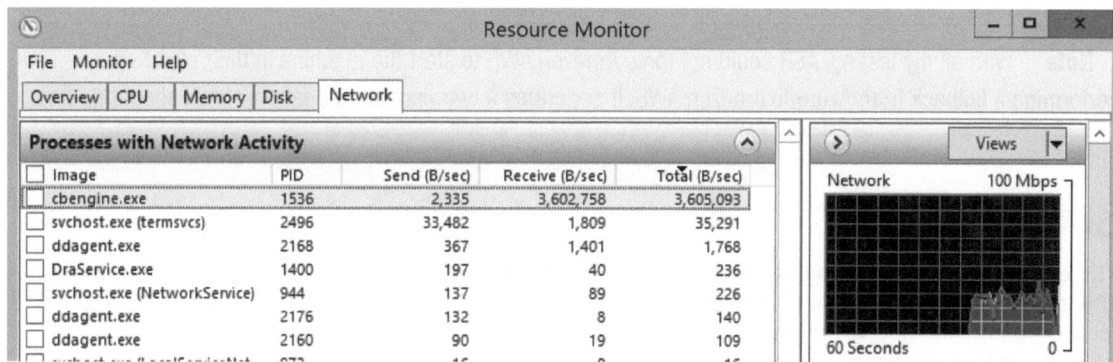

Figure 9-61. *Monitoring ASR replication service (cbengine.exe) for receiving data*

8. In meantime, ASR synchronized the protected virtual machine back to the on-premises Hyper-V host, and the job is waiting for "user input". Select the waiting line in the job list and click the Complete Failover button, as shown in Figure 9-62.

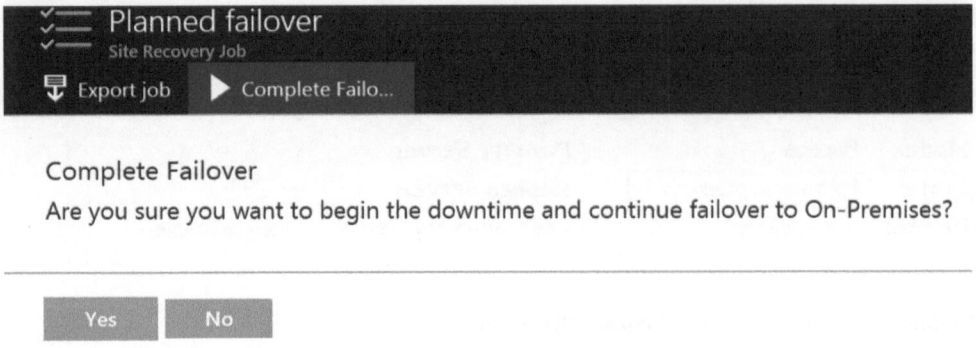

Complete Failover

Are you sure you want to begin the downtime and continue failover to On-Premises?

| Yes | No |

Figure 9-62. Confirming failover to on-premises

9. Wait for the failover job to complete. The failed back virtual machine should have a running status again on-premises.

■ **Note** With all my testing, ASR could not force Amazon AWS to start the machine in their cloud after performing a failback from Azure to Amazon AWS. It generates a warning, but the failover itself should go fine.

Summary

This chapter was dedicated to more advanced configurations of ASR, as well as fixing some common issues after failover. You learned about Azure OMS automation, how to integrate PowerShell scripts into your ASR recovery plans, and how to make the failover process more intelligent.

Next to that, you learned how to define a public IP address endpoint to a protected and failed over virtual machine, in order to allow direct RDP connections to it.

In the last section, you learned how to execute a full failback of a virtual machine from ASR back to the source environment.

This completes the three chapters dedicated to ASR. The following and last chapter will talk through some Azure licensing and budget best practices, with a focus on estimating the cost of using OMS, Azure Backup, and Azure Site Recovery.

Index

Get the eBook for only $4.99!

Why limit yourself?

Now you can take the weightless companion with you wherever you go and access your content on your PC, phone, tablet, or reader.

Since you've purchased this print book, we are happy to offer you the eBook for just $4.99.

Convenient and fully searchable, the PDF version enables you to easily find and copy code—or perform examples by quickly toggling between instructions and applications.

To learn more, go to http://www.apress.com/us/shop/companion or contact support@apress.com.